THE BOOK
OF THE GRADUAL SAYINGS

(ANGUTTARA-NIKĀYA)

OR

MORE-NUMBERED SUTTAS

𝔓𝔞𝔩𝔦 𝔗𝔢𝔵𝔱 𝔖𝔬𝔠𝔦𝔢𝔱𝔶

TRANSLATION SERIES, No. 24

THE BOOK OF THE
GRADUAL SAYINGS
(ANGUTTARA-NIKĀYA)
OR MORE-NUMBERED SUTTAS

VOL. II
(THE BOOK OF THE FOURS)

TRANSLATED BY

F. L. WOODWARD, M.A.

TRANSLATOR OF "MANUAL OF A MYSTIC," "THE BUDDHA'S PATH OF VIRTUE,"
"KINDRED SAYINGS, PTS. III., IV., V.," "GRADUAL SAYINGS, PT. I.," "SOME SAYINGS OF
THE BUDDHA," "BUDDHIST STORIES," ETC.

" Say on, sayers ! sing on, singers !
 Delve ! mould ! pile the words of the earth !
 Work on, age after age, nothing is to be lost,
 It may have to wait long, but it will certainly come
  in use ;
 When the materials are all prepared and ready, the
  architects shall appear !"
                                        WALT WHITMAN.

Published by the Pali Text Society

Distributed by

Routledge & Kegan Paul Ltd.

London and Boston

1973

First published	.	.	.	.	.	.	1933
Reprinted	.	.	.	.	.	.	1952
Reprinted	.	.	.	.	.	.	1962
Reprinted	.	.	.	.	.	.	1973

ISBN 0 7100 7616 9

PRINTED IN GREAT BRITAIN BY
STEPHEN AUSTIN AND SONS LTD., HERTFORD

TRANSLATOR'S PREFACE

I have not much to add here, except to thank Mrs. Rhys Davids for several notes and references, and for looking over the final proof-sheets of this volume, which I was prevented from doing by time and distance. I may, however, draw attention to one or two points of interest to Pāli scholars—viz., *akukkuccaka-jāta* (p. 212), and *ummagga* (pp. 184, 198). For these see an article in *J.R.A.S.*, July, 1931, where, among others, they are discussed by Mr. E. H. Johnston, with whose conclusions I agree. Also to words like *apaṇṇaka* (still a riddle), *assa (aṃsa)-puṭa* (p. 246), *kamm'oja* (p. 92), and several others which will be found listed in Index No. III. There is also a curious construction (p. 167), *so maṃ pañhena, ahaṃ veyyākaraṇena*, for which there is a solitary parallel at Mrs. Rhys Davids' *Sakya*, pp. 336-7.

I may add that a large number of the suttas in this volume appear in *Itivuttaka* and *Puggala-Paññatti*, with several differences in readings and form.

F. L. WOODWARD.

WEST TAMAR, TASMANIA,
1932.

CONTENTS

THE BOOK OF THE FOURS

PART II

(THE FIRST FIFTY SUTTAS)

Contents

(THE FIFTH FIFTY SUTTAS

INDEXES

THE BOOK
OF THE GRADUAL SAYINGS
(*ANGUTTARA NIKĀYA*)

Honour to that Exalted One, Arahant, the Fully Enlightened One

---

THE BOOK OF THE FOURS

PART II
(THE FIRST FIFTY SUTTAS)

CHAPTER I.—AT BHAṆḌAGĀMA.

§ i (1). *Understanding.*

THUS have I heard: On a certain occasion the Exalted One was staying among the Vajjians, at Bhaṇḍagāma.[1] Then the Exalted One addressed the monks, saying: 'Monks.'

'Yes, Lord,' replied those monks to the Exalted One. The Exalted One said:

'Monks, it is through not understanding, through not penetrating four things that we have thus gone on faring, thus gone on running this long time, both you and I. What four things ?

It is through not understanding, through not penetrating the Ariyan virtue, monks, the Ariyan concentration, the Ariyan wisdom: it is through not understanding, not penetrating the Ariyan release that we have thus gone on faring, thus gone on running this long time, both you and I.

Now, monks, when the Ariyan virtue, the Ariyan concentration, the Ariyan wisdom and the Ariyan release are understood and penetrated, cut off is the craving for becoming,

---

[1] *Cf. D.* ii, 122 (*M. Parinibbāna Sutta*). 'Becoming' stands at once for state, place and duration. The village seems not to be named elsewhere.

destroyed is the cord of becoming,[1] there is now no more again
of becoming.'

Thus spake the Exalted One.   So saying the Wellfarer added
this further as Teacher:

> ' Virtue and concentration, wisdom, release
> Beyond compare,—these things by Gotama
> Of famous name were fully understood.
> Thus, fully comprehending them, the Buddha,
> Ender of Ill, Teacher with opened eyes,
> Utterly calmed,[2] taught Dhamma to the monks.'

§ ii (2). *Fallen away.*

' Monks, he who possesses not four qualities is said to be
fallen away from this Dhamma-discipline.   What four ?

He who possesses not the Ariyan virtue . . . the Ariyan
concentration . . . the Ariyan wisdom . . . the Ariyan release is said to be fallen away from this Dhamma-discipline.
These are the four . . .

But, monks, he who possesses these four qualities is said
not to be fallen away from this Dhamma-discipline.   What
four ? (*repeat*).

> Ceasing they fall, and, falling from one life,
> Greedy for life renewed they come again.[3]
> Done is the task, enjoyed th' enjoyable:
> And happiness by happiness is won.'[4]

---

[1] *Bhava-netti=rajju*, ' by which beings are, like cattle, tied together
by the neck, led on to such and such becoming.' *Comy.*   In the *sutta* at
D. ii (Koṭigāma) it is the penetration of the Four Truths which leads to
this result, the words of the *gāthā* there being similar to those of our last §.

[2] *Parinibbuto.*

[3] At *Thag. v.* 63; *Brethr.*, p. 64: *cf. Gotama the Man*, 87.   Our *Comy.'s*
interp. differs from that on *Thag.* (where birds of prey pounce, *patanti*,
on fallen flesh (*cutā*) and pounce greedily again).   Here, however, *Comy.*
says: *Ye cutā, te patanti : ye patitā, te cutā : cutattā patitā, patitattā cutā ti
attho.*

[4] I quote Mrs. Rhys Davids's note on *Brethr. loc. cit.*: ' *i.e.*, says the
Commentary (ascribed to Dhammapāla): " By the happiness of the
attainment of fruition has Nibbāna, which is beyond happiness (or is

§ iii (3). *Uprooted* (a).

' Monks, possessed of four qualities the foolish, sinful, un-worthy[1] man carries about with him an uprooted,[2] lifeless self, is blameworthy, is censured by the intelligent and begets much demerit. What four ?

Without test or scrutiny he speaks in praise of what deserves not praise: likewise he speaks blaming things deserving praise. Without test or scrutiny he shows appreciation where there should be none. Likewise when appreciation should be shown he shows displeasure. These are the four qualities.[3]

But, monks, possessed of four qualities the wise, virtuous, worthy man carries about with him a self not uprooted, not lifeless, is not blameworthy, is not censured by the intelligent and begets much merit. What four ? (*The opposite qualities.*)

> Who praiseth him who should be blamed,
> Or blameth who should praisèd be,
> He by his lips stores up ill-luck
> And by that ill-luck wins no bliss.
> Small is the ill-luck of a man
> Who gambling loseth all his wealth.
> Greater by far th' ill-luck of him
> Who, losing all and losing self,
> 'Gainst the Wellfarers fouls his mind.

---

exceeding great happiness, *accanta-sukhaŋ*), been won, and by that happi-ness of insight, which has become a happy mode of *procedure*, has the bliss of Fruition, of Nibbāna, been reached." The latter interpretation, as Dr. Neumann has pointed out—winning happiness by happiness—is, in the *Majjhima-Nikāya* (i, 93 f.), contrasted with the Jain point of view: " Nay, friend Gotama, happiness is not to be got at by happiness, but by suffering,"—the ascetic standpoint (*cf. Further Dialogues*, i, 68).' Here our *Comy.* much less convincingly simply describes a series: ' By human happiness, heavenly happiness: by musing-happiness, the happiness of insight: by this, path-happiness: by path-happiness, fruition-happiness: by this, Nibbāna-happiness is won.'

[1] *A-sappuriso=anariya. Cf. infra*, text 32, § 31.

[2] *Cf. A.* i, 105 (of three things); *G.S.* i; *infra*, text 84 and § 222; iii, 139 (of five things). At p. 221 *attanā viharati.*

[3] As at § 83 *infra.*

> Whoso reviles the Worthy Ones,
> In speech and thought designing ill,
> For an hundred thousand periods,
> For six and thirty, with five more
> Such periods, to Purgatory's doomed.'[1]

§ iv (4). *Uprooted* (b).

' Monks, by wrong conduct towards four persons the foolish, sinful, unworthy man carries about[2] with him an uprooted, lifeless self, is blameworthy, is censured by the intelligent, and begets much demerit. Who are the four ?

Monks, it is by wrong conduct towards mother, father, a Tathāgata, and a Tathāgata's followers that the foolish, sinful, unworthy man . . . begets much demerit.

But, monks, by right conduct towards (these same) four . . . the wise, virtuous, worthy man carries about with him a self not uprooted, not lifeless: he is not blameworthy . . . he begets much merit.

> Mother and father and the Enlightened One,
> Tathāgata, and those who follow him,
> Whoso entreateth ill stores up much woe.
> For such ill deeds to parents, in this life
> The sages blame that man, and in the life
> That follows to the place of woe he goes.

> Mother and father and the Enlightened One,
> Tathāgata, and those who follow him,
> Whoso entreateth well stores up much merit.
> For such good deeds to parents, in this life
> The sages praise that man, and afterwards
> In the world of heaven he wins happiness.'

§ v (5). *With the stream.*[3]

' Monks, these four persons are found existing in the world. What four ?

The person who goes with the stream, he who goes against

---

[1] These verses are at *Sn. vv.* 657-60; *S.* i, 149; *A.* v, 171; *Netti*, 132.

[2] A lit. trans. of *attānaŋ pariharati, supra*, § 3; *infra*, § 121, etc.

[3] *Anusota.* At *Pugg.*, p. 62.

the stream, he who stands fast, and he who has crossed over, has gone beyond, who stands on dry land,—a brāhmin.

And of what sort, monks, is the person who goes with the stream ?

Here in the world, monks, a certain person indulges his passions and does wrong deeds. This one is called " a person who goes with the stream."

And of what sort, monks, is the person who goes against the stream ?

Here in the world, monks, a certain person indulges not his passions, he does no wrong deed, but with suffering and dejection, with tearful face and lamentation lives the God-life, complete and utterly fulfilled. This one is called " a person who goes against the stream."

And of what sort, monks, is the person who stands fast ?[1]

Here in the world, monks, a certain person, by destroying the five fetters that bind to the lower worlds, is reborn spon-taneously, there meanwhile to pass utterly away, of a nature to return from that world no more. This one is called " a person who stands fast."

And of what sort, monks, is the person who has crossed over,[2] gone beyond, who stands on dry land,—a brāhmin ?[3]

Here in this world, monks, a certain person, by the de-struction of the āsavas, realizes in this very life, by himself thoroughly comprehending it, the heart's release, the release by wisdom, which is free from the āsavas, and having attained it abides therein. This one, monks, is called " a person who has crossed over, gone beyond, who stands on dry land,—a brāhmin."

These four persons, monks, are found existing in the world.

> Whoso give rein to passions, in this world
> Not passion-freed, in sense-desires delighting,
> These oft and oft subject to birth and eld,
> Bondsmen to craving,[4] down the current go.

---

[1] *Thitatto = thita-sabhāvo.*   [2] *Tinno = oghaŋ taritvā thito. Comy.*
[3] *Cf. S.* i, 47; iv, 174; *Dhp.,* chap. 26 (*Brāhmaṇa-vagga*)=*settho, niddoso. Comy. Cf. Netti,* 157 (*ayaŋ asekho*).
[4] *Tanhādhipannā = ajjhotthatā, ajjhogalhā. Comy.*

Therefore the sage, here fixed in mindfulness,
Not following after lusts and evil deeds,
Tho' he may suffer, should abandon[1] passions.
'Tis he, men say, who 'gainst the current goes.

Who hath cast off the five depravities,[2]
A perfect pupil he, that cannot fail,[3]
Master of mind,[4] with faculties subdued,—
He is " the man who standeth fast," they say.[5]
He, comprehending all states, high and low,[6]
In whom all states are quenched, ended, exist not,—
He, knowing all,[7] the God-life having lived,
Is called " world-ender, who hath passed beyond ".'[8]

§ vi (6). *Of small learning.*[9]

' Monks, these four persons are found existing in the world.
What four ?

One of small learning, who profits not by his learning:[10]
one of small learning, who profits by his learning: one of wide
learning, who profits not thereby: one of wide learning, who
profits thereby.

And in what way, monks, is a person of small learning not
profited thereby ?

In this case, monks, a certain person has small learning in
Sutta, Geyya, Veyyākaraṇa, Gāthā, Udāna, Itivuttaka, Jātaka,

---

[1] Text *paheyya*; *Itv.* 115 (where lines 7 and last two occur); and
Sinh. eds. *jaheyya.*

[2] Text has *kilesāni pahāya pañca*, but *Sinh.* ed. *kilesāni sahaŋ pahāya.*

[3] Text *apahāna-dhammo*; *Sinh.* ed. *asahāna-dh.* (*Comy.* def. this as
aparihīna-sabhāvo).

[4] *Ceto-vasippatto*, see below, text, p. 36 and § 191.

[5] He is *anāgāmin. Comy.*

[6] *Parovarā = uttama-lāmakākusala-kusalā ti. Comy.*

[7] *Vedagu.*

[8] *Lokantagu.*

[9] *Appassuto*, lit. ' having heard little ' (there were no books). At
Pugg. 62.

[10] *Sutena anuppanno = anupagato. Comy.* Lit. ' arisen, come about.'
I take it to mean ' has come to nothing.'

Abbhutadhammā and *Vedalla*:[1] yet, as of that small learning
he knows not the letter, knows not the meaning,[2] he does not
live in accordance with Dhamma. That, monks, is how a
person of small learning profits not thereby.

And in what way, monks, is a person of small learning
profited thereby ?

In this case, monks, a certain person has small learning in
Sutta and the rest: but, as of that small learning he knows both
the letter and the meaning, he lives in accordance with Dhamma.
That, monks, is how a person of small learning profits thereby.

And in what way, monks, is a person of wide learning not
profited thereby ?

In this case, monks, a certain person'has wide learning in
Sutta and the rest: but, as of that wide learning he understands
neither the letter nor the meaning, he lives not in accordance
with Dhamma. That, monks, is how a person of wide learning
profits not thereby.

And in what way, monks, is a person of wide learning
profited thereby ?

In this case, monks, a certain person has wide learning in
Sutta . . . and the rest: but, as of that wide learning he
understands both the letter and the meaning, he is profited
thereby. That, monks, is how a person of wide learning
profits thereby.

So these are the four persons found existing in the world.

> If one have little learning, and withal[3]
> No concentration in his doing,[4] men
> Will blame him both in learning and in deeds.

---

[1] *Cf. Pugg.* 43; *Vin.* iii, 8; *M.* i, 133; *infra,* §§ 102, 186. A late insertion
of the ninefold Buddhist Scriptures, not collected at that time, classed
according to their contents—viz.: Discourses proper,discourses mixed with
verses, expository matter, verses proper, short stories illustrating the
' solemn sayings,' the logia, the birth-stories, the marvels, and certain
catechetical suttas. *Comy.* explains in detail.

[2] *Attha-dhamma.*

[3] These gāthas are quoted at *V.M.* i, 48 and trans. by Prof. Maung Tin
in *Path of Purity,* i, 54. The last two lines are at *Dhp.* 230.

[4] *Sīlena asamāhito.*

If one have little learning, and withal
Much concentration in his doing, men
Will praise his deeds, his learning not complete.

And if one have much learning, and withal
No concentration in his doing, men
Will blame his deeds, his learning being complete.
And if one have much learning, and withal
Much concentration in his doing, men
Will praise him both for learning and for deeds.

The Buddha's deeply learnèd follower,
One who is Dhamma-bearer,[1] who is wise
And, like the gold of Jambu,[2] without blame.—
Devas praise him, Brahmā too praiseth him.'

§ vii (7). *Illuminates*[3] *(the Order).*

' Monks, these four who are accomplished in wisdom, disciplined, confident,[4] deeply learned, Dhamma-bearers, who live according to Dhamma,—these four illuminate the Order. Which four ?

A monk who is accomplished in wisdom . . . who lives according to Dhamma, illuminates the Order: a nun who is accomplished in wisdom . . . illuminates the Order: so also do lay-disciples, both male and female. These are the four who, being accomplished in wisdom, disciplined, confident, deeply learned, Dhamma-bearers, living in accordance with Dhamma, illuminate the Order.

---

[1] *Dhamma-dharo.*

[2] *Nekkhaŋ Jambonadassa (cf. infra,* text 29), pure gold found acc. to some in the Jambu river. *Cf. UdA.* 416. *Comy. jāti-suvaṇṇa* : but from the *jambu*-tree acc. to *SA.* i, 125 (of an ornament or necklet of sterling gold), def. as *mahājambu-sākhāya pavatta-nadiyaŋ nibbattaŋ : mahājambu-palāse vā paṭhaviyaŋ paviṭṭhe suvaṇṇ.' ankurā uṭṭhahanti* (somewhat like Vergil's Golden Bough at *Æn.* vi).

[3] *Sobhati* is the uddāna-title; *cf. Dial.* ii, 114; *S.* iv, 375. *Comy. paññā-veyyattiyena* (accomplished) *samannāgato.*

[4] *Visārado.*

Whoso is wise and confident,
Of learning deep, a Dhamma-bearer,
And lives accordantly therewith,—
" Light of the Order " such is called.

The virtuous monk, the learnèd nun,
The layman and laywoman staunch,
These four illuminate the Order.
" Lights of the Order " they are called.'[1]

§ viii (8). *Confidence.*[2]

'Monks, these are the four confidences of a Tathāgata, possessed of which a Tathāgata knows his place as leader of the herd, utters his lion's roar in the companies and sets rolling the Brahma-wheel.[3] What are the four ?

As to the charge made: You who claim to be perfectly enlightened are not perfectly enlightened in these things,—I see no grounds, monks, for showing that any recluse or brāhmin, that any Deva or Māra or Brahmā, that anyone in the whole world can with justice make this charge. Since I see no grounds for such a charge, I abide in the attainment of peace, of fearlessness, of confidence.

As to the charge made: You who claim to have destroyed the āsavas have not destroyed these āsavas,—I see no grounds, monks, to show that any recluse or brāhmin . . . can with justice make this charge. Since this is so, I abide in the attainment of peace, of fearlessness, of confidence.

As to the charge made: The things declared by you to be hindrances[4] have no power to hinder him that follows them,—I see no grounds, monks, . . . Since this is so I abide in the attainment of peace, of fearlessness, of confidence.

As to the charge made: The Dhamma preached by you fails in its aim. It does not lead him who acts in accordance

---

[1] *Cf.* text, § 211 for those four who defile the company.

[2] *Vesārajjaŋ. Cf. M.* i, 71 (*Sīhanāda-sutta*), where the ten powers of a T. are detailed.

[3] *Brahma-cakka=Dhamma-c.*   Lit. God-wheel.

[4] *Antarāyikā dhammā .M.* i, 130 *ff.*

therewith to the perfect destruction of Ill,—I see no grounds,
monks, to show that any recluse or brāhmin, that any Deva
or Māra or Brahmā, that anyone in the whole world can with
justice make this charge. Since I see no grounds for such a
charge, I abide in the attainment of peace, of fearlessness, of
confidence.

These, monks, are the four confidences of a Tathāgata,
possessed of which a Tathāgata knows his place as leader of
the herd, utters his lion's roar in the companies and sets
rolling the Brahma-wheel.

> These widespread ways of talk, whate'er they be,
> On which recluse and brāhmin take their stand,—
> When they come near Tathāgata, 'tis said,
> Those utterances are not confident.[1]
> But he who conquering all[2] set rolling on
> The Dhamma-wheel in pity for all creatures,—
> To such, the best of Devas and mankind,
> All beings bow. He hath passed o'er becoming.'[3]

§ ix (9). *Craving*.[4]

' Monks, there are these four grounds for the arising of craving,
whereby craving, if it does so, arises in a monk. What four ?

Because of robes, monks, arises craving in a monk, if it
does arise: because of alms-food . . . because of lodging . . .

---

[1] The reading here is doubtful. Text:

> Tathāgataŋ patvāna te bhavanti
> Visāradaŋ vādapathā ti vuttaŋ.

But *Sinh.* ed.:

> Tathāgataŋ patvā na te bhavanti
> Visāradaŋ (? visāradā) vādapathā ti vattitaŋ.

Acc. to this latter I trans. (They are not *vesārajjāni* like those of the B.)
Comy. appears to follow the *Sinh.* reading, thus: *na te bhavanti*, ' they are
ruined (=*bhijjanti, vinassanti*),' but does not discuss the second of these
lines.

[2] Text *kevaliŋ*; v.l. *kevalo*; *Comy. kevalī*; *Sinh.* text, which I follow
here, *kevalaŋ=sabbaŋ* (*cf. sabbābhibhū* of *Vin.* i, 8, etc.).

[3] *Bhavassa pāraguŋ.*

[4] This sutta occurs at *Itiv.*, p. 109, the gāthas at p. 9. *Cf. Pts. of
Contr.* 69; *D.* iii, 228.

because of success or failure in this or that[1] arises craving in a monk.   These are the four grounds.

> Whoso hath craving as his mate[2]
> To age-long wandering is bound.
> He cannot cross saṃsāra's stream,
> Existence thus or otherwise.
> Knowing the danger of it all,
> Knowing how craving beareth woe,
> Freed from all craving let the monk,
> Ungrasping, mindful, wander forth.'

§ x (10). *Bonds.*

' Monks, there are these four bonds.   What four ?

The bond of passions, that of becoming,[3] that of view and the bond of ignorance.

And of what sort, monks, is the bond of passions ?

Herein a certain one understands not, as they really are, the arising, the passing away, the satisfaction, the disadvantage of and the escape from the passions.   In him who understands not these things as they really are, the passionate lust, the passionate delight, the passionate affection, the passionate greed, the passionate thirst, the passionate fever, cleaving and craving that is in the passions, which occupies his mind,—this, monks, is called " the bond of passions."

So much for the bond of passions.   And how is it with the bond of becoming ?

Herein, monks, a certain one understands not, as they really are, the arising of becomings . . . the escape from becomings.

---

[1] *Itibhavibhava; infra*, § 254. *Cf. D.* i, 8 (*-kathā*, 'talk of this or that ').   Acc. to *Comy.* it refers to loss or gain in food, but in the fuller *Comy.* at *Sn.* 6 *bhava* is contrasted with *vibhava* thus: ' becoming is success, not-becoming failure; becoming is eternality, not-becoming is annihilation; becoming is good, not-becoming is evil; *vibhava* and *abhava* are the same in meaning.'   However, the corresponding word in the gāthās is *ittha-bhāvaññathābhāvaŋ*, 'thus-state or otherwise-state.'

[2] *Taṇhā-dutiyo.   Cf. S.* iv, 37.

[3] ' Passionate desire for becoming in the form-and-formless worlds.' *Comy.*   Bond = *yoga.*

In him who understands not these things, as they really are,
the lust for becomings, the delight in becomings, the affection
for becomings, the greed for becomings, the thirst, fever,
clinging, the craving for becoming that is becomings, which
occupies his mind,—this, monks, is called "the bond of
becoming."

So much for the bond of passions and the bond of becoming.
And how is it with the bond of view ? (*The same is repeated
for view.*)

So much for the bonds of passions, becoming and view.
And what of the bond of ignorance ?

Herein, monks, a certain one understands not, as they
really are, the arising of the six spheres of sense . . . and
escape therefrom. In him who understands not (these things)
as they really are, the ignorance, the nescience of the six
spheres of sense which occupies his mind,—this, monks, is
called "the bond of ignorance."

In bondage to evil, unprofitable things which defile, which
lead to again-becoming, which are distressing and have sorrow
for their result, which are concerned with birth and decay,
he is therefore called "one who rests not from bondage."
These, monks, are the four bonds.

Monks, there are these four releases from the bonds. What
four ?

Herein, monks, a certain one understands, as they really
are, the arising . . . the passing away . . . of passions (*the
rest is the reverse of the above*).

Set free from evil, unprofitable things which defile . . .
which are concerned with birth and decay, therefore is he
called "one who rests from bondage." These, monks, are the
four releases from the bonds.

> Bound by the bond of passions and becoming,[1]
> Bound by the bond of view, by ignorance
> Circled about,[2] to birth and death returning
> Creatures go faring on saṇsāra's round.

---

[1] The first half of these gāthas is at *Itiv.* 95.
[2] *Purakkhatā=purato katā parivāritā vā. Comy.*

But they who, passions fully comprehending,
Have learned becoming's bond and have thrown off
The bond of view and ignorance abandoned,[1]
Freed from all bonds have surely bonds transcended.'

CHAPTER II.—DEPORTMENT.[2]

§ i (11). *Deportment.*

' Monks, if while he walks there arise in a monk thoughts sensual or malign or cruel, and that monk admits them, does not reject and expel them, does not make an end of them, does not drive them out of renewed existence, a monk who while walking becomes thus is called " void of zeal and unscrupulous, always and for ever sluggish and poor in energy."

If while he stands still . . . while he sits . . . while he lies awake there arise in a monk thoughts sensual, malign or cruel, and that monk admits them . . . a monk who while lying awake becomes thus is called " poor in energy."

But if, while he walks . . . stands . . . sits . . . lies awake, such thoughts arise and he does not admit them, but rejects, expels, makes an end of them, drives them out of renewed existence,—a monk who while walking . . . standing . . . sitting . . . lying awake becomes such an one is called " ardent, scrupulous, always and for ever strong in energy and resolute."

Whether he walk or stand or sit or[3] lie,
The monk who thinks of evil, worldly things,[4]
Walking the wrong path, by delusion blinded,
Can never touch supreme enlightenment.

---

[1] *Virājayaŋ* (part. of *virājeti*, where the gerund should be used: prob. for *virājiya*, as at *S.* i, 15, where *Comy.* expl. as *virājitvā)=virājento vā virājetvā vā. Comy.*

[2] The uddāna-title of this vagga is derived from § i, *caraŋ* (really ' walking '), which embraces the four bodily postures. The sutta occurs at *Itiv.* 115, where the readings of our text of *ce* after *caraŋ, ṭhito, nisinno* are rightly omitted; so also in *Sinh.* text.

[3] For gāthas (at *Itiv.* 82) *cf. Sn.* 193; *Ud.* 61. Text should read *uda vā.*

[4] *Geha-nissitaŋ =kilesa-n. Comy.*

Whether he walk or stand or sit or lie,
The monk, controlling thoughts, who takes delight
In ceasing from all thoughts,—sure such an one
Is fit to touch supreme enlightenment.'

§ ii (12). *Virtue.*[1]

'Monks, do ye live perfect in virtue, do ye live perfect in
the performance of the obligations,[2] restrained with the restraint of the obligations, perfect in the practice of right
behaviour; seeing danger in the slightest faults, undertake and
train yourselves in the training of the precepts. For him
who so lives . . . so restrained . . . who undertakes the
training of the precepts, what else remains to be done ?

If, as he walks, coveting-and-ill-will have vanished from a
monk: if sloth-and-torpor, excitement-and-flurry, doubt-and-
wavering are abandoned: if his energy be stout and unshaken:
if his mindfulness be established and unperturbed: if his body
be calm and tranquil, his mind composed and one-pointed,—a
monk become thus as he walks is called " ardent, scrupulous,
always and for ever strong in energy and resolute."

If, as he stands . . . sits . . . lies awake, he becomes thus,
he is so called.

Whether he walk or stand or sit or lie
Or stretch his limbs or draw them in again,
Let him do all these things composedly.
Above, across, and back again returning[3]—
Whatever be one's bourn in all the world[4]—
Let him be one who views[5] the rise and fall
Of all compounded things attentively.[6]
For mind's composure doing what is right,
Ever and always training,—" ever intent "—
That is the name men give to such a monk.'

---

[1] This sutta occurs at *Itiv.* 118.
[2] *Pāṭimokkha. Cf. D.* i, 63; *M.* i, 33; *VM.* i, 15; *Vibh.* 244.
[3] *Apācinaŋ*=back again.
[4] *Jagato gati=lokassa nipphatti. Comy.*
[5] Text should read *samavekkhitā.*   [6] Here *Itiv.* inserts a line.

§ iii (13). *Effort.*

'Monks, there are these four right efforts.[1] What four ?

Herein a monk generates desire for the non-arising of evil, unprofitable states that have not yet arisen. He makes an effort, sets going energy, he lays hold of and exerts his mind (to this end). He generates desire for the abandoning of evil, unprofitable states that have arisen: he makes an effort . . . He generates desire for the arising of profitable states not yet arisen: he makes an effort . . . He generates desire for the persisting, for the non-confusion, for the more-becoming, for the increase, cultivation and fulfilment of profitable states that have arisen: he makes an effort, sets going energy, he lays hold of and exerts his mind (to this end). These, monks, are the four right efforts.

By right exertion they have conquered Māra's realm:[2]
Freed, they have passed beyond the fear of birth and death:
Those happy ones have vanquished Māra and his host
And, from all power of Namuci escaping, are in bliss.'[3]

§ iv (14). *Restraint.*

'Monks, there are these four efforts. What four ?

The effort to restrain, the effort to abandon, the effort to make become, and the effort to watch over.

And of what sort, monks, is the effort to restrain ?

Herein[4] a monk, seeing an object with the eye, is not entranced by its general features or by its details. Inasmuch as coveting and dejection, evil, unprofitable states, might flow in upon one who dwells with this eye-faculty uncontrolled, he applies himself to such control, sets a guard over the eye-faculty, wins the restraint thereof. Hearing a sound with the

---

[1] The four *sammappadhānāni*, described at *D.* ii, 120; *M.* ii, 11 and elsewhere [*cf. VibhA.* 291 *ff.*) and called ' co-factors of struggling,' *K.S.* v, 173, 239 and *infra*, vii, § 9. *Samma* = *sundara, uttama, paripuṇṇa*. *Comy.*

[2] Text *Māradheyyādhibhuno*; *Sinh.* text -*abhibhūtā.*

[3] *Comy.* compares gāthas at *S.* iii, 83, *sukhino vata arahanto*, etc. Namuci, a name for Māra. *Comy.* on *S.* v, 1 explains it as *na-muñcati,* ' does not let one go.'

[4] *Cf. D.* i, 70; *Pts. of Contr.* 264; *K.S.* iv, 63; *SnA.* 7 *ff.*

ear, or with the nose smelling an odour, or with the tongue tasting a savour, or with body contacting tangibles, or with mind cognizing mental states, he is not entranced by their general features or by their details; but, inasmuch as coveting . . . might flow in upon one who dwells with this mental faculty uncontrolled, he applies himself to such control . . . wins restraint thereof. This, monks, is called "the effort to restrain."

And of what sort, monks, is the effort to abandon ?

Herein a monk does not admit sensual thought that has arisen, but abandons it, expels it, makes an end of it, drives it out of renewed existence. So also with regard to malign and cruel thought that has arisen. He does not admit evil, unprofitable states that arise from time to time . . . he drives them out of renewed existence. This, monks, is called "the effort to abandon."

And of what sort is the effort to make become ?

Herein a monk makes to become the limb of wisdom[1] that is mindfulness, that is based on seclusion, on dispassion, on ending, that ends in self-surrender. He makes to become the limb of wisdom that is investigation of Dhamma . . . the limb of wisdom that is energy, that is so based. He makes to become the limb of wisdom that is zest . . . that is tranquillity . . . that is concentration . . . that is equanimity, based on seclusion, on dispassion, on ending, that ends in self-surrender. This, monks, is called "the effort to make become."

And of what sort, monks, is the effort to watch over ?

Herein a monk watches over the favourable concentration-mark,[2] the idea of the skeleton,[3] the idea of the worm-eaten

---

[1] *Cf. K.S.* v, 51 *ff. The limbs of wisdom* (where in my trans. that of ' zest ' is by error omitted).

[2] *Bhaddakaŋ samādhi-nimittaŋ. Cf. A.* i, 115; *G.S.* i, 100; *VM.* i, 123; *Compendium,* 54 (the *dasa asubhāni*). This is the reflex image of the object of his exercise. *Comy.* calls it *bhaddakaŋ* and refers to the meditation on the repulsive things, *VM.* i, 173. Presumably, by concentrating on the unlovely, he realizes the lovely by contrast. See *Path of Purity,* ii, 147: ' To him who guards the sign there is no loss of what has been obtained. Whoso neglects to guard it loses all that he obtained.'

[3] *Aṭṭhika-saññā. Cf. S.* v, 129; *K.S.* v, 110. To meditate on these ideas is said to lead to *sukha-vihāraŋ.*

corpse, of the discoloured corpse, of the fissured corpse, the idea of the inflated corpse. This is called "the effort to watch over."

These then, monks, are the four efforts.

> Restraint, abandoning, making-become, watching o'er,
> These are the four (best) efforts taught by him,
> The Kinsman of the Sun.[1]   Herein a monk,
> Ardently striving, makes an end of Ill.'

§ v (15). *Types.*[2]

'Monks, there are these four chief types (of beings). What four ?

Chief of those who have personality is[3] Rāhu, lord of the Asuras. Chief of those who are given to the pleasures of sense is Mandhātā[4] the rājah. Chief of those who have lordship is Māra the Wicked One. In the world of Devas, Māras and Brahmās, together with recluses and brāhmins, devas and mankind, a Tathāgata is reckoned chief, an Arahant, a perfectly Enlightened One. These, monks, are the four chief types.

> Rāhu is chief of persons: chief of those
> Enjoying sense-delights is Mandhātā:
> Māra is chief of those who lordship own:
> With power and glory[5] is he radiant.
> Above, across, and back again returning,
> Whatever be one's bourn in all the world,[6]
> Of world and devas chief is held a Buddha.'

§ vi (16). *The subtle.*[7]

'Monks, there are these four powers over the subtle. What four ?

Herein a monk is possessed of the power to penetrate the

---

[1] *Ādicca-bandhu.*   *Cf. S.* i, 186, 192, iii, 142.

[2] *Paññattiyo.*   [3] *Attabhāvin.*

[4] *Cf. JA.* ii, 310; *Mil.* 115; *Thag.* 485.

[5] Text should read *yasasā* for *yassā.*   [6] *Cf. supra,* § 2.

[7] *Sokhummāni.* Uddāna calls the sutta *Sukhumaŋ. Comys.* read *sukhumāni* and def. as 'knowledge of how to penetrate the subtle characteristics.'

subtilty of body, and he beholds not any other power more
excellent or more refined than that one; he aspires not for any
other power to penetrate the subtilty of body more excellent
and refined than that. He is possessed of a like power with
regard to feeling . . . to perception . . . to the activities,[1]
and he beholds not, aspires not for any power of penetrating
subtilty more excellent and more refined than that. These
are the four.

> Knowing the subtilty of form and knowing
> How feelings come to be, and whence arises
> Perception, how it ends, knowing th' activities
> As other and as ill, but not as self:[2]
> (These things) if he do see aright, the monk,
> At peace, delighting in the place of peace,
> Beareth the final body (in the world),
> For he hath conquered Māra and his mount.'[3]

§ vii (17). *No-bourn.*[4]

'Monks, there are these four goings to the no-bourn. What
four ?

One goes to the no-bourn through desire, ill-will, delusion,
or fear.[5] These are the four.

> Led by desire, ill-will, delusion, fear,
> If one transgresses Dhamma, his good name
> Fades as the moon in the dark fortnight wanes.'

§ viii (18). *Bourn.*

'Monks, there are these four goings to the bourn. What
four ?

---

[1] *Sankhārā.* 'Synergies' has been suggested by Mrs. Rhys Davids.

[2] *Parato . . . dukkhato . . . no ca attato.* Cf. *S.* i, 188, *Sankhāre
parato passa, dukkhato mā ca attato. Cf. K.S.* i, 239.

[3] Māra is pictured as riding into battle on an elephant.

[4] *Agati,* not leading to the *gati* or bourn: sometimes taken as Nibbāna
(for one who has reached it there is no goal further, acc. to the orthodox
interpretation). Here def. by *Comy.* (as at *VM.* ii, 683) as wrong
action done under the influence of desire, hate or delusion.

[5] Quoted *Netti,* 129, 162, where it is added that the Teacher spoke
these gāthās.

One goes not to the no-bourn through desire, ill-will, delusion, fear. These are the four.

> Led by desire, ill-will, delusion, fear,
> If one transgress not Dhamma, his good name
> Waxes, as in the bright fortnight the moon.'[1]

§ ix (19). *Bourn and no-bourn*

(*A combination of* vii *and* viii.)[2]

§ x (20). *The food-steward.*

'Monks, possessed of four qualities a food-steward is put into Purgatory according to his deserts.[3] What are the four ?

He goes to the no-bourn through desire, ill-will, delusion and fear. Possessed of these four qualities a food-steward is put into Purgatory according to his deserts.

Monks, possessed of four qualities a food-steward is put into Heaven according to his deserts. What four ? (*The opposite of the above.*)

> Whatever folk are unrestrained in lusts,
> Not led by Dhamma or respect for Dhamma,[4]
> Led by desire, ill-will and fear they go:[5]
> " A blemish to the company "[6] they're called.
> Thus was it said by the Samaṇa who knows.[7]

> Therefore those worthy ones and worthy praise
> Who, fixed in Dhamma, do no evil deed,
> Not going by desire, ill-will and fear,—
> " Cream of the company " such ones are called.
> Thus was it said by the Samaṇa who knows.'

---

[1] *Cf. D.* iii, 182 (*Sigālovāda-sutta*).

[2] Spoken thus, says *Comy.*, for the sake of the ' intelligent.'

[3] *Yathābhataŋ. Cf. A.* i, 8; *G.S.* i, 6 *n.*; *infra*, Ch. VII, 4. For the food-steward or almoner (*bhattuddesako*) *cf.* Vin. i, 58; *A.* iii, 274; *JA.* i, 5. There were evidently ' unjust stewards ' in those days.

[4] *Dhammika* seems to be the equivalent of ' conscientious.'

[5] The gāthas omit the third quality, *moha*.

[6] *Parisa-kkasāvo. Cf. infra*, text 225 (*p. dussana*) and *Dhp.* v. 9. *Kasāva* is an astringent, opp. to *maṇḍa* below; *Comy.* paraphr. by *p-kacavara* (dust-heap).

[7] Here and below text should read *samaṇena jānatā*.

CHAPTER III.—URUVELĀ.

§ i (21). *At Uruvelā (a).*[1]

On a certain occasion the Exalted One was staying near Sāvatthī, at Jeta Grove in Anāthapiṇḍika's Park. Then the Exalted One addressed the monks, saying: 'Monks.'

'Yes, lord,' replied those monks to the Exalted One.

'On a certain occasion, monks, I myself was staying at Uruvelā, on the bank of the river Nerañjarā, under the Goatherds' Banyan,[2] just after I had become fully enlightened. To me then occurred this thought as I was meditating alone: Ill at ease dwells the man who reverences not, obeys not. What if[3] I were to dwell doing honour and paying reverence to some recluse or brāhmin, and serving him?

Then, monks, it was I who had this thought: For the perfection of the sum total of virtues[4] still imperfect I would dwell so doing honour, obeying, reverencing and serving a recluse or brāhmin: but not in this world with devas, Māras, Brahmās, not in the host of recluses and brāhmins, not in the world of devas and mankind do I behold any other recluse or brāhmin more perfect in virtue than myself, whom honouring I could dwell reverencing, obeying and serving him.

For the perfection of the sum total of concentration still imperfect I would dwell . . . for the perfection of the sum total of wisdom . . . for the perfection of the sum total of release still imperfect I would dwell so doing honour . . . but not in this world . . . not in the world of devas and mankind do I behold any other recluse or brāhmin more perfect in concentration, in wisdom, in release than myself, whom honouring I could dwell reverencing, obeying and serving him.

---

[1] In Magadha. *Cf. Asl.* 219; *Expos.* ii, 296; *UdA.* 26, where the name is said to mean 'sand-heap.' The well-known incidents here repeated occur at *S.* i, 138; *K.S.* i, 174.

[2] See *K.S.* i, 128 *n.*

[3] Text *kinnu kho*; Sinh. text *kannu kho*.

[4] *Sīla(-samādhi-paññā-vimutti)-khandha. Cf. A.* i, 125; *G.S.* i, 107, where it is said that one should worship, revere, follow, serve and honour one superior to oneself in these qualities.

Then, monks, it was I who had this thought: Suppose this Dhamma in which I have been perfectly enlightened,—suppose I were to dwell honouring, reverencing, obeying and serving this Dhamma ?

Thereupon, monks, Brahmā Sahampati, knowing the thought that was in my mind, just as a strong man might straighten out his bent arm or bend in his outstretched arm, just so did he vanish from the Brahma world and appear in front of me.

Then, monks, Brahmā Sahampati, placing his outer robe over one shoulder and with his right knee pressing the ground,[1] stretched out his joined palms towards me and said this:

"Even so, Exalted One! Even so, Wellfarer! Whosoever were in time past arahants, perfectly enlightened ones, lord, those reverend ones also dwelt honouring, reverencing, obeying and serving Dhamma. Whosoever, lord, in future time shall be arahants . . . shall also dwell honouring . . . and serving Dhamma. So also now, lord, let the Exalted One who is arahant, a perfectly enlightened one, dwell honouring, reverencing, obeying and serving Dhamma." Thus spake Brahmā Sahampati. So saying he added this further:

"The Perfect Buddhas who have passed,
The Perfect Buddhas yet to come,
The Perfect Buddha who is now,
And hath for many banished woe,—
All dwelt their dhamma[2] honouring,
Do dwell[3] and shall dwell: 'tis their way.[4]
So he to whom the self is dear,[5]

---

[1] In the *S.* version the Editor has read *attha-kāmo,* 'welfare is dear.'

[2] *Saddhamma.* See below, Ch. V, 3, 4, where occur both *saddhamma* and *dhamma.* It *may* mean *saka-dhamma,* the standard each one follows ('the voice of conscience,' § 246 *n.*).

[3] *Comy.* pointing out that there is only one Buddha at a time quotes:

Na me ācariyo atthi, sadiso me na vijjati.
Sadevakasmiṃ lokasmiṃ n' atthi me paṭipuggalo.
(*Vin.* i, 8=*M.* i, 171.)

[4] *Esa Buddhāna-dhammatā. Cf. M.* iii, 121.

[5] *Attakāma. Cf. S.* 1, 75=*Ud.* v, 1 (but *VM.* 297 quoting it prefers the reading *attha-k.*). The reading at *S.* is *attha* (weal).

Who longeth for the great Self[1]—he
Should homage unto Dhamma pay,
Remembering the Buddha-word."[2]

Thus spake Brahmā Sahampati, monks. So saying he saluted me and keeping me on his right side vanished there and then.

Then, monks, seeing that it was the wish of the Brahmā and proper for myself, I dwelt honouring, reverencing, obeying and serving that very Dhamma which had been well comprehended by me. Moreover, monks, since the Order has become possessed of greatness, I hold the Order also in strict regard.'[3]

§ ii (22). *At Uruvelā (b).*

'On a certain occasion, monks, I myself was staying at Uruvelā on the bank of the river Nerañjarā, under the Goatherds' Banyan, just after I had become perfectly enlightened.

Then, monks, a great number of brāhmins, broken-down old men, aged, far gone in years, who had reached life's end, came to visit me where I was. On reaching me they greeted me courteously, and after the exchange of greetings and courtesies sat down at one side. As they sat thus, monks, those brāhmins said this to me:

"We[4] have heard it said, master Gotama, that Gotama the recluse pays no respect to, does not rise up in presence of, does not offer a seat to brāhmins who are broken-down old men, aged, far gone in years, who have reached life's end.[5] Inasmuch, master Gotama, as[6] the worthy Gotama does none of

---

[1] *Mahattaŋ*; text *mahantaŋ*; v.l. *mahattiŋ=mahanta-bhāvaŋ. Comy.* But *cf. G.S.* i, 227.

[2] *Saraŋ* (part. nom. by poetic licence) *Buddhāna-sāsanaŋ.*

[3] *Tibba-gāravo.* This last § is not in *S.* i. It has the appearance of having been added to make up the 'Triple Gem' (*Buddha-dhamma-sangha*), a later conception. *Comy.* remarks: 'When was the Order honoured? It was when Mahāpajāpatī offered the set of robes to the Master (*M.* iii, 253), who then said: "Give them to the Order, Gotamid. If you do so, both I myself and the Order will be honoured."'

[4] Text should read *sutaŋ no* for *ne. Comy.* has *n' etaŋ=no etaŋ*; *Sinh.* text *m' etaŋ.* [5] As at *A.* i, 67=*G.S.* i, 63; *A.* iv, 173.

[6] *Yadidaŋ* here is preferable to *tayidaŋ* of text and *A.* iv.

these things, it is not the proper thing to do,[1] master Gotama."

Then, monks, I thought to myself: In truth these reverend ones understand not either the elder, or the things which make an elder.[2]

Though a man be old, monks, eighty or ninety or a hundred years of age, yet if he be one who speaks out of due season, who speaks things untrue and unprofitable, things contrary to Dhamma and contrary to Discipline: if he be one who utters words unworthy to be treasured in the heart,[3] words unseasonable and void of reason, words undiscriminating and not concerned with welfare,—then that one is reckoned just a foolish elder.

Though a man be young, monks,—a youth, a mere lad, black haired and blessed with his lucky prime, one in the first flush of life,—if he be one who speaks in due season, who speaks things true and profitable, things according to Dhamma and Discipline: if he be one who utters words worthy to be treasured in the heart, words seasonable, reasonable, discriminating and concerned with welfare,—then that one is reckoned a wise elder.

Now, monks, there are these four things which make the elder. What four ?

Herein a monk is virtuous, perfect in the obligations, restrained with the restraint of the obligations, perfect in the practice of right behaviour, seeing danger in the slightest faults. He undertakes and trains himself in the training of the precepts, he has learned,[4] is replete with learning, is a hoard[5] of learning. Those doctrines which, lovely at the beginning, lovely in the middle, lovely at the end (of life)

---

[1] *Na sampannaŋ=ananucchavikaŋ. Comy.* (at *A.* i, *na yuttaŋ*).

[2] *Thera* and *thera-karaṇe dhamme.*

[3] As at *D.* i, 4 and with *Comy.* text should read *anidhānavatiŋ vācaŋ bhāsitā* for *tanidāna.* (*Comy. na hadaye nidhetabba-yuttakaŋ.*) *Cf. infra,* § 198.

[4] *Suta. Cf. KhpA.* 102. *Comy.* likens him to a full pot which does not leak.

[5] *Sannicayo. Cf. A.* i, 94.

both in the meaning and the letter of them, which preach the
utterly fulfilled, the perfectly purified way of the God-life,—
such doctrines are much heard by him, borne in mind, repeated aloud,[1] pondered over and well penetrated by his
vision.[2] The four stages of musing which are of the clear
consciousness,[3] which are concerned with the happy life in
this very world,—these he wins easily, without effort. By
the destruction of the āsavas, in this very life thoroughly
understanding the heart's release, the release by wisdom, he
realizes it, attains it and dwells therein.

These, monks, are the four things which make the elder.

He who with swollen mind doth utter
Much idle talk, his purpose void
Of all restraint, nor takes delight
In very dhamma,[4] is a fool.
Far from the rank of elder he.
Evil his view, he lacks regard.

He who, in virtue perfect, learned,
Of ready wit, controlled, a sage,
With wisdom sees the sense of things,[5]
Of open heart,[6] of ready wit,
He hath transcended every state.

Who hath abandoned birth and death,
Who in the God-life perfect is,—
That is the man I elder call.
By ending of the āsavas
A monk is rightly elder called.'

---

[1] *Vacasā paricitā=vācāya sajjhayitā. Comy.*

[2] *Ditthiyā=paññāya. Comy.*

[3] *Abhicetasika=abhikkhanta-visuddha-cittaɳ. Comy.*

[4] *Asaddhamma-rato.* See above on § i of this chapter, and on
§ 246.

[5] *Paññāy' atthaɳ.* So *Comy.* and *Sinh.* text, but our text *paññāyattha.*
' With Way-insight [or wisdom] he sees the meaning of the four truths.'
Comy.

[6] *Akhila.*

§ iii (23). *The world.*

'Monks, the world[1] is fully comprehended by a Tathāgata. From the world a Tathāgata is released. Monks, the arising of the world is fully comprehended by a Tathāgata: the arising of the world is abandoned by a Tathāgata. The ending of the world is fully comprehended by a Tathāgata: the ending of the world is realized by a Tathāgata. Monks, the practice going to the ending of the world is fully comprehended by a Tathāgata: the practice going to the ending of the world is made to become by a Tathāgata.

Monks, whatsoever in the whole world, with the world of Māras, Brahmās, together with the host of recluses and brāhmins, of devas and mankind, is seen, heard, sensed, cognized, attained, searched into, pondered over by the mind,—all that is fully comprehended by a Tathāgata. That is why he is called "Tathāgata." Moreover, whatever a Tathāgata utters, speaks and proclaims between the day[2] of his enlightenment and the day on which he passes utterly away,—all that is just so[3] and not otherwise. Therefore is he called "Tathāgata."

Monks, as a Tathāgata speaks, so he does: as he does, so he speaks. That is why he is called "Tathāgata."

Monks, in the whole world, with the world of Devas, of Māras, of Brahmās . . . of devas and mankind, a Tathāgata is conqueror, unconquered, all-seeing,[4] omnipotent. Therefore is he called "Tathāgata."

> By comprehending all the world
> In all the world just as it is,
> From all the world is he released,
> In all the world he clings to naught.[5]

---

[1] *Comy.* takes *loko* to mean *dukkha-saccaŋ.* This § occurs at *Itiv.* 121 with slight differences. *Cf.* the First Utterance in *Vinaya*, i, 10; *D.* iii, 135.

[2] 'Night' acc. to the Indian use.   [3] *Tatth' eva.*

[4] *Añña-d-atthu-dasa*, lit. 'come-what-may-seeing.'

[5] *Anūpayo* (Windisch at *Itiv.* 122 prefers *anūpamo*); for *anūpaya cf. S.* i, 181 =*taṇhā-diṭṭhi-upāyehi virahito. Comy.*

He is the all-victorious sage:
'Tis he who loosens every bond:
By him is reached[1] the perfect peace
(Nibbāna) that is void of fear.[2]

The Enlightened One, the passion-free,
Sinless, who hath cut off all doubts,
Hath reached the end of every deed,
Freed by removal of the base.[3]

Exalted One, Enlightened he,
The lion he without compare.
For the deva-world and world of men
He caused the Brahma-wheel to roll.

Wherefore the devas and mankind
Who went for refuge to the Seer
Meeting shall pay him homage due,
The mighty one, of wisdom ripe.[4]

" Tamed, of the tamed is he the chief:
Calmed, of the calm is he the sage:
Freed, of the freed topmost is he:
Crossed o'er, of them that crossed the best ":

So saying shall they honour him
The mighty one, of wisdom ripe,—
" In the world of devas and mankind
None is there who can equal thee." '

§ iv (24). *Kāḷaka.*[5]

On a certain occasion the Exalted One was staying at Sāketa,
in Kāḷaka's Park. Then the Exalted One addressed the
monks, saying: ' Monks.'

---

[1] Text should read *phuṭṭhassa*, ' gen. for instrumental.' *Comy.* It
is, however, not gen. but dative.

[2] *A-kuto-bhaya.*

[3] *Upadhi*, substrate.

[4] *Vitasārada*, ' free from sprouting again.' *Cf. supra* on Ch. I, § 8;
Itiv. 76.

[5] Acc. to *Comy.* he was a rich man who gave a park to the Order.
Sāketa was a town in Kosala. *Cf. Buddh. India*, 39.

' Yes, lord,' replied those monks to the Exalted One.   The
Exalted One said:

' Monks, whatsoever in the world, with its devas . . . with
its host of recluses and brāhmins, of devas and mankind,—
whatsoever is seen, heard, sensed, cognized, attained, searched
into, pondered over by the mind,—all that do I know.   Whatsoever is seen, heard . . . pondered over by the mind,—that
have I fully comprehended: all that is understood by the
Tathāgata, but the Tathāgata is not subject to it.[1]

If I were to say: " I know whatsoever in the world is seen,
heard, and so forth," it would be a falsehood in me.   If I
were to say: " I both know it and know it not," it would be
a falsehood in me.   If I were to say: " I neither know it nor
am ignorant of it," it would be a falsehood in me, that would
be a fault in me.[2]

Thus, monks, a Tathāgata is a seer of what is to be seen,
but he has no conceit[3] of what is seen: he has no conceit of
what has not been seen, he has no conceit of what is to be seen,
he has no conceit about the seer.

Hearing what is to be heard, he has no conceit of what has
been heard or not heard or is to be heard, he has no conceit
about the hearer.   So also sensing what is to be sensed . . .
cognizing the cognizable . . . he has no conceit of the thing
cognized or to be cognized or of him who has cognition.

Thus, monks, the Tathāgata,[4] being such an one in things seen,
heard, sensed, cognized, is " such."   Moreover, than " he who
is such " there is none other greater or more excellent, I declare.

---

[1] *Taŋ Tathāgato na upaṭṭhāsi.   Comy.* has *na upagañchi* (by way of
the sense-doors).   This is expl. by next line of gāthas, *etaŋ ajjhositaŋ
n' atthi.*   The reading at *UdA.* 130, where this passage is quoted, is *taŋ
Tathāgatassa na upaṭṭhāsi,* ' did not occur to (? was not invented or
imagined by) the T.'

[2] *Kali=doso.   Comy.*

[3] Deeming, fancy: *maññati,* as at *S.* iv, 22; *K.S.* iv, 12.

[4] The text is confused here.   Comparing *Comy.* and *Sinh.* text and
punctuating, I get the reading *dhammesu tādiso yeva, tādī ; tamhā ca
pana tāditamhā* (abl. of *tādiso) añño tādī uttaritaro vā,* etc.   *Tādī =arahā,
ariya.*   (*Cf. Sn.* 522, *Nāgo tādi pavuccate tathattā.*)   Full comments on
Tathāgata will be found at *UdA.* 128, 130, where this sutta is quoted.

Whate'er is seen, heard, sensed or clung to is esteemed
As truth by other folk. 'Midst those who are convinced[1]
Not such am I, not one to claim that what they say,
Be it true or false, is ultimate.[2] I long ago[3]
Beheld this barb whereon mankind are hooked, impaled.
I know, I see, to that cling not Tathāgatas.'

§ v (25). *The God-life.*[4]

'Monks, this God-life is not lived to cheat or cajole people.
It is not concerned with getting gain, profit or notoriety. It
is not concerned with a flood of gossip nor with the idea of
"let folk know me as so-and-so." Nay, monks, this God-life
is lived for the sake of self-restraint, for the sake of abandoning,
for the sake of detachment from the passions, for the sake of
making to cease.

For self-restraint and for abandoning,
Heedless of what men say[5] of it, this God-life
Did that Exalted One proclaim as going
Unto the plunge[6] into Nibbāna's stream.

This is the Way whereon great ones, great seers
Have fared ; and they who, as the Buddha taught,
Attain to that, will make an end of ill,
E'en they who what the teacher taught perform.'

§ vi (26). *The cheat.*[7]

'Monks, whatsoever monks are cheats, stubborn, babblers,
astute,[8] insolent, uncontrolled, such are no followers of me.[9]

---

[1] *Saya-sayvutesu=diṭṭhi-gatikā. Comy.*

[2] *Paray=uttamay katvā. Comy.*, which quotes the common boast
'*idam eva saccay, mogham aññan' ti.*

[3] *Paṭigacca.* 'Under the Bodhi tree,' says *Comy.*

[4] As at *Itiv.* 28, which omits *itivāda-* and *virāga-nirodhatthay.*

[5] *Anītihay=iti-ha-parivajjitay, aparapattiyay. Comy.* (avoiding, in-
dependence of, mere talk).

[6] *Ogadha. Cf. A.* i, 168; *S.* v, 344=*K.S.* v, 298 n.

[7] This sutta occurs at *Itiv.* 113. *Cf. Thag.* 959.

[8] *Singī. Comy.* quotes the def. at *Vibh.* 351, lit. 'having a horn.'
VibhA. 476 explains 'in the sense of piercing: a name for the depraved
life of townsfolk.' Trans. at *Brethr.*, p. 337, 'skilled diplomatists.'

[9] *Māmakā=mama santakā. Comy.*

Such have fallen away from this Dhamma-discipline: nor do such monks win growth, increase, prosperity in this Dhamma-discipline.

But, monks, whatsoever monks are no cheats, not stubborn, no babblers, sages, tractable, well controlled, such indeed are followers of me. Such have not fallen away from this Dhamma-discipline: such monks win growth, increase and prosperity therein.

> Cheats, stubborn, babblers, crafty rogues,
> Insolent and uncontrolled,—
> They in Dhamma do not grow
> By the all-wise One declared.

> But honest ones, no babblers, sages,
> Tractable and well controlled,
> They verily in Dhamma grow
> By the all-wise One declared.'

§ vii (27). *Contented.*[1]

'Monks, these four things are trifling, easily gotten and blameless. What four ?

Among robes, monks, rag-robes are a trifling thing, easily gotten and blameless. Of food, monks, alms-food of scraps is a trifling thing . . . of lodgings, monks, the root of a tree is a trifling thing . . . of medicines, monks, ammonia[2] is a trifling thing, easily gotten and blameless too. These are the four trifling things. . . .

Indeed, monks, when a monk is content with trifles that are easily gotten, I declare this to be one of the factors of recluseship.[3]

> Contented with what brings no blame,
> A trifling, easy-gotten thing,
> His mind untroubled by the thought[4]
> Of lodging, robes, or food and drink,

---

[1] At *Itiv.* 102. *Cf. Path of Purity,* i, 76.   [2] *Pūtimutta.*

[3] Here text has *aññataraŋ sāmaññaŋ*, but *Itiv. sāmañ' aṅgaŋ* (factor of recluseship).

[4] To make sense with *vighāto cittassa* text should read *na* for *ca.*

He is not worried where to go.[1]
And thus the things declared to suit
The life of the recluse are won
By that contented, earnest monk.'[2]

§ viii (28). *Lineage*.[3]

' Monks, these four Ariyan lineages, reckoned as ancient, as
of long standing, as traditional, primeval, pure and unadulterated now as then, are not confounded, nor shall they be, are
not despised by discerning recluses and brāhmins. What
are the four ?

Herein, monks, a monk is content with any sort of robes,[4]
and speaks in praise of such content. For the sake of getting
robes he resorts not to unseemly and unbecoming conduct. . . .
If he gets not robes he is not dismayed thereat: and if he does
get them he is free from the bond of selfishness, of greed, of
craving for them. Seeing the danger therein and skilled in
the escape[5] therefrom he makes use of them. Yet does he not
exalt himself because of his content with any sort of robes,
nor does he disparage others (who are not content). Whoso,
monks, is skilled herein, not slothful, but mindful and heedful,
this monk is one who stands firm in the primeval, ancient,
Ariyan lineage.

Then again, a monk is content with any sort of alms-food

---

[1] *Disā na paṭihaññati*. So *Itiv.*, *Sinh.* ed., and *Comy.*—i.e., he is not
vexed by his destination. But our text reads unmetrically *na paṭi-
haññanti*, ' his bearings are not troubled.' *Comy.* apparently takes
disā as abl. sing., meaning ' the direction of a village, etc., where he
might expect alms, etc.'

[2] Text *sikkhato*, but *Comy.*, *Sinh.* ed., and *Itiv. bhikkhuno*.

[3] *Ariya-vaṃsa*. Most of this sutta is in the *Saṅgīti-sutta*, *D.* iii, 224.
Comy. states that it was preached at the Jetavana to forty (?) thousand
monks. This is reckoned the eighth ' lineage,' the seven others being
the Khattiya, Brāhmaṇa, Vessa, Sudda, Samaṇa, Kula and Rāja-
vaṃsas. It is also called *Ariya-tanti* and *Ariya-paveṇi*.

[4] *Comy.* as is natural treats the subject of monkish life in extra-
ordinary detail. Most of the matter will be found at *VM.* i, 62 *ff.*

[5] *Nissaraṇa-puñño*. *Comy.* takes this to mean ' knowing their use
for keeping him warm.'

and speaks in praise of such content. For the sake of getting alms-food he resorts not to what is unseemly and unbecoming. If he gets not alms-food he is not dismayed thereat: and if he does get it he is free from the bond of selfishness,[1] of greed, of craving for it. Seeing the danger therein and skilled in the escape therefrom, he makes use of it. Yet does he not exalt himself because of his content with any sort of alms-food, nor does he disparage others (who are not content). Whoso, monks, is skilled herein . . . this monk is one who stands firm in the primeval, ancient, Ariyan lineage.

Then again, a monk is content with any sort of lodging and speaks in praise of such content. For the sake of getting lodging he resorts not . . . If he gets not lodging he is not dismayed thereat. . . . Whoso, monks, is skilled herein . . . stands firm . . . in the Ariyan lineage.

Once more, monks, a monk delights in abandoning. So delighting he delights in making-become.[2] Yet because of his delight in the one and the other he exalts not himself because of that delight, nor does he disparage others (who delight not therein). Whoso, monks, is skilled herein, not slothful but mindful and heedful, this monk is one who stands firm in the primeval, ancient, Ariyan lineage.

These, monks, are the four Ariyan lineages reckoned as ancient, as of long standing, as traditional, primeval, pure and adulterated now as then; which are not confounded nor shall be, are not despised by discerning recluses and brāhmins.

Moreover, monks, possessed of these four Ariyan lineages, whether a monk dwell in the east or the west, north or south,— wherever he may dwell he masters discontent and content,[3] monks. He is a sage.

> No discontent compels the sage,
> The sage no discontent compels:[4]

---

[1] *Gathita*, lit. bound, tied.

[2] *Pahāna* and *bhāvanā*, *i.e.* in abandoning evil and developing good things.

[3] *Arati-rati-saho.*

[4] *Comy., Sinh.* text *vira-saŋhati* for text's *dhiraŋ sahati* (four times).

The sage doth discontent compel,
Compeller of discontent is he.
Him, that all kamma hath decided[1]
And scattered it, who shall restrain ?
Pure as the gold of Jambu he.
Who is there can speak blame of him ?
Even the devas praise that man:
Praised by Brahmā himself is he.'[2]

§ ix (29). *Factors of Dhamma.*[3]

' Monks, these four factors of Dhamma, reckoned as ancient,
of long standing, as traditional, primeval, pure and unadulterated now as then, are not confounded nor shall they be, are
not despised by discerning recluses and brāhmins. What are
the four ?

Not-coveting, monks, is a factor of Dhamma, reckoned as
ancient . . . not-malice, right mindfulness and right concentration . . . are not despised by discerning recluses and
brāhmins. These are the four factors of Dhamma. . . .

Not covetous, with heart of malice void,
A man should dwell, with concentrated mind,
With mind one-pointed, in the self controlled.'

§ x (30). *Wanderers.*

On a certain occasion the Exalted One was staying near
Rājagaha on Vultures' Peak Hill. Now at that time a great
number of notable Wanderers were in residence on the bank
of the Snake river,[4] in the Wanderers' Park, to wit: the
Wanderers Annabhāra, Varadhara, Sakuludāyin[5] and other
notable Wanderers.

Now at eventide the Exalted One, arising from his solitary

---

[1] *Sinh.* text and *Comy. sabba* (for *sammā* of text) *-kamma*; *Sinh.* text
and text *-vyākataŋ* (determined, settled). Text also reads *kho* for *ko*.

[2] This couplet occurs above, I, § 6. *Cf. Dhp.* 230; *Ud.* 77.

[3] Quoted at *Netti,* 170. *Cf.* D. iii, 229.

[4] *Sappiní :* S. i, 153; *Vin. Texts,* i, 254, n. 2; *infra,* text 176, where
the same Wanderers discuss the ' brāhmin truths '; and *G.S.* i, 168.

[5] The sutta at *M.* ii, 29 is named after this Wanderer.

musing, went towards the bank of Snake river, where was the
Wanderers' Park, and on reaching it sat down on a seat made
ready.   As he sat the Exalted One said this to those Wanderers :

Wanderers, these four factors of Dhamma, reckoned
ancient, of long standing, as traditional, primeval, pure and
unadulterated now as then, are not confounded nor shall
they be, are not despised by discerning recluses and brāhmins.
What are the four ?   (*Here he repeats the previous sutta.*)

Now, Wanderers, if one should thus object: " But I could
point to a recluse or brāhmin who, though he has realized[1] this
Dhamma-factor of not-coveting, is nevertheless covetous,
strongly passionate in his desires,"—of such an one I would
say: " Then let him speak out ! Let him utter speech, and
I shall behold his excellence." Indeed, Wanderers, it is a
thing impossible that such a recluse or brāhmin, so doing, could
be pointed to as covetous, strongly passionate in his desires.

Again, Wanderers, if one should thus object: " But I could
point to a recluse or brāhmin who, though he has realized this
Dhamma-factor of not-malice, is yet malevolent of heart, of
corrupt thoughts,"—of such an one I would say: " Then let
him speak out ! Let him utter speech, and I shall behold his
excellence." Indeed, Wanderers, it is a thing impossible that
such an one, so doing, could be pointed to as malevolent of
heart, as of corrupt thoughts.

Again, Wanderers, if one should thus object: " But I could
point to a recluse or brāhmin who, though he has realized this
Dhamma-factor of right mindfulness, is nevertheless distracted and uncontrolled,"—of such an one I would say:
" Let him speak out then and so forth. . . ."

Again, Wanderers, if one should thus object: " But I could
point to a recluse or brāhmin, who, though he has realized
this Dhamma-factor of right concentration, is nevertheless
not concentrated but flighty-minded,"—of such an one I
would say: " Then let him speak out ! Let him utter speech,
and I shall behold his excellence."

---

[1] *Paccakkhāya* (ger. of *paccakkhāti*) means ' by personal experience,'
not *paṭikkhipitvā* as *Comy.* takes it, for it does not make sense.

Now, Wanderers, whoso should think he ought to censure and despise these four Dhamma-factors of not-coveting, not-malice, right mindfulness and right concentration,—I say that in this very life four righteous reproaches,[1] occasions for censure, come upon that man. What four ?

Thus: If your reverence despises, censures the Dhamma-factor of not-coveting, then (it follows that) those recluses and brāhmins who are covetous, strongly passionate in desires, must be honoured by your reverence, they must be praised by your reverence. And if your reverence censures, despises the Dhamma-factor of not-malice, then (it follows) that those recluses and brāhmins who are malevolent of heart, corrupt in thought, must be honoured by your reverence, they must be praised by your reverence. And if your reverence censures, despises the Dhamma-factor of right mindfulness, then (it follows that) those recluses and brāhmins who are distracted and uncontrolled . . . must be praised by your reverence. And if your reverence censures, despises the Dhamma-factor of right concentration, then (it follows that) those recluses and brāhmins who are not concentrated but flighty-minded must be honoured by your reverence, must be praised by your reverence.

Indeed, Wanderers, whosoever[2] should think he ought to censure and despise these four factors of Dhamma, I say that in this very life these four righteous reproaches, occasions for censure, come upon that man.

Why, Wanderers, even the men of Ukkala, Vassa and Bhañña,[3] who were deniers of the cause, deniers of the deed, deniers of reality,—even they did not judge it fit to censure and despise these four Dhamma-factors. Why so ? Because they feared blame, attack, reproach.

---

[1] *Sahadhammikā vādānupātā. Cf. S.* ii, 33.

[2] Text should read *yo kho.*

[3] This para. occurs at *S.* iii, 72; *K.S.* iii, 63; *Pts. of Contr.* 95; *M.* iii, 78 (which reads *Okkalā*). *Comy.* cites the men as types of extreme views. Trans. at *K.S.* ' Keepers of the retreat (in the rains) and preachers,' which it might mean; but the word *Vassa-Bhañña* is probably a doublet, like *Sāriputta-Moggallānā,* etc.

Without ill-will and mindful ever,
Who in the self (*ajjhattaŋ*) is well composed,
Who trains to discipline his greed,—
He is the one called " diligent." '

CHAPTER IV.—THE WHEEL.

§ i (31). *The wheel.*

' Monks, there are these four wheels,[1] possessed of which on devas and mankind there rolls a four-wheeled prosperity: possessed of which both devas and mankind in no long time attain greatness and increase in prosperity. What are the four wheels ?

They are: dwelling in a fitting place, association with the worthy ones,[2] perfect application of the self,[3] and merit done aforetime. These are the four wheels . . . possessed of which both devas and mankind in no long time attain greatness and increase in prosperity.

If one dwells in a fitting dwelling-place
And friendship makes with Ariyans,[4]
And perfectly applies the self,
And hath aforetime merit done,
There rolls[5] upon him wealth of crops,
Fame, good report and happiness.'

---

[1] *Cf.* D. iii, 276: quoted *Asl.* 58; *Expos.* i, 77; *VibhA.* 399. Here *Comy.* merely def. as *sampattiyo.* 'The four wheels have been declared, but should be classed as the one moment, in the sense of occasion (or, conjuncture), for they are the occasion for the production of merit. *Expos.* These are among the blessings described in *Mahāmangala-sutta, Sn.* 258.

[2] *Sappurisā=ariyā.*

[3] *Atta-sammā-paṇidhi*, lit. ' perfect self-adjustment ' (*Dial.* iii, 254). *Comy.* has *attano sammā-ṭhapanaŋ. KhpA.* 132, *atta-*=' the mind, or, the whole personality.' *Cf. Sammā paṇihitaŋ cittaŋ, Dhp.* 43 and *UdA.* 16 (where *cakka* is discussed).

[4] *Ariya-mitta-karo* (a word not in *Pāli Dict.*).

[5] *Adhivattati*, metaphor of a rolling wheel.

§ ii (32). *Sympathy.*[1]

'Monks, there are these four bases of sympathy. What four ?

Charity, kind speech, doing a good turn and treating all alike.[2] These are the four.

> Charity, kind words, and doing a good turn[3]
> And treating all alike as each deserves:
> These bonds of sympathy are in the world
> Just like the linchpin of a moving car.[4]
> Now if these bonds were lacking, mother who bore
> And father who begat would not receive
> The honour and respect (which are their due).
> But since the wise rightly regard these bonds,
> They win to greatness[5] and are worthy praise.'[6]

§ iii (33). *The lion.*[7]

'Monks, the lion, king of beasts, at eventide comes forth from his lair. Having come forth from his lair he stretches himself. Having done so he surveys the four quarters in all directions. Having done that he utters thrice his lion's roar. Thrice having uttered his lion's roar he sallies forth in search of prey.

Now, monks, whatsoever brute creatures[8] hear the sound of the roaring of the lion, king of beasts, for the most part they are afraid: they fall to quaking and trembling. Those that dwell in holes seek them: water-dwellers make for the

---

[1] *Sangaha*, what holds together (the linchpin of the gāthas). *Cf. D.* iii, 152; *infra*, text 248 and *n.* on § 9 of Ch. IV.

[2] *Samānattā*='impartiality,' but *Comy.* takes it as 'imperturbability' (*samāna-sukha-dukkha-bhāvo*).

[3] *Attha-cariyā*, lit. conduct in or for welfare.

[4] *Cf. Sn.* 654, *kamma-nibandhanā sattā rathass' āṇī va yāyato.*

[5] Read *mahattaŋ* for text's *mahantaŋ*.

[6] Gāthas at *JA.* v, 330 (*Sona-Nanda J.*), where Fausböll's punctuation has misled the translator of the Cambridge ed. volume. They are continued *infra*, text 70=*A.* i, 132; *Itiv.* 109.

[7] At *S.* iii, 84=*K.S.* iii, 70 (a Sāvatthī discourse).

[8] *Tiracchāna-gatā pāṇā*, those which go horizontally, not erect.

water: forest-dwellers enter the forest: birds mount into the air.

Then, monks, whatsoever rājah's elephants in village, town, or rājah's residence are tethered with stout leathern bonds, such burst and rend those bonds asunder, void their excrements and in panic run to and fro. Thus potent, monks, is the lion, king of beasts. over brute creatures: of such mighty power and majesty is he.

Just so, monks, when a Tathāgata arises in the world, an Arahant, a Perfectly Enlightened One, perfect in lore and conduct, Wellfarer, a world-knower, the trainer unsurpassed of men who can be trained, teacher of devas and mankind, a Buddha, an Exalted One,—he teaches Dhamma: "Such is the person-pack: such the origin of the person-pack: such is the ending of the person-pack: such is the practice going to end the person-pack."[1]

Then, monks, whatsoever devas there be, long-lived, lovely, and become happy, for a long time established in lofty palaces,[2] —they too, on hearing the Dhamma-teaching of the Tathāgata, for the most part[3] are afraid: they fall to quaking and trembling, saying: "It seems, sirs, that we who thought ourselves permanent are after all impermanent: that we who thought ourselves stable are after all unstable: not to last, sirs, it seems are we: and lasting we thought ourselves. So it seems, sirs, that we are impermanent, unstable, not to last, compassed about with a person-pack.

Thus potent, monks, is a Tathāgata over the world of devas and mankind: of such mighty power and majesty is he.

---

[1] *Sak-kāya, i.e.* the pack or group or cluster (*kāya* is prob. derived from *ci,* to heap up. *Pāli Dict.*) of oneself. *Cf. nikāya,* etc. *Cf. K.S.* iii, 134 *ff.* At the *Sīha-sutta* of *S.* iii, it is *rūpā, vedanā,* etc., that are mentioned.

[2] *Uccesu vimānesu* (? auras). *Cf. G.S.* i, 164, where the B. claims the power to get ' high seats, the deva-seat and the Ariyan seat.'

[3] *Comy.* remarks: ' Whom does he except ? Devas who are Ariyan followers. These are not afraid because of their having destroyed the āsavas. . . .' It may refer to those who had been followers on earth.

When a Buddha, fully knowing,[1]
Sets the Dhamma-wheel a-rolling—
Teacher he without a rival
Of the devas and the world—
Teaching that the framework[2] ceases
And the framework comes to be,
And the Ariyan Eightfold Way
That leads to calming of all Ill,—
Devas, they who live for ages,
Beauteous, of great renown,
Like the beasts before the lion,
Fall a-trembling, are afraid;
For they have not done with framework.[3]
" Transient, friends," say they, " are we,"
Whenas they hear the Arahant's words,
Of such an one who well is freed.'

§ iv (34). *Faiths.*[4]

' Monks, there are these four best faiths. What four ?

Monks, as compared with creatures, whether footless, bipeds, quadrupeds, or those with many feet, with form or void of form, with sense or void of sense or indeterminate in sense, a Tathāgata, an Arahant, a Fully Enlightened One is reckoned best of them.[5] They who have faith in the Buddha have

---

[1] *Abhiññāya = jānitvā. Comy.*   [2] *Sakkāya. Cf. supra, n.*

[3] *Avītivattā sakkāyaŋ.*

[4] *Pasādā.* This sutta occurs at *Itiv.* 87 (and is included at *A.* iii, 36) in three sections; but to make it a Four the Eightfold Way is here inserted, but this is not in the gāthas, which are the same in all three books. The gāthas deal with the ' triple gem ' and charity (four bests). It is also curious that *Comy.* does not mention the gāthas either here or at *A.* iii. Have they been added from *Itivuttaka* (which for several reasons I conclude to be an older collection than *Anguttara*) ? Or does this show that the prose part is later than, or written up to, the gāthas (a thing which evidently has been done in some cases, not to mention the *Jātaka Comy.*)? *Comy.* on *Ratana-sutta* of *Khuddaka-P.* (*KhpA*) quotes our sutta several times.

[5] *Quoted Vis. Mag.* i, 293, where *yāratā* (an adverb) is incorrectly taken as a pronoun, as also in our *Comy.* Text omits ' that is ' (*yadidaŋ*), which is in the *Itiv.* text.

faith in the best: of those who have faith in the best the result
is best.

Monks, as compared with things compounded, the Ariyan
eightfold way is reckoned best of them. They who have faith
therein have faith in the best: of those who have faith in the
best the result is best.

Monks, as compared with things compounded or not compounded, freedom from passion is reckoned best of them, to
wit: the subduing of pride in self,[1] the restraint of thirst, the
removal of clinging, the cutting off of the base of rebirth, the
destruction of craving, freedom from passion, ending, Nibbāna.
They who have faith in Dhamma (which is passionless)[2] have
faith in the best: of those who have faith in the best the result
is best.

Monks, as compared with orders and companies, the Order
of a Tathāgata's disciples is reckoned best, to wit: the four
pairs of men, the eight types of men,[3] that is, the Exalted
One's Order of disciples. Worthy of honour are they, worthy
of reverence, worthy of offerings, worthy of salutations with
clasped hands,—a field of merit unsurpassed for the world.

Monks, they who have faith in the Order have faith in the
best: of those who have faith in the best the result is best.
These are the four faiths.[4]

> Of those who have faith at its best,
> Who comprehend best Dhamma,
> Of those who have faith in the Buddha,
> Gift-worthy, unsurpassed:
> Of those who have faith in Dhamma,
> Passionless, calming, blissful:

[1] *Mada-nimmadana =māna-mada-purisa-mada*, acc. to *VM. loc. cit.*;
but our *Comy. rāga-mada.* We cannot help noting that all these negative
virtues are regarded as the best things.

[2] *Virāge (dhamme)*, not in text, but at *A.* iii, 36 and *Itiv. Cf. Vimāna
V.* 51, *rāga-virāgam anejam asokaŋ dhammaŋ.*

[3] *Purisa-puggalā. Comy.* does not notice this either here or at
A. iii, 36. *Cf. Dial.* iii, 238: those on the four paths, together with
those who have won the fruits thereof.

[4] *Cf. K.S.* v, 296 *ff.*, where the Buddha remarks that the winning of
four continents is not worth one-quarter of a quarter of these four.

Of those who have faith in the Order,
The field of merit supreme:
Of those who give gifts of their best[1]
The merit doth increase.
Best is their life and beauty,
Fame, good report, bliss, strength.
The sage who gives of his best,
In best of dhammas calmed,
Deva-become or human,
Winning the best rejoiceth.'

§ v (35). *Vassakāra.*[2]

On a certain occasion the Exalted One was staying near
Rājagaha, in Bamboo Grove at the Squirrels' Feeding-ground.

Now on that occasion Vassakāra the brāhmin, a great
official of Magadha, came to visit the Exalted One, and
on coming to him greeted him courteously, and after the
exchange of greetings and courtesies sat down at one side.
As he sat thus Vassakāra the brāhmin said this to the Exalted
One:

'Master Gotama, we brāhmins proclaim a man, if he possesses four qualities, as one of great wisdom, as a great man.
What are the four qualities ?

Herein, master Gotama, he is learned. Of whatsoever he
hears he understands the meaning as soon as it is uttered,
saying: "This is the meaning of that saying. This is the
meaning of that saying." Moreover, he has a good memory,
he can remember and recall a thing done long ago, said long
ago. Again, in all the business of a householder he is skilled
and diligent, and therein he is resourceful and capable of
investigating what is proper to be done, what should be
arranged. Now, master Gotama, if a man possess these
qualities, we proclaim him as one of great wisdom, as a great
man. If the worthy Gotama thinks me worthy of commenda-

---

[1] *Aggassa dātā* is taken by *Comy.* on *Sn.* 217 (*SnA.* ii, 270) as ' off the
top,' ' first-fruits.' *Cf. A.* iii, 42, 51 (*agga-dāyī*).

[2] ' Rain-maker.' *Cf. infra,* text 172; *D.* ii, 72, 87; *M.* iii, 8.

tion herein, let him commend me. On the contrary, if he thinks me blameworthy, let him blame me therefor.'

' Well, brāhmin, I neither commend you nor blame you herein. I myself proclaim a man possessed of four qualities to be one of great wisdom, to be a great man. What are the four ?

Herein, brāhmin, we have a man given up to the welfare of many folk, to the happiness of many folk. By him are many folk established in the Ariyan Method,[1] to wit: in what is of a lovely nature, in what is of a profitable nature. To whatsoever train of thought[2] he wishes to apply himself, to that train of thought he applies himself: to whatever train of thought he desires not to apply himself, to that train of thought he applies not himself. Whatever intention[3] he wishes to intend, he does so or not if he so wishes. Thus is he master of the mind[4] in the ways of thought. Also he is one who attains at will,[5] without difficulty and without trouble the four musings which belong to the higher thought,[6] which even in this very life are blissful to abide in. Also by destruction of the āsavas, in this very life thoroughly comprehending it of himself, he realizes the heart's release, the release by wisdom, and attaining it abides therein.

No, brāhmin, I neither commend nor blame you herein, but I myself proclaim a man possessed of these four qualities to be one of great wisdom, to be a great man.'

' It is wonderful, master Gotama ! It is marvellous, master Gotama, how well this has been said by the worthy Gotama ! I myself do hold the worthy Gotama to be possessed of these same four qualities. Indeed, the worthy Gotama is given up to the welfare of many folk, to the happiness of many folk. By him are

---

[1] *Ñāya. Cf. S.* ii, 68, etc.   [2] *Vitakka.*

[3] *Sankappa.* For the many attempts to translate this word see the table at *Sakya,* p. 85 (Mrs. Rhys Davids).

[4] *Ceto-vasippatto. Cf. supra,* text 6.

[5] *Nikāma-lābhī (MA. attano iccha-vasena. Pāli Dict.* ' giving pleasure ' [?]), *M.* i, 33, 354; *S.* v, 316; *K.S.* v, 280.

[6] *Abhicetasikānaŋ (MA.=visuddha-citta).* Our *Comy.* has nothing to say here of this fairly frequent phrase or at *S.* v.

many folk established in the Ariyan Method, to wit: in what is
of a lovely nature, in what is of a profitable nature. Indeed,
the worthy Gotama, to whatever train of thought he wishes to
apply himself, to that train of thought applies himself. . . .
Surely the worthy Gotama is master of the mind in the ways
of thought. Surely the worthy Gotama is one who attains
at will . . . the four musings . . . Surely the worthy Gotama
by destruction of the āsavas . . . realizes the heart's release,
the release by wisdom . . . and attaining it abides therein.'

' Indeed, brāhmin, your words come close and challenge me
to a statement.[1] Nevertheless I will satisfy you by replying.
I am indeed given up to the welfare of many folk, to the
happiness of many folk. By me are many folk established in
the Ariyan Method, to wit: in what is of a lovely nature, in
what is of a profitable nature. To whatsoever train of
thought I desire to apply myself, to that I apply myself or
not as I please. Whatever intention I wish to intend, I do
so or not as I please. Indeed, brāhmin, I am master of the
mind in the ways of thought. Indeed, I am one who attains
at will . . . the four musings. . . . Indeed, brāhmin, by the
destruction of the āsavas . . . I realize the heart's release . . .
and attaining it abide therein.

> He who for all things found release from Death,
> Who showed their weal to devas and mankind,
> Who taught the Method, Dhamma,[2] seeing which
> And hearing which full many folk are calmed;
> Skilled (guide) of what is right way and what wrong,[3]
> Task-ended he, who hath no āsavas,
> Enlightened One who weareth his last body,—
> He " great in wisdom " and " great man " is called.'

---

[1] *Āsajja upaniya-vācā bhāsitā.* As at *A.* i, 172=*G.S.* i, 156, where
see *n.*

[2] *Cf. D.* ii, 151, *ñāyassa dhammassa padesa-vattī*; *M.* ii, 181, *ñāyaŋ
dhammaŋ kusalaŋ = saka-vipassanakaŋ maggaŋ.* *Comy.*

[3] I read with *Sinh.* text *kusalo katakicco anāsavo* (our text applies
these epithets to *ñāyaŋ*). *Cf. Sn.* 627 (of the brāhmin), *maggāmaggassa
kovidaŋ.*

§ vi (36). *As to the world.*[1]

On a certain occasion the Exalted One was journeying along
the highroad between Ukkaṭṭhā and Setabbya.[2] Now the
brāhmin Doṇa[3] was also journeying along the highroad
between Ukkaṭṭhā and Setabbya. Then the brāhmin Doṇa
beheld on the footprints of the Exalted One the wheel-marks[4]
with their thousand spokes, with their rims and hubs and all
their attributes complete. On seeing these he thought thus:
It is wonderful indeed! It is marvellous indeed! These
will not be the footprints of one in human form.

Just then the Exalted One stepped aside from the highroad
and sat down at the root of a certain tree, sitting cross-legged,
holding his body upright and setting up mindfulness in front
of him. Then the brāhmin Doṇa, following up the Exalted
One's footprints, beheld the Exalted One seated at the foot
of a certain tree. Seeing him comely, faith-inspiring,[5] with
senses calmed, tranquil of mind, in the attainment of composure by masterly control, (like) a tamed, alert, perfectly
trained[6] elephant,[7] he approached the Exalted One and draw-
ing near to him said this:

---

[1] *Loke,* given in the *uddāna.* See Introduction, p. vi.

[2] In Kosala. *Cf. Brethr.* 67; *M.* i, 326. *Comy.* expl. the name of
the former thus: ' built by torchlight (*ukkā*).' At the latter Kassapa
Buddha was said to have been born.

[3] This may be the brāhmin to whom the Buddha's bowl was given
after his death, *D.* ii, 166. *Comy.* pictures him as a master of the three
Vedas, journeying along with 500 youths and teaching them.

[4] For the marks of the ' Superman ' see *Introd.* to *Dial.* iii, 132 *ff.*
(*Lakkhana-sutta*). They seem to have been a brāhmin, not Buddhist,
legend, or part of it, and point to a later period when the Buddha's
quasi-divinity had become established. Of these footprints *Comy.*
remarks: ' The Buddha's footprints, being *sukhumāni,* are invisible,
but on this occasion he purposely allowed the impressions to be seen
by the brāhmin.' *Cf. The Life of Buddha,* by Dr. Thomas, p. 215 *ff.*

[5] *Pasādaniya.* At *Ud.* 7, *dassaniya.*

[6] Text repeats *santindriyaŋ,* which should read *yatindriyaŋ* (*UdA.* 87)·
Comy. has *saŋyatindriyaŋ.*

[7] *Nāga.* *Comy.* fancifully derives the word from (*puna*) *anāgacchati*
and *na āguŋ karoti.*

' Your worship will become[1] a deva ?'

' No indeed, brāhmin. I'll not become a deva.'

' Then your worship will become a gandharva ?'

' No indeed, brāhmin, I'll not become a gandharva.'

' A yakkha, then ?'

' No indeed, brāhmin, not a yakkha.'

' Then your worship will become a human being ?'

' No indeed, brāhmin, I'll not become a human being.'

' When questioned thus: " Your worship will become a deva . . . a gandharva . . . a yakkha . . . a human being ?" you reply: " Not so, brāhmin, I'll not become a deva . . . a gandharva . . . a yakkha . . . I'll not become a human being." Who then, pray, will your worship become ?'

' Brāhmin, those āsavas whereby, if they were not abandoned, I should become a deva,—those āsavas in me are abandoned, cut off at the root, made like a palm-tree stump, made non-existent, of a nature not to arise again in future time. Those āsavas whereby, if they were not abandoned, I should become a gandharva, a yakkha, a human being,— those āsavas in me are abandoned . . . not to arise again in future time. Just as, brāhmin,[2] a lotus, blue, red or white, though born in the water, grown up in the water, when it reaches the surface stands there unsoiled by the water,—just so, brāhmin, though born in the world, grown up in the world, having overcome the world,[3] I abide unsoiled by the world. Take it that I am a Buddha, brāhmin.

---

[1] *Bhavissati.* This passage has hitherto been mistranslated. The brāhmin does not ask ' Are you ?' but uses the future tense common to the verbs *be* and *become.* The Buddha replies, not ' I am not (these things),' but ' shall not become,' also using the future. The gāthas clearly imply that he will not again ' become' any one of these creatures, having destroyed the basis of rebirth; nor do they hint at any supernatural or superhuman marks or appearance. Probably the sentence about the ' wheels,' as well as the last prose paragraph, is a later insertion, being an editorial attempt to lend the plausibility of later values to a fragmentary, half-forgotten ' saying.' We meet with apparently the same Doṇa in the next Nipāta.

[2] Text wrongly *bhikkhave* for *brāhmaṇe.*

[3] *Cf. St. John's Gospel*, xvi, 33.

The āsavas whereby would be
A deva-birth or airy sprite,[1]
Gandharva, or whereby myself
Would reach the state of yakkhahood,
Or go to birth in human womb,[2]—
Those āsavas now by myself
Are slain, destroyed and rooted out.[3]

As a lotus, fair and lovely,
By the water is not soiled,
By the world am I not soiled;
Therefore, brāhmin, am I Buddha.'[4]

§ vii (37). *Incapable of falling away.*

' Monks, possessed of four qualities a man is incapable of falling away; he is near to Nibbāna. What are the four ?

Herein a monk is perfect in virtue, he is guarded as to the doors of the sense-faculties, he is moderate in eating, he is given to watchfulness.

And in what way is a monk perfect in virtue ?

Herein a monk is virtuous,[5] he dwells restrained with the restraint of the obligations: perfect in the practice of right conduct he sees danger in the slightest faults: he takes up and

---

[1] Text should read *devūpapatty*. *Vihangamo* is described by *Comy.* as *ākāsa-caro gandhabba-kāyika-devo*.

[2] Text here and at *MA*. i, 61, *abbaje* (optative of a supposed *abbajati*, ' would go '). *Pāli Dict.* suggests *andaje* (but what case would this be and how would one translate ?). I adopted this reading at *UdA*. 17⁶, and in Mr. Jayasundara's trans. of *A*. ii, with *Sinh*. text. But now I propose to read *abbude* (the fœtus). I took the gāthas wrongly. *Comy.* says nothing.

[3] *Vinaḷikatā*=*vigata-naḷā*, *vigata-bandhanā katā*. *Comy.* and at *Sn*. 542, *vigata-naḷa*, *ucchinnā*.

[4] The brāhmin's question is not unique. In another story also of this legendary type, the Sonananda Jātaka (*J*. v, 317), we read: ' Art devatā, gandharva or Sakka, giver to men ? Art human of magic potency ? As what may we know thee ?'

[5] *Cf. G.S.* i, 59.

trains himself in the stages of training. Thus a monk is perfect in virtue.

And how is a monk guarded as to the doors of the sense-faculties ?

Herein[1] a monk, seeing an object with the eye, does not grasp at the general features or at the details thereof. Since coveting and dejection, evil, unprofitable states, might flow in upon one who dwells with the faculty of the eye uncontrolled, he applies himself to such control, he sets a guard over the faculty of the eye, attains control thereof. When he hears a sound with the ear, or with the nose smells a scent, or with the tongue tastes a savour, or with the body contacts tangibles; when with the mind he cognizes mental states, he does not grasp at the general features or details thereof. But since coveting and dejection, evil, unprofitable states, might flow in upon . . . he sets a guard over the faculty of mind, attains control thereof. That is how a monk has the doors of the sense-faculties guarded.

And how is a monk moderate in eating ?

Herein a monk takes his food thoughtfully and prudently,[2] not for sport, not for indulgence, not for personal charm or adornment, but just enough for the support, for the continuance of body, for its resting unharmed, to help the living of the God-life, with this thought: My former feeling I check and I set going no new feeling. Thus maintenance[3] shall be mine, blamelessness and comfort in life. Thus a monk is moderate in eating.

And how is a monk given to watchfulness ?

By day a monk walks up and down and then sits, thus cleansing his heart of conditions that should be checked.[4] By night for the first watch he does likewise. In the middle watch of the night, lying on his right side he takes up the lion

---

[1] *Cf. G.S.* i, 98.   [2] *Cf. infra*, § 159.   [3] *Yātrā.*

[4] *Āvaraṇīyā.* At *G.S.* i, 98 I trans. 'that hinder.' *Cf. M.* i, 55, iii, 3 (*Pāli Dict.* wrongly states that it is used only negatively). *Comy.* at *A.* i, 114 says ' the five hindrances.' However, the form of the word seems to imply that there are states to be checked, *not* ' which may hinder,' as gen. translated.

posture,[1] resting one foot on the other, and thus collected and composed fixes his thoughts on rising up again.[2] In the last watch of the night, at early dawn, he walks up and down, then sits, and so cleanses his heart of conditions that should be checked. That is how a monk is given to watchfulness.

Possessed of these four qualities a monk is incapable of falling away: he is near to Nibbāna.

> Stablished in virtue, faculty-controlled,
> Moderate in eating, given to watchfulness,
> Thus dwelling day and night unwearièd,
> Making become good dhamma[3] for to win
> Peace from the toil,[4] in earnestness delighting,
> In slackness seeing danger,—such a monk
> Incapable of failure nears the Goal.'[5]

§ viii (38). *Withdrawn.*

' Monks, a monk who has shaken off individual beliefs, who[6] has utterly given up quests, whose body-complex is calmed, is called " withdrawn." '[7]

And how is a monk one who has shaken off individual beliefs ?

Herein, monks, whatsoever individual beliefs generally prevail among the generality of recluses and brāhmins, to wit: The world is eternal or The world is not eternal: The world is finite or The world is infinite: What is life, that is

---

[1] *Cf. D.* ii, 134; *infra*, text 244.

[2] *Uṭṭhāna-saññaŋ manasikaritvā* (or ? ' exertion ').

[3] *Cf. Bhāvento maggam uttamaŋ, Sn.* 1130.

[4] *Yoga-kkhemassa. Comy.* takes it to mean the four *yogā* (or *oghā*) of *kāma-bhāva, diṭṭhi, avijjā.*

[5] =*Dhp.* ver. 32.

[6] *Panuṇṇa-pacceka-sacco.* At *D.* iii, 269=*Dial.* iii, 247, these three items form part of the ' ten Ariyan methods of living ' (*Ariya-vāsā*), and are recorded in Asoka's *Bhabra Edict.* [Text inserts *vā* after -*sambhāro*, which is not in *Sinh.* MS. or below at § 4 of this sutta.]

[7] *Paṭilīna. Comy. nilīno eki-bhāvaŋ upagato.*

body; or One thing is life, another thing is body; A Tathāgata
is beyond death or A Tathāgata is not beyond death; or, He
both is and is not; or, He neither is nor is not beyond death,—
all these beliefs of his are given up, vomited up, dropped,
abandoned, and renounced.[1] That, monks, is how a monk has
shaken off individual beliefs.

And how is a monk one who has utterly given up quests ?

Herein, monks, the quest after sense-pleasure is abandoned
by a monk, the quest after becoming is abandoned, the quest
after the holy life has become allayed.[2] That, monks, is how
a monk is one who has utterly given up quests.

And how is a monk one whose body-complex is calmed ?

Herein a monk, by abandoning pleasure and abandoning
pain, by the coming to an end of the ease and discomfort which
he had before, attains and abides in a state of neither pain nor
pleasure, an equanimity of utter purity, which is the fourth
musing. That, monks, is how a monk is one whose body-
complex is calmed.[3]

And how is a monk " withdrawn " ?[4]

Herein, monks, the conceit of " I am " is abandoned in
a monk, cut off at the root, made like a palm-tree stump,
made not to become again, of a nature not to arise again
in future time. That, monks, is how a monk is withdrawn.

Monks, a monk who has shaken off individual beliefs . . .
is called " withdrawn."

> The quests of sense, becoming, God-life—
> (These three) accumulations of wrong view

---

[1] *Cf. S.* iii, 257, iv, 391.

[2] Acc. to *Comy.* the first quest is abandoned on the path of non-
return, the second on the Arahant path, whereon also the desire for
the God-life (having been satisfied) is abandoned; but the *diṭṭhi* held
about it is dropped by the Stream-winner. At *Dial.* iii, 209, it is taken
as the quest of ' problems connected with ' the God-life, such as the self
and its origin, nature and ending, etc. *Cf K.S.* v, 43 *n.*

[3] Treated more fully in suttas *On the Faculties, K.S.* v, 188 *ff.*

[4] *SA.* i, 106 quotes this sutta and passage.

Become perversion of the truth. In him
Who from all sensual lust is purified,
Who by destroying craving is set free,
Quests are renounced, wrong views are rooted out.
That monk at peace, composed and tranquil-minded,
Unconquered one, by comprehending pride
Awakened one,—'tis he is called " withdrawn." "¹

§ ix (39). *Ujjaya.*²

Now the brāhmin Ujjaya came to visit the Exalted One,
and on coming to him greeted him courteously, and after
the exchange of greetings and courtesies sat down at one
side. So seated the brāhmin Ujjaya said this to the Exalted
One:

' Pray, does the worthy Gotama praise sacrifice ?'³

' No, brāhmin, I do not praise every sacrifice. Yet I would
not withhold praise from every sacrifice. In whatever
sacrifice, brāhmin, cows are slaughtered, goats and sheep are
slaughtered, poultry and pigs are slaughtered and divers
living creatures come to destruction,—such sacrifice, brāhmin,
which involves butchery I do not praise. Why so ?

To such a sacrifice, brāhmin, involving butchery neither
the worthy ones nor those who have entered on the worthy
way⁴ draw near. But in whatever sacrifice, brāhmin, cows are
not slaughtered . . . and living creatures come not to destruction, such sacrifice not involving butchery I do praise;
such as, for instance, a long-established charity, an oblation for
the welfare of the family.⁵ Why so ? Because, brāhmin,
the worthy ones, those who have entered on the worthy
way, do draw near to such a sacrifice which involves not
butchery.

---

¹ First four lines at *Itiv.* 48.
² This brāhmin questions the B. at *A.* iv, 285.
³ *Yañña.*
⁴ *Araha-magga,* not *arahatta-magga* (as in *Pāli Dict.*).
⁵ This would be the *pitri-yajna,* acc. to *Comy.*

The sacrifice of horse and human life,[1]
The throwing of the peg,[2] the drinking-rite;[3]
The house unbarred, with all their cruelty
Have little fruit. Where goats and sheep and kine
Of divers sorts are sacrificed, go not
Those sages great who've travelled the right way.[4]

But sacrifices free from cruelty
Which men keep up for profit of the clan,
Where goats and sheep and kine of divers sorts
Are never sacrificed,—to such as these
Go sages great who've travelled the right way.
Such should the thoughtful celebrate: and great
The fruit of such; profit they bring, not loss.
Lavish the offering, devas therewith are pleased.'

§ x (40). *Udāyin*.[5]

Now the brāhmin Udāyin came to visit the Exalted One
. . . as he sat at one side the brāhmin Udāyin said this to the
Exalted One:

---

[1] Part of these gāthas occurs at *A*. iv, 151; *Itiv*. 21, in a set on ' culti-
vating amity '; *Sn. v.* 303; the whole at *S*. i, 76=*K.S*. i, 102, where see
notes. Our *Comy*., which=*SnA*. 321, differs somewhat from *SA*.
i, 145 *ff*., where the primitive form of these sacrifices is explained as
harmless before the time of the rājah Okkāka. The *assa-medha* was
then *sassa-m*. (sacrifice for a good harvest); the *purisa-m*. was a general
feed of six months' duration, *medha* being called *medhāvitā*, shrewdness
(in social functions). The *sammā-pāsa* was then called ' a bond to bind
men's hearts.' The word *vāja-peyya* was originally *vāca-peyya*, affabil-
ity in address, calling a person ' dear ' or ' uncle ': it was in short
piya-vācā. Such security prevailed that all kept open doors, unbolted
(*niraggala*). These older phrases are called by *SA*. ' the four bases of
sympathy '; *cf. supra*, § 2 and *AA*. on *A*. iv, 151. But, as said above,
they had now degenerated into bloody sacrifices and orgies. The
whole story of Okkāka and the brāhmins will be found at *Sn*., p. 50
(*Brāhmaṇa-dhammika-sutta*).

[2] *Comy*. ' Every day they threw a *sammā*, pin of a yoke or a peg,
and where it fell they built an altar for sacrifice.'

[3] Text should read *vāja-* for *vāca-*.

[4] *Sammaggatā=samyak gatā ; cf. supra, araha-magga*.

[5] *Cf. K.S*. v, 72; *G.S*. i, 208.

' Pray, does the worthy Gotama praise sacrifice ?'
(*The Buddha repeats the previous sutta, but the gāthas are
different.*)

> Fit sacrifice performed in season due
> And free from cruelty,[1]—to such draw near
> Those well trained in the God-life, even those
> Who have the veil rolled back while (yet) on earth,[2]
> Who have transcended time and going.[3]   Such
> Do the enlightened praise, those skilled in merit,[4]

> Whether in sacrifice or act of faith,[5]
> Oblation[6] fitly made with heart devout
> To that good field of merit,—those who live
> The God-life, they who offerings most deserve—
> Well offered, sacrificed, conferred,—so given
> Lavish the offering; devas therewith are pleased.
> Thus offering, the thoughtful, faithful one[7]
> With heart released, thereby becoming wise,
> Wins to the blissful world from suffering free.'[8]

Chapter V.—Rohitassa.

§ i (41). *Concentration.*

' Monks, there are these four ways of making-concentration-
to-become.[9] What four ?

There is, monks, the making-concentration-to-become
which, when developed and made much of, conduces to happy

---

[1] *Nirārambhaŋ=pāṇa-samārambha-rahitaŋ. Comy.*

[2] *Vivatta-cchadā. Cf. D.* i, 89 (-*chadda*). *Comy.* does not notice.

[3] *Kālaŋ gatiŋ* (text *gati*)=*vatta-kāle c' eva vatta-gatiñ ca atikkantā.
Comy.* Some MSS. read -*kathaŋ-kathī. Sinh.* text *vitivatta-kālaŋ-gatiŋ.*

[4] Text should read *kovidā.*

[5] The brāhmin *shraddhā* ceremony, like the Buddhist *Peta-dāna =
mataka-dāna. Comy.*

[6] *Havyaŋ.* So *Comy.* and *Sinh.* text, but our text *bhavyaŋ=bhabbaŋ.*
Cf. Sn. 464; *S.* i, 169, *Hunitabbaŋ* (from *juhati*). *Comy.*

[7] There seems to be a play on the words, contrasting *medha, medhāvī*;
saddha, shraddha.

[8] *Avyāpajjhaŋ,* here a noun, as at *Itiv.* 16, 52='non-injury' (*ahiŋsa*
[9] *Samādhi-bhāvanā* at *D.* iii, 222=*Dial.* iii, 215.

living in this very life. There is, monks, the making-concentration-to-become which, when developed and made much
of, conduces to winning knowledge-and-insight.[1] There is,
monks, the making-concentration-to-become which . . . conduces to mindfulness and well-awareness. There is, monks,
that which, when developed and made much of, conduces
to the destruction of the āsavas.

Now, monks, what sort of making-concentration-to-become
. . . conduces to happy living in this very life ?

Herein a monk, aloof from sense-desires . . . attains the
first musing; by the calming down of thought directed and
sustained . . . he attains the second musing; by the fading
out of zest . . . he attains the third musing; by rejecting
pleasure and pain alike . . . he attains the fourth musing[2]
and abides therein. . . . This is called "the making-concentration-to-become which conduces to happy living in this
very life."

And of what sort is that which conduces to winning knowledge-and-insight ?

Herein a monk pays attention to consciousness of light,
he concentrates on consciousness of daylight,[3] as by day,
so by night, as by night, so by day. Thus with wits alert,
with wits unhampered, he cultivates the mind to brilliance.
This, monks, is called "the making-concentration-to-become
which, when developed and made much of, conduces to winning knowledge-and-insight."

And what sort of making concentration to become . . .
conduces to mindfulness and well-awareness ?

Herein, monks, the feelings which arise in a monk are evident[4]

---

[1] *Comy.* calls this (*dibba-cakkhu*) clairvoyance or the light of knowledge (*ñāṇáloko*). *Cf.* the phrase ' knowledge arose, light arose,' *K.S.*
v, 157; *G.S.* i, 149.

[2] Text abridges thus. For the full details see *G.S.* i, 165, etc. *Cf. The
bases of psychic power*, *K.S.* v, 235.

[3] *Comy.* expl. ' the consciousness that it is daytime.' It means that
he is always wide awake at his task. *P. Dict.* has ' consciousness of sight.'

[4] *Cf. The four stations* (*or arisings*) *of mindfulness*, *K.S.* v, 157.
Comy. says *viditā=pākaṭā* (evident).

to him, the feelings which abide with him are evident to him, the feelings which come to an end in him are evident to him. The perceptions which arise in him . . . the trains of thought which arise in him, which abide with him, which come to an end in him are evident to him. This, monks, is called "the making-concentration-to-become which conduces to mindfulness and well-awareness."

And what sort of making-concentration-to-become, if developed and made much of, conduces to the destruction of the āsavas ?

Herein a monk dwells observing the rise and fall in the five factors of grasping, thus: Such is material, such is the arising of material, such its vanishing. Such is feeling . . . such is perception . . . such are the activities, such the arising of the activities, such their vanishing. Such is consciousness . . . such the vanishing of consciousness. This, monks, is called "the making-concentration-to-become which conduces to the destruction of the āsavas." These are the four forms of it. Moreover, in this connexion I thus spoke in *The Chapter on the Goal* in (the sutta called) *The Questions of Puṇṇaka* :[1]

By searching in the world things high and low,[2]
He who hath naught to stir him[3] in the world,
Calm[4] and unclouded, cheerful, freed of longing,
He hath crossed over birth and eld, I say.'

§ ii (42). *Questions.*[5]

' Monks, there are these four ways of answering a question. What four ?

---

[1] In *Pārāyana-Vagga* of *Sutta Nipāta*, v. 1048.   The lines are also quoted at *G.S.* i, 116, and other verses from this ancient poem are found in the Nikāyas.   See *Buddhist India*, 178.

[2] *Parovarāni = uccāvacāni, uttamādhamāni (Comy.)*, and on *A.* i, 132, *parāni ca ovarāni ca* (but *SnA. orāni*).

[3] Text should read *yass' iñjitaṃ*.   [4] Text should read *santo*.

[5] *Cf. Dial.* iii, 221 *n.*; *A.* i, 197 (*G.S.* i, 178 *ff.*) in the *Mahāvagga* (which may be what *Comy.* on *D.* iii refers to under the name *Mahāpadesa-kathā*), but in a different order, followed by the gāthas *infra*.

There is the question which requires a categorical reply; that which requires a counter-question; that which requires to be waived; and there is the question which requires a discriminating reply. These are the four.

> The downright answer first, then qualified;[1]
> The third he'll counter, set the fourth aside.
> " Skilled in the questions four " they call a monk
> Who knows to answer fitly thus and thus.
> Hard to o'ercome, to vanquish hard, profound,
> Invincible is such an one, and skilled
> To see the meaning, be it true or false;
> Wise to reject the false, he grasps the true.
> " Sage in the grasp of truth "[2] that wise one's called.'

§ iii (43). *Wrath*[3] (a).

' Monks, these four persons are found existing in the world. What four ?

He who pays regard to wrath, not to true dhamma; he who pays regard to hypocrisy, not to true dhamma; he who pays regard to gain, not to true dhamma; and he who pays regard to honours, not to true dhamma. These are the four persons . . .

Monks, these four persons are found existing in the world. What four ?

He who pays regard to true dhamma, not to wrath; to true dhamma, not to hypocrisy; to true dhamma, not to gain; and he who pays regard to true dhamma, not to honours. These are the four persons . . .

---

[1] Reading with *Sinh.* text *vacanâparaŋ.*

[2] *Atthâbhisamayā* =*attha-samāgamena. Comy.*

[3] *Cf. infra,* text 84; *S.* i, 169, 240. *Kodha* is reckoned a serious obstacle to progress. It would seem to mean a tendency to flare up on any occasion, like a smouldering fire. *Lābha-sakkāra-siloka* is the name of a *vagga* in *S.* ii, 225 *ff.* These defects are reckoned ' a terrible thing ' and ' a hindrance to winning *yoga-kkhema.*'

Who pay regard to wrath, hypocrisy,
To gain and honours,—such monks do not grow
In Dhamma taught by him the Fully Waked.
They who have lived and do live honouring
True Dhamma,—such as these do grow indeed
In Dhamma taught by him the Fully Waked.'

§ iv (44). *Wrath* (*b*).

' Monks, these four (qualities) are not according to true
dhamma. What four ?

Regard for wrath, not for true dhamma; for hypocrisy . . .
for gain . . . for honours, not for true dhamma. These are
the four qualities . . .

Monks, these four qualities are according to true dhamma.
What four ?

Regard for true dhamma, not for wrath; regard for true
dhamma, not for hypocrisy; for true dhamma, not for gain;
regard for true dhamma, not for honours. These are the
four . . .

Paying regard to wrath, hypocrisy,
To gain and honours, like a rotten seed
In good soil sown, a monk can make no growth.
They who have lived and do live honouring
True dhamma,—such do grow indeed in Dhamma,
As, after use of oil, drugs have more power.'[1]

§ v (45). *Rohitassa*[2] (*a*).

On a certain occasion the Exalted One was staying near
Sāvatthī at Jeta Grove in Anāthapiṇḍika's Park. Then
Rohitassa, of the devas,[3] when the night was waning, came,

---

[1] *Sneham anvāy' iv' osadhā ti.* (*Sinh.* text has an unintelligible reading.) The words *sneham anvāya* at *Sn.* 36 mean ' following affection '; but
here *sneha* undoubtedly means oil. *Osadha* at *PvA.* 198 is called *ārogya-
vahaŋ agadaŋ*, ' healing drug.' It is curious that *Comy.* has nothing to
say of this phrase.

[2] This sutta occurs at *S.* i, 61 = *K.S.* i, 85.

[3] *Deva-putto*, like *kula-putto*; *putto* means ' membership of a body.'

lighting up all Jeta Grove with surpassing brilliance, to see
the Exalted One, and saluting him stood at one side. So
standing Rohitassa of the devas said this to the Exalted One:[1]

'Pray, lord, is it possible for us, by going, to know, to see,
to reach world's end,[2] where there is no more being born or
growing old, no more dying, no more falling (from one existence)
and rising up (in another) ?'

'Your reverence, where there is no more being born or
growing old, no more dying, no more falling from one existence
and rising up in another,—I declare that that end of the world
is not by going to be known, seen, or reached.'

'It is wonderful, lord ! It is marvellous, lord, how well
it is said by the Exalted One: "Where there is no more being
born . . . that end of the world is not by going to be known,
seen or reached "'!

Formerly, lord, I was the hermit[3] called Rohitassa, Bhoja's
son, one of psychic power, a sky-walker.[4]   Such, lord, was my
speed,—just as if a stout bowman,[5] for instance, a skilled
archer, a practised hand, a trained man could with a light
shaft shoot easily across a palm-tree's shadow,—such was my
speed.   The extent of my stride was as the distance between
the eastern and the western ocean.   To me, lord, possessed
of such speed and of such a stride,[6] there came a longing
thus: I will reach world's end by going.

But, lord, not to speak of (the time spent over) food and

---

[1] *Cf.* Introduction.

[2] *Lokass' antaŋ* (*cf. K.S.* iv, 58)=*sankhāra-loka.   Comy.*

[3] *Isi* =Skt. *ṛishi*, anchorite, bard, seer, sage.

[4] *Iddhimā vehāsangamo.   Comy.* says nothing here or at *S.* i, 61.
See *VM.* i, 382, quoting *Pṭs.* ii, 213; *Path of Purity*, ii, 443: ' Which is
the psychic power inborn as the result of karma ?   (The traversing of
the sky) by all birds, all devas, some men, and some denizens of purgatory . . . some men at the beginning of the world-cycle . . . by
universal monarchs. . . .   Jotika the householder has it.   Jaṭilaka
the householder . . . Ghosita . . . Meṇḍaka has it.   The five persons
of great merit have it. . . .   The fourth jhāna is the original stage for
its attainment.'

[5] *Cf. S.* ii, 266; *M.* i, 82; *A.* iv, 429, for the simile.   The text of *S.* i
alone inserts *katayoggo* after *katahattho.*

[6] This phrase is omitted by *S.* i and inserted in the next sentence.

drink, eating, tasting[1] and calls of nature, not to speak of
struggles to banish sleep and weariness, though my life-span
was a hundred years, though I lived a hundred years, though
I travelled a hundred years, yet I reached not world's end
but died ere that. Wonderful indeed, lord ! Marvellous it
is, lord, how well it has been said by the Exalted One: " Your
reverence, where there is no more being born or growing old,
no more dying, no more falling (from one existence) and
rising up (in another), I declare that that end of the world is
not by going to be known, seen or reached."'

'But,[2] your reverence, I declare not that there is any
making an end of Ill without reaching world's end. Nay,
your reverence, in this very fathom-long body, along with
its perceptions and thoughts, I proclaim the world to be,
likewise the origin of the world and the making of the world
to end, likewise the practice going to the ending of the world.

> Not to be reached by going is world's end.
> Yet there is no release for man from Ill
> Unless he reach world's end.   Then let a man
> Become[3] world-knower, wise, world-ender,
> Let him be one who liveth the God-life.
> Knowing the world's end by becoming calmed[4]
> He longeth not for this world or another.'

§ vi (46). *Rohitassa (b)*.

Now when that night was spent the Exalted One addressed
the monks, saying:

---

[1] *Asita-pīta-khāyita-sāyita.*   S. text has *pīta*; A. text *khāyita.*
Trans. at *K.S.* i takes *sāyita* as ' resting,' and implies that he abstained
from all these things for a hundred years (?).

[2] Here our text repeats the previous phrase *Yattha kho . . . vadāmi.*
I follow the more likely reading of S. i, *Na kho paṇ' ahaŋ.* At S. iv, 93
the two declarations are made by the Buddha and the solution reached
by Ānanda.   Here 'world' is defined by him and his definition approved
by the Buddha. *Cf. Buddh. Psychology,* 75; *Dialog.* i, 273; *VM.* i, 204.

[3] Reading *bhave* of S. text for *have* (verily) of A. and *Sinh.* texts.
Perhaps *have* in the next sutta (gāthas) has influenced the reading here.

[4] *Samitāvī* (=*samita-pāpo.   Comy.*) *ñatvā.*   S. text reads *samitāvi-
ñatvā.*

'Monks, this night Rohitassa of the devas, when night was waning, came to visit me, lighting up the whole Jeta Grove with surpassing brilliance, and on coming to me stood at one side. So standing Rohitassa of the devas said this to me:

"Pray, lord, is it possible for us by going to know, to see, to reach world's end, where there is no more being born or growing old, no more dying, no more falling (from one existence) and rising up (in another) ?"

At these words, monks, I said this to Rohitassa of the devas: "Your reverence, where there is no more being born . . . I declare that that end of the world is not by going to be known, seen or reached." Whereupon, monks, Rohitassa of the devas said this to me: "Wonderful it is, lord ! It is marvellous, lord, how well this has been said by the Exalted One : 'Your reverence, where there is no more being born . . . no more rising up . . . I declare that that end of the world is not by going to be known, seen or reached'" (*and he repeated his words of the previous sutta*).

At these words, monks, I said this to Rohitassa of the devas:

"But, your reverence, I declare not that there is any making an end of Ill without reaching world's end. Nay, your reverence, in this fathom-long body, along with its perceptions and thoughts, I proclaim the world to be, likewise the origin of the world and the making the world to end, likewise the practice going to the ending of the world." '
(*The gāthas are repeated.*)

§ vii (47). *Very far away.*[1]

'Monks, these four things are very far away from each other. What four ?

The sky,[2] monks, and the earth; this is the first pair of things very far away from each other. This shore of ocean, monks, and that shore of ocean: this is the second pair. The place, monks, where the blazing one[3] comes up and the place where

---

[1] This sutta is quoted at *KV*. 344=*Pts. of Contr.* 203, to prove that opposite things or qualities are side by side.

[2] Text *nabhā*, but all the rest *nabhaŋ*; so also gāthas.

[3] *Verocana*, the sun. 'Son of Agni (fire).'

he goes to setting: this is the third pair. Dhamma of the
good, monks, and dhamma[1] of the bad: that is the fourth
pair of things very far away from each other. These are the
four . . .

> Far is the sky from earth and far, men say,
> The further side of ocean; far the place
> Where the blazing one, light-maker, riseth
> From where he goeth down; but further still
> Are dhamma of the good and of the bad.[2]
> Not transient is union of the good:
> As long as it remains it is just so.
> Soon wanes[3] the union of the bad.   Wherefore
> Far from the bad is dhamma of the good.'

§ viii (48). *Visākha.*[4]

On a certain occasion the Exalted One was staying near
Sāvatthī in Jeta Grove at Anāthapiṇḍika's Park. Now
on that occasion the venerable Visākha of the Pañcālas[5]
was in the assembly-hall[6] instructing, inciting, enlightening
and inspiring the monks with a dhamma-talk in language
polished, distinct and free from hoarseness, unfolding the
meaning, comprehensive and unbiassed.[7]

Now at eventide the Exalted One, rising from his solitary
meditation, approached the assembly-hall, and on coming

---

[1] Here apparently the same as *saddhamma* (' own way '), as in § 43
above.

[2] Gāthas quoted at *J.A.* v, pp. 483 and 508.

[3] *Veti. Cf. Dialog.* ii, 251 *n.*

[4] *Cf. Brethr.* 152; *K.S.* ii, 190, where the Buddha praises his manner
of speaking and pronounces the gāthas here following.

[5] East of the Kurus. *Cf. Buddhist India*, 27, 203. *Comy.* ' son of
Pañcālī, a brāhmanī.'

[6] *Upaṭṭhāna-sālā*, def. at *UdA.* 102 as ' a preaching-pavilion . . .
hall of service . . . where monks determine discipline, speak Dhamma,
engage in discussion, and gather for general purposes.'

[7] *Cf. S.* i, 189 (of Sāriputta's way of speech), where the last term,
anissitāya, is omitted. This means, acc. to *Comy.*, ' unattached to
saṃsāra, wheel of involution or devolution,' but more probably it means
' unhesitating.'

there sat down on a seat made ready.   On sitting down he
addressed the monks, saying:

'Pray, monks, who was it that was in the assembly-hall
instructing . . . the monks . . . in language polished . . .
comprehensive and unbiassed ?'

'Lord, it was the venerable Visākha of the Pañcālas.'

Then the Exalted One said this to the venerable Visākha
of the Pañcālas:

'Well said, well said, Visākha ! Well have you instructed
the monks in the assembly-hall . . . in language . . . comprehensive and unbiassed.'

(So said the Exalted One. The Wellfarer, having thus
spoken, as Teacher added this further:)[1]

'If he utter no word men know him not—[2]
A wise man mixed up with fools.
If he open his mouth men know him
When he teaches the Deathless Way.
Let him speak out,[3] light up Dhamma;
Let him hoist the banner of seers;
Seers have bright speech for their banner,
Dhamma's the banner of seers.'

§ ix (49). *Perversions.*[4]

'Monks, there are these four perversions of perception,
four perversions of thought, four perversions of view. What
four ?

To hold that in the impermanent there is permanence is
a perversion of perception, thought and view. To hold that
in the not-Ill there is Ill is a perversion of perception, thought

---

[1] This passage is not in our text, but at *S.* ii. Gāthas at *JA.* v, 509.

[2] At *K.S.* ii, 280, and in my verses at p. 71 of Mr. Jayasundara's
trans. of *A.* ii, the first couplet is taken wrongly. *Na abhāsamānaɱ
jānanti* (as *Comy.* remarks) means 'if he speak not, they know him
not'; *not* 'though he speak not they know him.' All texts read *nābh.,*
not *na bh.*

[3] *Bhāsati* = 'speak' and 'illuminate.'

[4] *Vipallāsā.*

and view. To hold that in the not-self[1] there is self is a perversion of . . . view. To hold that in the foul there is the fair is a perversion of perception, thought and view. These are the four perversions of perception, thought and view.

Monks, there are these four non-perversions of perception, thought and view. What four ?

To hold that in the impermanent is impermanence . . . that in Ill is Ill . . . that in the not-self is not-self . . . that in the foul is the foul,—these are the non-perversions of perception, thought and view.

> They who in change perceive the permanent
> And happiness in Ill,[2] and see the self
> In what is not-self, in the foul the fair,—
> Such wander on the path of view perverse,
> Creatures of mind distraught, of mind unsound.
> Bond-slaves to Māra,[3] not free from the bond,
> To the round of birth and death do beings go.
> But when the wakened ones, makers of light,
> I' the world arise, they show this dhamma forth,
> Which goeth to Ill's calming. Hearing them
> Men become wise, get back their sense[4] and see
> Th' impermanent as being such, and Ill
> As being Ill, and what is not-self see
> As not-self, and behold the foul as foul,
> Thus by right view transcending every Ill.'

§ x (50). *Stains.*[5]

' Monks, there are these four stains of moon and sun, stained by which stains moon and sun burn not, shine not, blaze not. What are the four ?

---

[1] Viz., in body or mind. *Cf. Vinaya Texts*, i, 100.

[2] Note the discrepancy.

[3] Text should read *-yutta.*

[4] Text and *Sinh.* text *paccalatthu. Comy. paccaladdha=saka-cittaṇ paṭilabhitvā.*

[5] 'This sutta occurs at *Vin.* ii, 295.

Cloud, monks, is a stain of moon and sun . . . fog[1] . . .
smoke-and-dust . . . Rāhu, monks, is a stain of moon and
sun, stained by which stain moon and sun burn not, shine
not, blaze not. These are the four stains . . .

Just so, monks, there are four stains of recluses and brāhmins,
stained by which stains some recluses and brāhmins burn
not, shine not, blaze not. What four ?

Monks, there are some recluses and brāhmins who drink
fermented liquor, who drink liquor distilled, who abstain
not from liquor fermented and distilled. This, monks, is
the first fault of recluses and brāhmins, stained by which
stain some recluses and brāhmins . . . blaze not.[2]

Monks, there are some recluses and brāhmins who are
given to things sexual, who abstain not from things sexual
This, monks, is the second stain of recluses and brāhmins,
stained by which stain some recluses and brāhmins . . .
blaze not.

Monks, there are some recluses and brāhmins who take[3]
gold and silver, who abstain not from accepting gold and silver.
This, monks, is the third stain, stained by which stain some
recluses . . . blaze not.

Monks, there are some recluses and brāhmins who live by
a wrong means of living, who abstain not from a wrong means
of living. This, monks, is the fourth stain of recluses and
brāhmins, stained by which stain some recluses and brāhmins
burn not, shine not, blaze not.

> Some samaṇas and brāhmaṇas are snared[4]
> By lust and ill-will. Clothed in ignorance,

---

[1] *Mahikā.* So *Comy., Sinh.* text and MSS. There seems no authority
for *mahiyā* of text (perhaps a misprint).

[2] It is noticeable that monks are not mentioned. But probably
'recluses' includes them. At *S.* iv, 325 monks are called 'recluses
who are *Sakya-puttā*' in a charge of this sort made against them by
laymen. For the effects of drink see *Expositor*, ii, 487; *Asl.* 380.

[3] *Sādiyanti=gaṇhanti. Comy. Cf. K.S.* iv, 230.

[4] Reading *-parikkhitta (parikkhipati)* for *-paṭikkiṭṭhā* of our text
(*-parikkiliṭṭhā* of *Vin.* ii) and *-parikkiṭṭhā* of *Sinh.* text. (The Sinhalese
almost invariably pronounce *t* as *th.*) *Comy.* does not remark. The
MS. is probably dictated, which accounts for many errors.

Beings delight in pleasure-giving shapes;
Liquor fermented and distilled they drink;
They follow sexual lust; by folly blinded[1]
Some samaṇas and brāhmaṇas take gifts
Of gold and silver and live wrongfully.
These are called " stains " by the Enlightened One,
The Kinsman of the Sun. Tainted by these
Some samaṇas and brāhmaṇas burn not,
They shine not, tarnished, dust-soiled, utter fools,[2]
Shrouded in darkness; slaves of craving they,
Led by the cord of craving, and they swell
The dreadful charnel-field[3] and reap rebirth.'

(THE SECOND FIFTY SUTTAS)

CHAPTER VI.—FLOOD OF MERIT.

§ i (51). *Flood of merit (to laymen) (a).*

Sāvatthī was the source (of this sutta).[4]

' Monks, there are these four floods of merit, floods of things
profitable, bringing happiness, giving the best things,[5] whose
fruit is happiness, leading to the heaven world, leading to
what is dear, delightful and pleasant, to profit and happiness.
What are the four ?

To him, monks, who is the giver of the robe, using which a
monk is able to attain and abide in unbounded concentration

---

[1] *Aviddasū=andhabālā. Comy.*

[2] Reading *magā=bālā* (*cf. JA.* vi, 206, 209) with *Vin.* ii, 295. *Pabhā*
of text is impossible in the context. *Comy.* does not notice.

[3] *Cf. S.* ii, 278; *Thag.* 456 (which reads *ācinanti* for our *ādiyanti*);
expl. at *UdA.* 352.

[4] This sutta is the only one in this volume so derived. *Cf. S.* v, 391,
400 (also a Sāvatthī-n.)=*K.S.* v, 336, 343; it is also quoted at *Pts. of
Contr.* 202 (*KV.* 345). At *A.* iv, 245 eight such floods are given. For
the term see *DA.* i, 303. It occurs at *A.* iii, 51 as a Five.

[5] *Sovaggika=suṭṭhu aggānaŋ rūpādīnaŋ dāyakā. Comy.* It is generally taken as ' belonging to heaven.'

of mind, to him comes a flood of merit, a flood of things
profitable, bringing happiness.

To him, monks, who is the giver of alms-food, using which
a monk is able to attain and abide in . . .

To him, monks, who is the giver of lodging, using which a
monk is able to attain and abide in . . .

To him, monks, who is the giver of requisites and medicines
for use in sickness, using which a monk is able to attain and
abide in unbounded concentration of mind,—to him comes a
flood of merit, a flood of things profitable, bringing happiness,
giving the best things, whose fruit is happiness, leading to
the heaven world, leading to what is dear, delightful and
pleasant, to profit and happiness. These, monks, are the four
floods of merit, floods of things profitable . . .

Moreover, monks, if an Ariyan disciple be possessed of these
four floods of merit, floods of things profitable, it is no easy
thing to take the measure of his merit, (so as to say):—" Such
and such is the extent of the flood of merit and so forth,"
nay, it is to be reckoned as an incalculable, immeasurable,
mighty mass of merit.

Just as, monks, it is no easy thing to take the measure of
the water[1] in the mighty ocean (so as to say):—" So many
gallons of water, so many hundred, so many thousand, so
many hundreds of thousands of gallons of water,"—nay, it
is to be reckoned as an incalculable, immeasurable, mighty
mass of merit.

> To boundless mighty ocean, mighty pool,
> Fearsome, the resting-place of divers gems,
> As rivers bearing multitudes of men[2]
> Flow broadly down and to that ocean come;
> Just so to him that giveth food, drink, clothes,
> Who bed and seat and coverlet provides,
> Torrents of merit flood that mortal wise,
> As rivers, bearing water, reach the main.'[3]

---

[1] *Cf. K.S.* iv, 267.   [2] *A.* iii, 52 reads *maccha-*.
[3] Gāthas at *S.* v, 400=*K.S.* v, 267.

§ ii (52). *Flood of merit (to laymen) (b).*[1]

'Monks, there are these four floods of merit . . . (*as in previous sutta*).

Herein, monks, the Ariyan disciple is possessed of unwavering loyalty to the Buddha, thus: He it is, the Exalted One, Arahant, a fully Enlightened One, perfect in lore and conduct, Wellfarer, a world-knower, the trainer unsurpassed of men who can be trained, teacher of devas and mankind, a Buddha, an Exalted One. This, monks, is the first flood of merit which . . . leads to profit and happiness.

Then again, monks, the Ariyan disciple is possessed of unwavering loyalty to Dhamma, thus: Well proclaimed by the Exalted One is Dhamma, to be seen in this life, not a thing of time, (inviting to) come and see,[2] leading onward, to be understood by the wise, each for himself. This, monks, is the second flood of merit . . .

Then again, monks, the Ariyan disciple is possessed of unwavering loyalty to the Order of monks, thus: Walking the Way well is the Exalted One's Order of disciples, walking uprightly, walking according to the Method, walking dutifully is the Exalted One's Order of disciples: namely, the four pairs of men, the eight types[3] of men. That is the Exalted One's Order of disciples. Worthy of honour are they, worthy of reverence, worthy of salutations with clasped hands,—a field of merit unsurpassed for the world. This, monks, is the third flood of merit . . .

Then again, monks, the Ariyan disciple is possessed of the virtues dear to the Ariyans, virtues unbroken, whole, unspotted, untarnished, giving freedom, praised by the wise; virtues untainted, which lead to concentration of the mind. This, monks, is the fourth flood of merit, flood of things profitable, bringing happiness, giving the best things, whose fruit is happiness, leading to the heaven world, leading to what is dear, delightful and pleasant, to profit and happiness.

Thus, monks, these are the four floods of merit, floods of

---

[1] *Cf. S.* v, 330, 397.   [2] *Ehi-passiko,* lit. ' come-see-ish.'
[3] *Cf.* iv, § 4, *supra.*

things profitable . . . which . . . lead to profit and happiness.

> Whoso hath faith in the Tathāgata
> Unwavering and firm, whose life is good,
> Praised by the Ariyans and dear to them;
> Whoso is likewise loyal to the Order
> And looks straight forth,—" He is not poor "[1] they say,
> " Not (lived) in vain the life of such a man."
> So let the wise man cultivate (these four)
> Faith, virtue, piety and seeing Dhamma,
> Bearing the Buddha's message in his mind.'[2]

§ iii (53). *Living together* (a).

On a certain occasion the Exalted One was journeying along the highroad between Madhurā[3] and Verañja, and a large number of housefathers and housewives were also journeying along that road.

Now the Exalted One, stepping off the highroad, sat down at the root of a certain tree upon a seat made ready. When they saw the Exalted One so doing the housefathers and housewives came up to him, and on reaching the Exalted One saluted him and sat down at one side. As they sat thus the Exalted One said this to those housefathers and housewives:

' Housefathers, there are these four ways of living together. What four ?

A vile[4] man lives along with a vile woman; a vile man lives

---

[1] Text should read *adaliddo ti tam āhu*.

[2] These gāthas are favourites and occur at *S.* i, 232, v, 384, 405; *A.* iii, 54.

[3] For Madhurā on the Jumna see *Buddhist India*, 36; but another is mentioned at *A.* iii, 256, noted for its ruggedness, dust, mad dogs, malicious yakshas, and it was hard to beg in; also at *A.* iv, 172. Suttas are named after these places at *M.* i, 290, ii, 83. Our text reads *Verañji*. At the former (*Verañjaka-sutta*) the Buddha also talks to householders and in a similar strain.

[4] *Chavo*, a corpse, or vile thing. *Cf. supra* I, § 3, ' a lifeless uprooted thing.'

along with a devī;[1] a deva lives along with a vile woman; a deva lives along with a devī.

And in what way, housefathers, does a vile man live along with a vile woman ?

In this case, housefathers, a husband is one who takes life, steals, is a wrong-doer in sense-desires, a liar, one given to the use of liquor fermented and distilled which causes sloth; he is a wicked man, an evil-doer, he lives at home with a heart soiled by the taint of stinginess,[2] he abuses and reviles recluses and brāhmins. His wife also is one who takes life, steals and so forth. Thus it is, housefathers, that a vile man lives with a vile woman.

And how, housefathers, does a vile man live along with a devī ?

In this case the husband is one who takes life, steals and so forth; he abuses recluses and brāhmins. But the wife is one who abstains from (all these things); she is virtuous, of a lovely nature, she lives at home with a heart freed from the taint of stinginess, she is no abuser or reviler of recluses and brāhmins. Thus, housefathers, does a vile man live along with a devī.

And how does a deva live along with a vile woman ?

In this case the husband is one who abstains from taking life, stealing and so forth . . . but the wife is one who abstains not . . . Thus does a deva live along with a vile woman.

And how does a deva live along with a devī ?

In this case both husband and wife are abstainers from taking life, stealing and so forth. . . . Thus it is, housefathers, that a deva lives along with a devī. These are the four ways of living together.

> Both vicious, mean, abusing others, these—
> Husband and wife, a vile pair linked together.

> A vicious husband, mean, abusing others;
> A virtuous wife, not stingy, but well-spoken—
> A devī she, paired with a partner vile.

---

[1] These are of course honorific terms, and are titles given to a king and queen.

[2] *Cf. G.S.* i, 260.

A husband good, not stingy, but well-spoken,
A vicious wife, stingy, abusing others—
A woman vile is partnered with a deva.

If both, believers, self-controlled, well-spoken,
Living as dhamma bids, use loving words
One to the other,—manifold the blessings[1]
That come to wife and husband, and to them
The blessing of a pleasant life[2] is born;
Dejected are their foes, for both are good.
So in this world living as dhamma bids,
The pair, in goodness match'd, i' the deva-world
Rejoicing win the bliss that they desire.'

§ iv (54). *Living together*[3] (b).

' Monks, there are these four ways of living together.
What four ?

A vile man lives along with a vile woman; a vile man lives
along with a devī; a deva lives along with a vile woman; a
deva lives along with a devī.

And in what way, monks, does a vile man live along with
a vile woman ?

In this case, monks, the husband is one who takes life, steals,
is a wrong-doer in sense-desires, a liar, given to harsh, bitter
speech and idle babble, one covetous, of a malevolent heart,
of perverted view, a wicked man, an evil-doer; he lives at
home with heart soiled by the taint of stinginess, he abuses
and reviles recluses and brāhmins.   And his wife is of a like
nature. . . .

---

[1] *Atthā sampacurā honti. Cf. S.* i, 110; *SA.* i (*sampacurā=bahavo.
Comy.*).   Here *vaḍḍhi-sankhātā atthā etesaŋ bahū honti. Comy. Cf.*
also *A.* iii, 172, *pacur' attha*; iv, 94; *UdA.* 165, 363, *pacura-jana=
puthujjana.*

[2] Text has *vās' atthaŋ*, but *Sinh.* text and *Comy.* and MSS. *phās'
atthaŋ* (explained by *Comy.* as *phāsu-vihāra-atthaŋ*).

[3] This sutta is much the same as (a) above, but has substitutes for the
fifth offence of drinking liquor. *Comy.* remarks that both are concerned with *kamma-patha*, and the householders' method of attaining
the first two paths of Stream-winning and Once-return.

And in what way, monks, does a vile man live along with a devī ?

In this case the husband is one who takes life, steals, and so forth. . . . But the wife is one who abstains (from all these things) . . . she is virtuous, of a lovely nature . . . she is no reviler of recluses and brāhmins. Thus, monks, does a vile man live along with a devī.

And in what way, monks, does a deva live along with a vile woman ?

In this case the husband is one who abstains from taking life, stealing, and so forth, but the wife abstains not from these things. Thus does a deva live along with a vile woman.

And in what way, monks, does a deva live along with a devī ?

In this case both husband and wife are abstainers from taking life, from stealing and the rest. . . .

These, monks, are the four ways of living together.'

(*Gāthas as before.*)

§ v (55). *Well matched*[1] *(a)*.

On a certain occasion the Exalted One was staying among the Bhaggā near Crocodile Haunt, at Bhesakalā Grove in Antelope Park.[2]

Now in the forenoon the Exalted One robed himself, and taking outer robe and bowl set out for the dwelling of the housefather, Nakula's father. On coming there he sat down on a seat made ready. Then the housefather, Nakula's father, and the housewife, Nakula's mother, came to see the Exalted One, and on coming to him saluted him and sat down at one side. So seated the housefather, Nakula's father, said this to the Exalted One:

---

[1] *Samajīvino* in the uddāna. At *A.* i, 26 this couple are reckoned as the best of lay-disciples, male and female, in ' intimate conversation.' At *AA.* i, 400 they are described as having been for 500 births parents or relatives of the Buddha, and still treat him as a son, and this conversation is there quoted. *Cf. K.S.* iii, 1, where the old man asks for consolation.

[2] The same places are mentioned at *M.* i, 95, 332; *S.* iv, 116. At *A.* iii, 295, N. is sick.

' Lord, ever since the housewife, Nakula's mother, was
brought home to me when a mere lad, she being then a mere
girl, I am not conscious of having transgressed[1] against her
even in thought, much less in person. Lord, we do desire to
behold each other not only in this very life but also in the life
to come.'

Then also the housewife, Nakula's mother, said this to the
Exalted One:

' Lord, ever since I, a mere girl, was led home to the housefather, Nakula's father, when he was a mere lad, I am not
conscious of having transgressed against him even in thought,
much less in person. Lord, we do desire to behold each other
not only in this very life, but also in the life to come.'

[Then said the Exalted One:] ' Herein, householders, if
both wife and husband desire to behold each other both in
this very life and in the life to come, and both are matched
in faith, matched in virtue, matched in generosity, matched
in wisdom,[2] then do they behold each other in this very life
and in the life to come.

> If both, believers, self-controlled, well-spoken,
> Living as dhamma bids, use loving words
> One to the other, manifold the blessings
> That come to wife and husband, and to them
> The blessing of a pleasant life is born.
> Dejected are their foes, for both are good.
> So in this world, living as dhamma bids,
> The pair, in goodness matched, i' the deva-world
> Rejoicing win the bliss that they desire.'

§ vi (56). *Well matched (b).*

(*This sutta with the gāthas is the same as the one above,
beginning with the Buddha's words, but was addressed to the
monks.*)

---

[1] Same phrase at *A.* iv, 66 (of Nanda's mother), with reading *ati-
carittā* (as also *Comy.*) for *aticaritā* of our text.

[2] To these four are often added *suta* (learning). At *K.S.* v, 339 these
virtues conduce to Stream-winning. See below, Ch. VII, § 1.

§ vii (57). *Suppavāsā.*[1]

On a certain occasion the Exalted One was staying among the Koliyans at a township of the Koliyans called Sajjanela.

Then the Exalted One in the forenoon, robing himself and taking outer robe and bowl, approached the dwelling of Suppavāsā of the Koliyans, and on reaching it sat down on a seat made ready. Then Suppavāsā of the Koliyans with her own hand satisfied and served the Exalted One with choice food, both hard and soft. And seeing that[2] the Exalted One had eaten his fill and had washed both hand and bowl,[3] Suppavāsā of the Koliyans sat down at one side. As she sat thus the Exalted One said this to Suppavāsā of the Koliyans:

'Suppavāsā, the Ariyan woman-disciple who gives food gives four things[4] to the receiver thereof. What four?

She gives life, she gives beauty, she gives happiness, she gives strength. Moreover, giving life she is a partaker of life,[5] be it as deva or human: giving beauty she is a partaker of beauty, be it as deva or human : giving happiness . . . giving strength she is a partaker of strength, be it as deva or human. Yes, Suppavāsā, the Ariyan woman-disciple who gives food gives these four things to the receiver thereof.

If she give food well prepared, pure, choice, possessing
　　flavour,
She by her offering made to those who walk upright,

---

[1] *Cf. G.S.* i, 25, where she is reckoned ' best of those who give choice alms-food,' and is called 'mother of Sīvali'; but she is not named in *Apadāna* or *Therigāthā*. At *Thag.* 60 she is called daughter of the Koliyan rājah. *Cf. Ud.* II, 8 for the account of her seven meals given to the Buddha.

[2] The construction is elliptical and requires the use of 'seeing' or 'knowing' to explain the acc. case. *DA.* i, 272 expl. *evaŋ bhūtaŋ Bhagavantaŋ ñatvā.*

[3] *Onīta-patta-pāṇiŋ.* This common phrase is expl. by *Comy.* at *DA., UdA.* 242, etc., as 'withdrawn-bowl-hand' (Skt. *oṇ.*); or 'washed-bowl-hand' (*onitta,* Skt. *avanij.*). Both incline to the latter interpretation. The right hand only is used in eating.

[4] *Ṭhānāni,* occasions.

[5] *Bhāginī.* There may be a word-play here on *bhaginī* (sister).

Who are well practised in the Way and lofty are,
On merit heaping merit, hath great fruit, and she
Is praised by that World-knower.   They who bear in mind
An offering such as this and gladsome[1] roam the world,
By tearing up the weed of meanness, root and branch,
Such are not blamed and come to reach the heaven-place.'

§ viii (58). *Sudatta.*[2]

Now the housefather Anāthapiṇḍika came to visit the
Exalted One, and on coming to him saluted him and sat down
at one side.   As he thus sat the Exalted One said this to the
housefather Anāthapiṇḍika:

' Housefather, the Ariyan disciple who gives food gives four
things to the receiver thereof.   What four ?

He gives life, beauty, happiness and strength.   (*As in the
previous sutta.*)

> To those well trained, who live on others' alms,
> Whoso gives zealously in season due
> Their daily food, on them confers four things:
> Long life and beauty, happiness and strength.
> Who giveth life, strength, beauty, happiness,
> Hath long and honoured life, wherever born.'

§ ix (59). *Food.*

' Monks, a supporter by giving food gives these four things
to the receiver thereof.   What four ?

He gives life, he gives beauty, he gives happiness, he gives
strength.   Moreover, giving life he is a partaker of life, be it
as deva or human.   Giving beauty he is a partaker of beauty
. . . giving happiness . . . giving strength he is a partaker
of strength, be it as deva or human.   Indeed, monks, a supporter by givi   food gives these four things.'

(*The gāthas are as at* § 8.)

---

[1] *Vedajātā.   Comy. tuṭṭhi-jātā.*   At *SA.* i, 120 equal to *hāsa-bahulo,
pāmojja-bahulo.*

[2] The personal name of A. (not in the text but acc. to the *uddāna*),
' feeder of the helpless.'   *Cf. Vin.* ii, 64; *S.* i, 211.

§ x (60). *The householder's duty.*

Now the housefather Anāthapiṇḍika came to visit the
Exalted One . . . As he sat at one side the Exalted One
said this to him:

'Housefather, possessed of four things the Ariyan disciple
has entered on the householder's path of duty,[1] a path which
brings good repute and leads to the heaven world. What are
the four ?

Herein, housefather, the Ariyan disciple waits upon the
Order of monks, he waits upon the Order of monks with the
offer of a robe, alms-food . . . lodging . . . requisites and
medicines for use in sickness. These are the four things.

> They are wise folk who enter on the path
> Of duty which becomes the householder,
> Serving the virtuous ones who on the Way
> Have rightly trod[2] with offerings of robes,
> Of alms-food, lodging, comforts, requisites.
> By day and night their merit groweth ever;
> Doing the lucky deed one reaches[3] heaven.'

CHAPTER VII.—DEEDS OF MERIT.

§ i (61). *Four deeds of merit.*[4]

Now the housefather Anāthapiṇḍika came to visit the
Exalted One . . . As he sat at one side the Exalted One
said this to him:

---

[1] *Gihī-sāmīci-paṭipadā,* called at *S.* v, 333 *gihī-sāmīcikāni* (=*anuc-
chavikāni, Comy.*), obligations which A. claimed to have kept fulfilled;
whereon the Buddha declares him to have won the fruits of S*f*ream-
winning.

[2] *Sammaggatā. Cf. supra,* text 43.

[3] *Kamati=vahati, pavattati, SA.* on *S.* iv, 283 =*carati, pavisati,
SnA.* 177. The line is at *Petavatthu,* p. 1; *cf. PvA.* 9 (*uppajjati upagac-
chati*).

[4] *Patta-kummāni* (in last line of the sutta)=*yutta-k., anucchavika-k.*
(*Comy.*), but it might be taken in the sense of *patta-dhamma, patta-mānasa,*
etc.—*i.e.,* mastery, as at *M.* i, 4; *S.* ii, 229, v, 326; *Itiv.* 76, 96; *infra,*
§ 90.

'Housefather, there are these four conditions (to realize which is) desirable, dear, delightful, hard to win in the world. What four?

(The wish:) O may wealth by lawful means come to me! This is the first condition . . .

Wealth being gotten by lawful means, may good report attend me[1] along with my kinsmen and teachers! This is the second condition . . .

Wealth being gotten by lawful means, and good report being gotten by me along with my kinsmen and teachers, may I live long and reach a great age! This is the third condition . . .

Wealth being gotten . . . and good report . . . and long life, when body breaks up, on the other side of death may I attain the happy bourn, the heaven world! This is the fourth condition . . .

These, housefather, are the four conditions (to realize which is) desirable, dear, delightful, hard to win in the world.

Now, housefather, to the winning of these four conditions . . . four conditions conduce. What four?

Perfection of faith, perfection of virtue, perfection of generosity and perfection of wisdom.[2]

And what, housefather, is perfection of faith?

Herein the Ariyan disciple is faithful, he has faith in the enlightenment of the Tathāgata, thus: He it is, Exalted One, Arahant, perfectly enlightened, and so forth, a Buddha is the Exalted One. This, housefather, is called " perfection of faith."

And what is perfection of virtue?

Herein the Ariyan disciple abstains from killing . . . from liquor fermented and distilled which causes sloth. This is called " perfection of virtue."

And what is perfection of generosity?

Herein the Ariyan disciple lives at home with heart free from the taint of stinginess, he is open-handed, pure-handed, delighting in self-surrender, one to ask a favour of, one who

---

[1] *Abbhugacchatu maŋ.*   [2] Above, Ch. VI, § 5.   Perfection = *sampadā.*

delights in dispensing charitable gifts.[1]   This, housefather, is called "perfection of generosity."

And what is perfection of wisdom ?

Housefather, living with his heart overcome by coveting and wrongful desire, one does what he should not, fails to do what he should; so doing, so failing to do, he falls[2] from good report and happiness.   Living with his heart overcome by malice . . . by sloth-and-torpor . . . by distraction-and-flurry . . . by doubt-and-wavering, he does what he should not, fails to do what he should; so doing, so failing to do, he falls from good report and happiness.

Now, housefather, that Ariyan disciple, knowing coveting and wrong desire to be a depravity of the mind, casts out the mind's depravity of coveting and wrong desire . . . casts out the mind's depravities of malice . . . sloth-and-torpor . . . distraction-and-flurry . . . doubt-and-wavering.   Now, housefather, in so far as the Ariyan disciple, knowing coveting (and the rest) to be depravities of the mind . . . is one who has cast out these depravities, this Ariyan disciple is called "of great wisdom, of far-spread wisdom, of clear range of vision,[3] one perfect in wisdom."

These four conditions, housefather, conduce to (the realization of the aforesaid) four conditions which are desirable, dear, delightful and hard to win in the world.

Now, housefather, that same Ariyan disciple, with the wealth acquired by energetic striving, amassed by strength of arm, won by sweat, lawful and lawfully gotten, is the doer of four deeds.   What are the four ?

Herein, housefather, with the wealth acquired by energetic striving and so forth the Ariyan disciple makes himself happy and cheerful,[4] he is a contriver of perfect happiness;[5] and

---

[1] *Cf. K.S.* v, 340, one of the 'limbs of Stream-winning.'

[2] *Dhaŋsati.*

[3] *Āpātha-daso* (not in *Index* or *P. Dict.*).   *Comy. taŋ taŋ atthaŋ āpāthe ti tam eva passati; sukhumam pi 'ssa attha-jātaŋ āpāthaŋ āgacchati yevā ti attho.*

[4] As at *D.* i, 51, etc.

[5] *Sammā sukhaŋ pariharati.*   This may mean 'he carries about with him.'

makes his mother and father, his children and wife, his servants
and workmen, his friends and comrades cheerful and happy,
he is a contriver of perfect happiness. This, housefather, is
the first opportunity seized by him, turned to merit and fittingly[1] made use of.

Then again, housefather, the Ariyan disciple with the wealth
acquired by energetic striving, amassed by strength of arm,
won by sweat, lawful and lawfully gotten,—with that wealth
he makes himself secure against all misfortunes whatsoever,
such as may happen by way of fire, water, the rājah, a robber,
an ill-disposed person or an (expectant) heir. He takes steps[2]
for his defence, he makes himself secure. This, housefather,
is the second opportunity seized by him, turned to merit and
fittingly made use of.

Again, housefather, with the wealth acquired by energetic
striving . . . lawfully gotten, the Ariyan disciple is a maker
of the fivefold offering,[3] namely: to relatives, to guests, to
departed petas, to the rājah and to the devatā. This is the
third opportunity seized by him, turned to merit and fittingly
made use of.

Then again, housefather, with the wealth acquired by
energetic striving, amassed by strength of arm, won by sweat,
lawful and lawfully gotten, the Ariyan disciple offers a gift to
all such recluses and brāhmins as abstain from sloth and
negligence, who are bent on kindness and forbearance, who
tame the one self, calm the one self, cool[4] the one self,[5]—
to such he offers a gift which has the highest results, a gift
heavenly, resulting in happiness and leading to heaven.[6] This

---

[1] *Āyatanaso* (not in *Index* or *P. Dict.*), 'in its proper sphere.' *Comy.*
has *kāraṇen' eva.*

[2] Text reads *vattanti* (? *vattan ti*), but *Sinh.* text and *Comy. vattati*
(he proceeds).

[3] *Bali. Cf. Petavatthu* and *Khuddaka-P.* Petas are those still in
purgatory; devatā those in *deva-loka.*

[4] As at *D.* iii, 61 (among the duties of the Wheel-turning Monarch),
and at *A.* i, 168, where I should translate thus.

[5] On this phrase *cf.* Vol. I, 151, where it fits the context far better
than it does here.

[6] *Cf. D.* iii, 66.

is the fourth opportunity seized by him, turned to merit and
fittingly made use of.

So, housefather, this same Ariyan disciple, with the wealth
acquired by energetic striving . . . lawfully gotten, is a doer
of these four deeds of merit.   If the wealth of anyone be spent[1]
without these four deeds of merit, such wealth is called " wealth
that has failed to seize its opportunity, failed to win merit,
unfittingly[2] made use of."   But, housefather, if the wealth of
anyone be spent on these four deeds of merit, then it is called
" wealth that has seized its opportunity, turned to merit, and
is fittingly made use of."

> I have enjoyed my wealth.   Those serving me
> And those dependent on me have escaped
> From dangers.   I have made the best of gifts,
> Nay, done th' oblations five.   The virtuous,
> Composed, who live the good life, I've supported.
> That aim[3] the which to win householders wise
> Should long for wealth, I've won.   I've done a deed
> Never to be regretted,—pondering thus
> A mortal man in Ariyan dhamma firm
> Is praised in this world, then in heaven rejoices.'[4]

§ ii (62). *Debtless.*

Now the housefather Anāthapiṇḍika came to visit the
Exalted One . . .   As he sat at one side the Exalted One
said this to the housefather Anāthapiṇḍika:

' Housefather, there are these four kinds of bliss to be won
by the householder who enjoys the pleasures of sense from
time to time and when occasion offers.   What four ?   The
bliss of ownership,[5] the bliss of wealth, the bliss of debtlessness,
the bliss of blamelessness.

And what, housefather, is the bliss of ownership ?

---

[1] *Parikkhayaŋ gacchati* = ' runs out.'
[2] Text should read *anāyatanaso*.
[3] Text should read *attho*.   [4] The gāthas are at *A*. iii, 46.
[5] *Atthi-sukhaŋ :* ' the bliss of " there-is." '

In this case a clansman has wealth acquired by energetic striving, amassed by strength of arm, won by sweat, lawful and lawfully gotten. At the thought: Wealth is mine acquired by energetic striving . . . lawfully gotten, bliss comes to him, satisfaction comes to him. This, housefather, is called " the bliss of ownership."

And what is the bliss of wealth ?

In this case, housefather, a clansman by means of wealth acquired by energetic striving . . . both enjoys his wealth and does meritorious deeds therewith. At the thought: By means of wealth acquired . . . I both enjoy my wealth and do meritorious deeds, bliss comes to him, satisfaction comes to him. This, housefather, is called " the bliss of wealth."

And what is the bliss of debtlessness ?

In this case a clansman owes no debt great or small to anyone. At the thought: I owe no debt, great or small, to anyone, bliss comes to him, satisfaction comes to him. This, housefather, is called " the bliss of debtlessness."

And what is the bliss of blamelessness ?

In this case, housefather, the Ariyan disciple is blessed with blameless action of body, blameless action of speech, blameless action of mind. At the thought: I am blessed with blameless action of body, speech and mind, bliss comes to him, satisfaction comes to him. This is called "the bliss of blamelessness."

Such, housefather, are the four kinds of bliss to be won by the householder who enjoys the pleasures of sense from time to time when occasion offers.

> Winning the bliss of debtlessness a man
> May then recall the bliss of really having.
> When he enjoys the bliss of wealth, he sees
> 'Tis such[1] by wisdom. When he sees he knows.
> Thus is he wise indeed in both respects.
> But these have not one-sixteenth of the bliss
> (That cometh to a man) of blamelessness.'

---

[1] Text *tatho*; *Sinh.* text *tato*.

§ iii (63). *Equal with Brahmā.*[1]

'Monks, those families where mother and father are worshipped in the home are reckoned like unto Brahmā.   Those
families where mother and father are worshipped in the home
are ranked with teachers of old.   Those families where mother
and father are worshipped in the home are ranked with the
devas[2] of old.   Worthy of offerings, monks, are those families
where mother and father are worshipped in the home.

"Brahmā," monks, is a term for mother and father.
"Teachers of old," monks, is a term for mother and father.
"Devas of old," monks, is a term for mother and father.
"Worthy of offerings," monks, is a term for mother and father.
Why so?   Because mother and father do much for children,
they bring them up, nourish and introduce them to the world.[3]

> Parents are "Brahmā" called, "teachers of old,"[4]
> Worthy of gifts are they, compassionate
> Unto their tribe of children.   Thus the wise
> Should worship them and pay them honours due,
> Serve them with food and drink, clothing and bed,
> Anoint their bodies, bathe and wash their feet.
> For service such as this to parents given
> In this life sages praise a man, and he
> Hereafter has reward of joy in heaven.'[5]

---

[1] *Cf. A.* i, 132=*G.S.* i, 114; *Itv.*, p. 109   The similar Upanishadic
context, Taittirīya 1, 11, 1.(misprinted in *G.S.* i as ii) runs as follows:
> One should not be negligent of duties to devas and fathers:
>> Become one to whom mother is as deva.
>> Become one to whom father is as deva;
and so for 'teacher' and for 'guest.'   *Cf.* also *Jāt.* No. 532.

[2] *A.* i omits this sentence.   *Pubbadevā*, like *pubbapetā*, would seem
to mean those who have lived on earth (ancestors) and are now worshipped as pitris, whereas petas are still earth-bound.   But it may
refer to the ancient Vedic gods.   Texts have *sapubbadevatāni*, but
Comy. -devakāni.

[3] *Dassetāro.   Comy.* takes this term to mean 'point out objects
desirable and undesirable.'

[4] The gāthas are a continuation of those of sutta 32, and the whole
poem is at *J.A.* v, 330 (*Sona-Nanda-Jātaka*).

[5] *Cf. S.* i, 182.

§ iv (64). *Purgatory.*[1]

' Monks, possessed of four qualities one is put into purgatory according to his deserts. What four ?

He is one who takes life, steals, is a wrong-doer in sensual desires, he is a liar. These are the four qualities possessed of which . . .

> To kill, to steal, to lie,—these three, and going
> After another's wife the wise commend not.'[2]

§ v (65). *Outer form.*

' Monks, these four persons are found existing in the world.[3] What four ?

He who measures according to (outward) form and is satis-fied therewith; he who measures according to (others') words and is satisfied therewith; he who measures according to austerity and is satisfied therewith; he who measures accord-ing to dhamma[4] and is satisfied therewith.

> If they have measured by the form and go by what folk say,
> Desire-and-passion-led, they do not know that man.
> If the very man he know not, nor things external see,
> Hedged in on every side that fool by words is swayed.
> If the very man he know not, but things external see,[5]
> The outward fruits observing, he too by words is swayed.
> But if he know the very man and see externals too,
> Clear-sighted without hindrance,[6] by words he is not
>   swayed.'[7]

---

[1] *Cf. supra,* I, § 10.

[2] From *Sigālovāda, D.* iii, 182; *cf. KhpA.* 143.

[3] *Cf. Pugg.,* p. 53; *Human Types,* 73, where each term is explained.

[4] One's own standard of right and wrong, not the later '*Dhamma.*'

[5] *Vi-nīvaraṇa-dassāvī*—i.e., freed from the five hindrances of sen-suality, ill-will, sloth-and-torpor, flurry-and-worry, doubt-and-wavering.

[6] Here *Sinh.* text wrongly reads *na passati.*

[7] These gāthas occur, with slight differences, at *Thag.* 469; *Brethr.* 230, where they are ascribed to Bhaddiya the Dwarf, the sweet-voiced teacher, and are there more fittingly applied. He says: ' People see my misshapen *rūpa,* and misjudge me; but on hearing my voice (*ghosa*) they are entranced. It looks as if our version is derived from those at *Thag.,* for in the former there is no reference to austerity or dhamma.

§ vi (66). *Lustful.*[1]

' Monks, these four persons are found existing in the world. What four ?

The lustful, the hateful, the deluded, the proud. These four . . .

In love with lustful things, enamoured of fair forms,
Vile creatures by delusion bound increase their bonds.
E'en clever men do evil deeds that spring from lust,
From hatred and delusion, painful, sorrow-fraught.
Blind creatures, clothed in ignorance, not having sight,
Being by nature such as this, in their conceit
Consider not: Perhaps it may be so with us.'[2]

§ vii (67). *Lord of snakes.*

On a certain occasion the Exalted One was staying near Sāvatthī, in Jeta Grove in Anāthapiṇḍika's Park. Now at that time at Sāvatthī a certain monk had been bitten by a snake and had died.[3] So a great number of monks came to visit the Exalted One, and on coming to him saluted him and sat down at one side. So seated those monks said this to the Exalted One:

' Lord, a certain monk here in Sāvatthī has been bitten by a snake and has died.'

' Then, monks, that monk did not suffuse with heart of amity the four royal families of snakes. Had he done so that monk would not have died of snake-bite. What are the four royal families of snakes ?

The royal family of snakes called Virūpakkha, that called Erāpatha, that called Chabyāputta and the royal family of

---

[1] *Cf. Pugg.*, p. 84.

[2] A difficult line owing to various readings. That of our text *yathā dhammā tathā santā na tass' evan ti maññā.* is obviously wrong. *Comy.* and *Sinh.* text read *na nassevan ti maññare.* MSS. have *kass' evaṃ : na sevaṃ : na ssevanti*, etc. Acc. to *Comy.*'s interpretation we should read *na n' ass' evan ti=na no assa.* For the form *maññare* (=*maññanti*), *cf. supra*, § 3, *vuccare.*

[3] *Cf. Vin.* ii, 109; *JA.* ii, 144.

snakes called Kanhā-gotamaka. Monks, that monk did not
suffuse with heart of amity these four royal families of snakes;
had he done so he would not have died of snake-bite. Monks,
for self-warding, for self-guarding, for self-protection I do
enjoin that ye suffuse with heart of amity[1] these four royal
families of snakes, thus:

> May I have kindness with Virūpakkhas,
> May I have kindness with Erāpathas,
> With Chabyāputtas may I kindness have,
> With Kaṇhā-gotamakas may I have kindness.

> May I have kindness with the footless,
> With those of two feet may I kindness have,
> With quadrupeds may I have kindness,
> May I have kindness with the many-footed.

> Let not the footless do me harm,
> Nor those that have two feet;
> Let not four-footed ones me harm,
> Nor those with many feet.

> All creatures, living things,—may all that has become,—
> May one and all see luck, and may no harm befall.

> Infinite the Buddha, infinite is Dhamma, infinite the Order.
> Finite are creeping things, snakes, scorpions, centipedes;
> Finite are spinning spiders,[2] house-lizards, rats and mice.

> Done by me is warding, done by me is protection.
> Let all things living now depart in peace.
> I, even I, before the Exalted One bow down;
> Before the seven fully Enlightened Ones I bow.'

---

[1] For the subject of *metta-bhāvanā* and *parittā cf.* Mrs. Rhys Davids
at *Dial.* iii, 185 *f.* and *Sakya*, 221 *ff.*; also *J.P.T.S.*, 1893.

Virūpakkha was regarded as regent of the western quarter (*D.* iii, 199).
Comy. can tell us nothing of the other three. *Jātaka Comy.* says that
the Bodhisattva promised long life to those who observed this *parittā*
or charm, and that thereafter the monks lived long, while the B. himself ' by developing the divine moods (*brahmavihāre*) was bound for the
Brahma world.' For *Metta-Sutta* see *KhpA.* ix and *Manual of a Mystic*,
p. 4 *ff.*

[2] *Uṇṇānabhi*, ' belly-spinners.' *JA. Comy.*

§ viii (68). *Devadatta.*

On a certain occasion the Exalted One was staying near Rājagaha, on the hill Vultures' Peak, not long after Devadatta had left (the Order).[1] Then the Exalted One addressed the monks thus concerning Devadatta:[2]

'To the ruin of self, monks, did (love of) gains, favours and flattery come upon Devadatta; to the misfortune of others, monks, did these come upon Devadatta. Just as, monks, the plantain gives fruit to the ruin of self, gives fruit to the misfortune of others, so did love of gains, favours and flattery come upon Devadatta to his own ruin, to the misfortune of others. Just as, monks, a bamboo . . . just as a reed . . . just as a mule conceives to her own ruin, to the misfortune of others, even so, monks, did love of gains, favours and flattery come upon Devadatta to the ruin of self, to the misfortune of others.

> Truly its fruit the plantain doth destroy,
> Their fruit destroys the bamboo and the rush;
> So homage doth destroy the fool,
> Just as its embryo the mule.'

§ ix (69). *Effort.*[3]

'Monks, there are these four efforts. What four?

The effort to restrain, that to abandon, that to make-become, and the effort to preserve.

And of what sort, monks, is the effort to restrain?

Herein a monk generates desire for the non-arising of evil, unprofitable states that have not yet arisen; he makes an effort, sets going energy, he lays hold of and exerts his mind (to this end). This, monks, is called "the effort to restrain."

And of what sort, monks, is the effort to abandon?

Herein a monk generates desire for the abandoning of evil,

---

[1] *Cf. Vin. Texts,* iii, 256.
[2] *Cf. K.S.* i, 192; ii, 163; *Milinda, trans.* i, 236; *Dhp. v.* 164; *Netti,* 130; *VM.* ii, 633; Thomas, *Life of Buddha,* 132.
[3] *Cf. K.S.* v, 219, *Right Efforts,* and above, I, §§ 3, 4.

unprofitable states that have arisen; he makes an effort . . .
exerts his mind (to this end). This is called "the effort to
abandon."

And of what sort, monks, is the effort to make-become ?

Herein he generates desire for the arising of profitable
states not yet arisen; he makes an effort . . . exerts his mind
(to this end).[1] This is called "the effort to make-become."

And of what sort, monks, is the effort to preserve ?

Herein a monk generates desire for the establishing, for
the non-confusion, for the more-becoming, for the increase,
cultivation and fulfilment of profitable states that have arisen;
he makes an effort, sets going energy, he lays hold of and exerts
his mind (to this end). This is called "the effort to preserve."
So these, monks, are the four efforts.

> Restraint, leaving, making-become, preserving—
> These are the four exertions taught by him,
> The Kinsman of the Sun. Herein a monk
> Ardently striving makes an end of Ill.'[2]

§ x (70). *Unrighteous.*

' At such time, monks, as rājahs are unrighteous, the ministers[3] of rājahs also are unrighteous. When ministers are unrighteous, brāhmins and householders also are unrighteous. Thus
townsfolk and villagers are unrighteous. This being so, moon
and sun go wrong in their courses.[4] This being so, constellations and stars do likewise; days and nights, months and
fortnights, seasons and years are out of joint; the winds
blow wrong, out of season. Thus the devas are annoyed.[5]
This being so, the sky-deva bestows not sufficient rain. Rains
not falling seasonably, the crops ripen in wrong season.

---

[1] *Cf. The Four Right Efforts, K.S.* v, p. 219 *f.*

[2] Gāthās as at I, § 14 above.

[3] Reading *rāja-yuttā* with *Comy.* and *Sinh.* text for text's *-puttā.*

[4] *Comy.* gives no reason for this. Probably it is meant that devas, in
warding men, are warning them. Text should read *candima-*, here and
below.

[5] According to *Comy.* tree-devas, etc., who live in trees, find their
homes gone.

Monks, when crops ripen in wrong season, men who live on
such crops are short-lived, ill-favoured, weak and sickly.

But, monks, when rājahs are righteous, the ministers of
rājahs also are righteous. When ministers are righteous,
brāhmins and householders also are righteous. Thus townsfolk and villagers are righteous. This being ş̣o, moon and
sun go right in their courses. This being so, constellations
and stars do likewise; days and nights, months and fortnights,
seasons and years go on their courses regularly; winds blow
regularly and in due season. Thus the devas are not annoyed
and the sky-deva bestows sufficient rain. Rains falling
seasonably, the crops ripen in due season. Monks, when
crops ripen in due season, men who live on those crops are
long-lived, well-favoured, strong and free from sickness.[1]

When kine are crossing, if the old bull swerve,
They all go swerving, following his lead.[2]
So among men, if he who's reckoned best
Live not aright, much more do other folk.
If the rājah be unrighteous, the whole realm dwells in woe.

When kine are crossing, if the bull go straight,
They all go straight because his course is straight.
So among men, if he who's reckoned best
Live righteously, the others do so too.
The whole realm dwells in happiness if the rājah lives aright.'

CHAPTER VIII.—THE SURE.[3]

§ i (71). *Effort.*

' Possessed of four things, monks, a monk has entered on
the path to surety, and he is determinedly bent on[4] the
destruction of the āsavas. What are the four ?

---

[1] Gāthās at *JA.* iii, 111; *Netti*, 130, 134; *cf.* also *JA.* v, No. 521, where
the story is told to the Kosalan rājah.

[2] *Nette* ; so also all MSS., but *Comy. nete.*

[3] *Apaṇṇaka* at *A.* i, 111=Nibbāna. See *n.* to *G.S.* i, 97. At *A.* i,
270 it is applied to a die (*maṇi*) which is ' true.' In the sutta the
noun *apaṇṇakatā* is used; *Comy.* expl. as *aviruddha,* unobstructed
Cf. K.S. iv, 253 *n.* Mrs. R. D. suggests 'not green, immature: trustworthy.'

[4] =*K.S.* iv, 110. *Text* has *yoni c' assa āraddhā*; at *A.* i, 113,
yoni c' assa āraddho. At *Itv.* 30, *yoniso āraddho hoti,* chosen by the

Herein a monk is virtuous, learned, of ardent energy and wise. Possessed of these four things a monk has entered on the path to surety . . .'

§ ii (72). *View.*

' Possessed of four things, monks, a monk has entered on the path to surety, and he is determinedly bent on the destruction of the āsavas. What are the four ?

Dispassionate thinking, benevolent thinking, harmless thinking and right view.[1] Possessed of these four things a monk has entered on the path to surety . . .'

§ iii (73). *Worthy.*

' Monks, possessed of four things a man is to be understood as being unworthy.[2] What four ?

Herein, monks, the unworthy man, even unasked, speaks out what is discreditable to another. What then (would he say) if asked ?

If, however, he is obliged to speak on being questioned, then without reserve or equivocation[3] he utters dispraise of another to the full and in all details. This, monks, is to be understood as the meaning of the saying: " This worthy[4] is an unworthy one."

Then again, the unworthy one, even when asked, does not speak out what is to another's credit; much less when unasked.

If, however, he is obliged to speak on being questioned, then with reserve and equivocation he utters praise of another grudgingly and in brief. ⸱This, monks, is to be understood as the meaning of the saying: " This worthy is an unworthy one."

---

editor out of many variants—*e.g., yoniso, yonissa, yonissayā, yoni so, yonicassa, yonicassa* and *yoniso c' assa. Yoniso* is abl., and it seems best to read *yoniso c' āraddho,* according to which I translate.

[1] The first three at *A.* i, 275. *Cf. K.S.* ii, 106 *n.*; again below, text 252.

[2] *Asappurisa, cf. A.* i, 61; at *SnA.* 479=*anariya.*

[3] Text and *Comy. alampetvā; Sinh.* text *alambetvā (Comy. alampitaŋ katvā* ?). The word does not seem to occur elsewhere. *P. Dict.* suggests *alambhetvā; cf. palambheti.*

[4] *Bhavaŋ,* sometimes ironical, as here.

Again, monks, the unworthy one, even when asked does not speak out what is discreditable to himself; much less does he do so when unasked.

If, however, he is obliged to speak on being questioned, then with reserve and equivocation he utters grudgingly and in brief what is to his own discredit.   This, monks, is to be understood as the meaning of the saying: " This worthy is an unworthy one."

Once more, monks, the unworthy one, even unasked, speaks out what is creditable to himself.   What then does he do when asked ?

If, however, he is obliged to speak on being questioned, then without reserve or equivocation he sings his own praises to the full and in all details.   This, monks, is to be understood as the meaning of the saying: " This worthy is an unworthy one."

Thus, possessed of these four things one is to be understood as an unworthy one.

Now, monks, possessed of four things one is to be understood as a worthy one.   What four things ?'   (*The opposite of the foregoing are detailed.*)

§ iv (74). *The young wife.*[1]

' Just as, monks, when a young wife is first led home (to her husband) either by day or night, she at first feels exceeding great fear and bashfulness in the presence of her mother-in-law, her father-in-law, her husband, and even towards servants and work-people; but as time goes on, owing to living together and intimacy, she addresses mother-in-law, father-in-law and husband thus: " Away with you !   What do you know ?"

Just in like manner, monks, a certain monk here maybe, when he first goes forth, whether by day or night, from the home to the homeless life, feels exceeding great fear and bashfulness in the presence of monks and nuns, disciples male

---

[1] *Comy.* and *Sinh.* text take this as part of the previous §, and the next § as §§ 4, 5, but the uddāna as separate.   *Vadhukā=sunisā* or *sunhā*, daughter-in-law.

and female, even of novices who serve[1] in the monastery,
but as time goes on, owing to living together and intimacy, he
addresses teacher and preceptor thus: "Away with you!
What do you know?"

Wherefore, monks, thus must ye train yourselves: I will
dwell in mind like a young wife newly arrived. That is how
ye must train yourselves.'

§ v (75). *Perfections.*[2]

'Monks, there are these four perfections. What four?

Perfection of virtue, perfection of concentration, of wisdom
and release.

Monks, there are these four perfections. What four?

Perfection of bodily form, of feeling, perception and becoming.[3] These are the four perfections.'

§ vi (76). *Kusinārā.*[4]

On a certain occasion the Exalted One was staying at
Kusinārā, at the Bend[5] in the Sāl-grove of the Mallas, between
the twin sāl-trees, at the time of his final passing away. Then
the Exalted One addressed the monks, saying: 'Monks.'

'Yes, lord,' replied those monks to the Exalted One. The
Exalted One said this:

'It may be, however, monks, that some one of you has
doubt or misgiving as to the Buddha or Dhamma or Order or
the Way or the Practice (going to the Way). Ask, monks!

---

[1] *Ārāmika-saman' uddesesu.* *Cf. A.* iii, 109.

[2] Text has *angāni* for *aggāni* of *Comy.* and *Sinh.* text, but is right
in the uddāna.

[3] *Bhav' aggaŋ. Comy.* takes this and the foregoing to be 'the
personality' in which one attains arahantship (*uttama-sarīra*).

[4] At *D.* ii, 154; *Dial.* ii, 172, but the introductory paragraph is at
D. ii, 137.

[5] *Upavattana* (branching off), so always, but at *DA.* i, *Upavattaṃ
Mallānaŋ.* It is not the name of a place proper. *Comy.* 'At a place
midway between the eastward row of sāl-trees where it turns north-
ward.' *UdA.* 238; *SA.* i, 222, *uttarena nivattati ; tasmā upavattanan ti
vuccati. Cf.* also *DA.* ii, 573.

Be not hereafter remorseful (at the thought): Face to face with us was the Teacher and we could not question the Exalted One face to face.'

At these words those monks were silent.

Then a second time the Exalted One addressed the monks (in the same words) and a second time those monks were silent.

Then for the third time the Exalted One addressed the monks (in the same words) and a third time those monks were silent.

Then said the Exalted One to the monks:

' It may be, however, monks, that out of respect for the teacher ye ask not. Then let one ask as friend of a friend.'[1]

At these words those monks were silent.

Thereupon the venerable Ānanda said this to the Exalted One:

' It is wonderful, lord! It is marvellous, lord! Thus convinced am I of the Order of monks that there is not in this Order of monks in a single monk any doubt or misgiving as to the Buddha, Dhamma, the Order, the Way or the Practice.'

' You, Ānanda, speak out of faith, but the Tathāgata has knowledge therein. There is indeed in this Order of monks no doubt or misgiving in a single monk as to the Buddha, the Order, Dhamma, the Way, or the Practice. Of these five hundred monks here, Ānanda, the most backward[2] is a Stream-winner, one saved from the Downfall, assured, bound for enlightenment.'

§ vii (77). *Unthinkable.*

' Monks, there are these four unthinkables, not to be thought of, thinking of which one would be distraught and come to grief.[3] What are the four ?

---

[1] The meaning here is obvious, but *Comy.* says ' Ask *each other,* as friend of friend, and I will solve your doubts,' which seems a strained interpretation. See *Gotama the Man,* 246-50.

[2] *Pacchimaka. Comy.* thinks this refers to Ānanda, and was said to encourage him to persevere, but this is open to doubt. It is improbable, also, that a large number of monks was present.

[3] *Cf. Expos.* i, 31, ' The bhikkhu who is ill-trained in Abhidhamma makes his mind run to excess in metaphysical abstractions and thinks of the unthinkable.'

Of Buddhas, monks, the range is unthinkable, not to be thought of . . . Of one who is musing, monks, the range of his musing is unthinkable, not to be thought of. The fruit of action, monks, is unthinkable, not to be thought of . . . World-speculation,[1] monks, is unthinkable, not to be thought of, thinking of which one would be distraught and would come to grief. These, monks, are the four unthinkables, thinking of which . . .'

§ viii (78). *Gifts*.[2]

' Monks, there are these four purities in gifts. What four ?

There is a gift, monks, which is made pure on the part of the giver, not of the receiver. There is a gift, monks, which is made pure on the part of the receiver, not of the giver. There is a gift which is made pure on neither side, and there is a gift which is made pure on both sides.

Now, monks, how is a gift made pure on the part of the giver, not of the receiver ?

In this case the giver is virtuous, of a lovely nature; the receivers are immoral and of a wicked nature. Thus the gift is made pure on the part of the giver, not of the receiver.[3]

And how is a gift made pure on the part of the receiver, not of the giver ?

In this case, monks, the giver is immoral, of a wicked nature, while the receivers are of the opposite nature. Thus the gift . . .

And how is a gift made pure neither on the part of the giver nor of the receiver ?

In this case, monks, both giver and receiver are immoral, of a wicked nature. Thus the gift . . .

---

[1] *Loka-cintā*. *Cf. K.S.* v, 377. *Comy.* on both passages, 'Such as: Who made the moon and sun ? Who made the earth, ocean, beings, mountains, mangoes, coconuts, etc. ?'

[2] *Cf. D.* iii, 231, but in different order; *M.* iii, 256, which has gāthās on the subject and a fifth set; *Pts. of Contr.* 322.

[3] *Comy.* illustrates (i) by Vessantara's gift, *JA.* vi, 487, and that of Kevaṭṭa to Dīgha-sammatthera; (iii) by that of a hunter at Vaḍḍhamāna, at a *peta-dāna*. ' Made pure ' is explained by *Comy.* as ' one of great fruit.'

And how is a gift made pure both on the part of the giver and of the receiver ?

In this case, monks, the giver is virtuous, of a lovely nature, and the receiver is one of a like nature. Thus the gift is made pure on both sides.

These are the four purities in gifts.'

§ ix (79). *Trade.*

Now the venerable Sāriputta came to visit the Exalted One. As he sat at one side the venerable Sāriputta said this to the Exalted One:

' Pray, lord,what is the reason, what is the cause why such and such a trade practised[1] by some person turns out a failure ? Again, lord, what is the reason, what is the cause why such and such a trade practised by some person does not turn out as he intended ? Pray, lord, what is the reason why such and such a trade . . . does turn out as he intended ? Again, lord, what is the reason, what is the cause why such and such a trade practised by some person prospers beyond[2] his intention ?'

' In this matter, Sāriputta, (suppose) someone comes to a recluse or brāhmin and makes him an offer,[3] saying: " Sir, say what you want by way of support." But he does not give him what he offered. If this man deceases from that life and returns to this sort of life, whatever trade he may practise, it turns out a failure.

Again in this matter, Sāriputta, suppose someone comes to a recluse or brāhmin and makes him an offer, saying: " Sir, say what you want by way of support." But he does not give him what he intended to give. Then, if this man deceases

---

[1] *Payutta,* not ' wasted,' as this passage is translated in *P. Dict. Cf. Sn.* v. 404, *payojaye dhammikaŋ so vaṇijjaŋ* (in order to prosper the householder should practise a lawful trade).

[2] *Parádhippāya.* (*Comy. par' ajjhāsayā, ajjhāsayato adhikatara-phalā hoti.*)

[3] Quoted *SnA.* ii. 171 on *Sn.* v. 101, *yo brāhmaṇaŋ vā samaṇaŋ vā aññaŋ vâpi vanibbakaŋ musāvādena vañceti . . .*

from that life and returns to this sort of life, whatever trade he may practise, it does not turn out as he intended.

Then again, Sāriputta, suppose someone comes to a recluse or brāhmin and makes him . . . a similar offer . . . and gives him what he intended to give. Then, if this man deceases . . . whatever trade he may practise turns out as he intended.

Once more, Sāriputta, suppose someone comes to a recluse or brāhmin and makes him a similar offer . . . and gives him more than he intended to give. Then if this man deceases from that life and returns to this sort of life, whatever trade he may practise, it prospers beyond his intention.

This, Sāriputta, is the reason, this is the cause why such and such a trade practised by some person turns out a failure . . . does not turn out as he intended . . . does turn out as he intended . . . prospers beyond his intention.'

§ x (80). *Essence of the deed.*

On a certain occasion the Exalted One was staying at Kosambī in Ghosita Park. Then the venerable Ānanda came to the Exalted One. . . . As he sat at one side the venerable Ānanda said this to the Exalted One:[1]

'Pray, lord, what is the reason, what is the cause why womenfolk neither sit in a court (of justice), nor embark on business, nor reach the essence of the deed ?'[2]

---

[1] Ānanda is often found interested in women. But *cf. K.S.* iv, 165 *ff.*

[2] Text *kamm' ojaŋ* (so also MSS. Adyar), the only instance of the word I have found; but *Sinh.* text and *Comy. Kambojaŋ* (?), the country in N.W. India next to Afghanistan. I follow our text's reading as there seems no reason for thus naming this country as a goal for woman's ambition. At *JA.* vi, 208 its natives are accounted barbarians. It may, however, have been on one of the great caravan routes. *Comy.* adds ' in search of wealth.' *Cf. Dhamm' oja*, ' essence of dhamma.' I think my rendering (pith of the matter) suits better with the fourth quality, *duppañño*, given for their shortcomings. (*Oja* is generally named in the series of *dhātuyo*; *vaṇṇa, gandha, rasa, oja*.) It is named as something extra—*e.g.*, as when devas put *oja* into the milk-rice of Sujātā or the truffles of Cunda, etc. (*cf. SnA.* ii, 154)—whereas certain yakkhas called *ojohārā* take it away.

'Womenfolk are uncontrolled, Ānanda. Womenfolk are envious, Ānanda. Womenfolk are greedy, Ānanda. Womenfolk are weak in wisdom, Ānanda. That is the reason, that is the cause why womenfolk do not sit in a court of justice, do not embark on business, do not reach the essence of the deed.'

CHAPTER IX.—UNSHAKEN.[1]

§ i (81). *Stealing.*

' Monks, possessed of four qualities one is put into purgatory according to his deserts.[2] What are the four ?

He takes life, steals, is a wrong-doer in things sensual, a liar. Possessed of these four qualities . . .

Monks, possessed of four qualities one is put into heaven according to his deserts. What are the four ?

He abstains from taking life, from stealing, from wrong-doing in things sensual, and from lying. These are the four.'

§ ii (82). *Lying.*

(*The same for one who is* a liar, malicious speaker, of harsh speech, an idle babbler; *and for one* who abstains from these things.)

§ iii (83). *Praise.*

' Monks, possessed of four qualities one is put into purgatory according to his deserts. What four ?

Without test or scrutiny he speaks in praise of what deserves not praise. Without test or scrutiny he speaks in blame of things deserving praise. In like manner he shows appreciation where there should be none. Likewise, where appreciation should be shown, he shows displeasure.[3] Such, monks, are the four qualities . . .

---

[1] Text, *Comy.* and MSS. give this title as *Macala* (there is no such word). The *m* is merely euphonic, as *Comy.* notes, and occurs first in this *vagga* at § 7 (*samana-m-acalo*).

[2] *Cf.* I, § 10 and *n.* The sutta = § 64 above, only the titles being different.

[3] As at I, § 3 above and *A.* i, 89 = *G.S.* i, 80. *Cf. Pugg.* 49.

Monks, possessed of four qualities one is put into heaven
according to his deserts. What four ?' (*The opposite of the
above.*)

§ iv (84). *Wrath.*[1]

' Monks, possessed of four qualities one is put into purgatory
according to his deserts. What four ?

He pays regard to wrath, not to saddhamma. He pays
regard to hypocrisy, not to saddhamma . . . to gain, not to
saddhamma. He pays regard to honours, not to saddhamma.'

(*The possessor of the opposite qualities is put into heaven* . . .)

§ v (85). *Darkness.*[2]

' Monks, these four persons are found existing in the world.
What four ?

He who is in darkness and bound for darkness; he who is
in darkness but bound for light; he who is in light but bound
for darkness; he who is in light and bound for light.

And how, monks, is a person in darkness bound for darkness?

In this case a certain person[3] is born in a low family, the
family of a scavenger or a hunter or a basket-weaver or wheel-
wright or sweeper,[4] or in the family of some wretched man
hard put to it to find a meal or earn a living, where food and
clothes are hard to get. Moreover, he is ill-favoured, ugly,
dwarfish, sickly, purblind, crooked, lame or paralysed, with
never a bite or sup, without clothes, vehicle, without perfumes
or flower-garlands, bed, dwelling or lights. He lives in the
practice of evil with body, speech and thought; and so doing,
when body breaks up, after death, he is reborn in the waste, the

---

[1] The same qualities as at I, § 43 above, except for the gāthās.

[2] As at *Pugg.* 51 (*Types*, 70-1), but without the address ' monks.'
At *S.* i, 93=*K.S.* i, 118 it is addressed to Pasenadi, rājah of Kosala,
and a number of gāthās are added. The framework is quoted at
Netti, 153.

[3] *Cf. A.* i, 107=*G.S.* i, 92.

[4] *Pukkusa,* originally one of a despised tribe of this name. *Cf.*
Dial. ii, 141 *n.* *Comy.* explains ' those who sweep up flowers,' which
are offered at shrines and are never removed by the devotees themselves.
For the others *cf Dial.* i, 100, ' aboriginal tribesmen who were hereditary
craftsmen in these three crafts.'

way of woe, the downfall, in purgatory. Thus, monks, is the person who is in darkness and bound for darkness.

And how, monks, is a person in darkness but bound for light ?

In this case a certain person is born in a low family . . . without bed, dwelling or lights. He lives in the practice of good with body, speech and thought . . . and so doing, when body breaks up, after death he is reborn in the happy bourn, in the heaven-world.

And how, monks, is a person in light but bound for darkness?

In this case a certain person is born in a high family, a family of wealthy nobles or a family of wealthy brāhmins or of wealthy householders, in a family that is rich, exceeding rich, of great possessions, with the support of abounding wealth, in a family that abounds in wealth of crops. And that man is well-built, comely and charming, possessed of supreme beauty of form. He is one able to get clothes, vehicle, perfumes and flower-garlands, bed, dwelling and lights. But he lives in the practice of evil with body, speech and thought. So doing, when body breaks up, after death he is reborn in the waste, the way of woe, the downfall, in purgatory. Thus, monks, is the person who is in light but bound for darkness.

And how, monks, is a person who is in light and bound for light ?

In this case a person is born in a high family . . . able to get clothes . . . bed, dwelling and lights. He lives in the practice of good with body, speech and thought. So doing, when body breaks up after death, he is reborn in the happy bourn, in the heaven-world. Thus, monks, is one who is in light and bound for light.

These, monks, are the four persons found existing in the world.'[1]

§ vi (86). *Of low estate.*[2]

' Monks, these four persons are found existing in the world. What four ?

---

[1] The sutta at *S.* i, 94 adds a simile to each character.

[2] This sutta also is at *Pugg.* 52 and in brief at *Pugg.* 7. *Comy.* explains that in each case it is meant that he is such and such, but may or will become such and such.

He who is low and low; he who is low and high; he who is high and low, and he who is high and high.'

§ vii (87). *Kinds of recluses*[1] (a).

' Monks, these four persons are found existing in the world What four ?

The unshaken recluse, the blue-lotus recluse, the white-lotus recluse, and the recluse who is exquisite among recluses.

And how, monks, is a person an unshaken recluse ?

Herein, monks, a monk is a pupil, one who has entered the way;[2] he dwells aspiring for the unsurpassed rest from the toil. Just like a rājah's eldest son, a noble duly anointed, one who is not yet anointed and has not come to security,[3] even so,

---

[1] I give this title to the four next suttas. The uddāna of our text calls the first two *Anno* (?) *sayyojanañ ca,* which is nonsense. The *Sinh.* text has *Putto sayyojanañ ca* (the word *putta* does occur in § 2, but without significance). The framework is again at *Pugg.* 63. As the qualifications differ in *A.* and *Pugg.,* I tabulate the four sorts of recluses:

 i. In *Ang. Samana-m-acala* =a pupil aspiring for *yoga-kkhema.*
    In *Pugg.* =a Stream-winner.
 ii. In *Ang. Samana-pundarīka* =one who has destroyed the āsavas, but not realized the eightfold release; a Non-returner.
    In *Pugg.* =a breaker of the five lower fetters; a Non-returner.
 iii. In *Ang. Samana-paduma* =destroyer of the āsavas; and has realized the eightfold release.
    In *Pugg.* =destroyer of three fetters; a Once-returner.
 iv. In *Ang. Samana-sukhumāla* =one who has every blessing in this life, and all powers; is absolutely happy.
    In *Pugg.* =destroyer of āsavas; Arahant.

Thus there is some confusion here, Nos. ii and iii being different in this sutta and in Abhidhamma versions. Our next sutta gives the same set of recluses in the usual order of Stream-winner, Once-returner, Non-returner and Arahant.

[2] *Patipado* (not in *A. Index* or *P. Dict.*)=*patipannako* (*Comy.*), but we have *pāṭipado* at *M.* i, 354; *It.* 79, which seems the more correct form.

[3] *Cf. A.* i, 108; *G.S.* i, 92 (of the unanointed prince), where I translate ' has reached the age of discretion,' but it must mean ' is secure in the succession.' As there, our text should read *abhisekh' anabhisitto.*

monks, is the pupil who has entered the Way, one who dwells aspiring for the unsurpassed rest from the toil.

And how, monks, is a person a blue-lotus recluse ?

Herein a monk, by destroying the āsavas, has reached the heart's release, the release by wisdom that is free from the āsavas, and having realized it abides therein.   Yet does he not abide experiencing with his own person[1] the eight deliverances.

Thus, monks, is a person a blue-lotus recluse.

And how, monks, is a person a white-lotus recluse ?

Herein a monk, by destroying the āsavas . . . (*as before*) . . . abides therein, and abides experiencing with his own person the eight deliverances.

And how, monks, is a person a recluse exquisite among recluses ?

Herein a monk when invited enjoys a plentiful supply of robes,[2] but he gets little if uninvited; . . . so also as regards alms-food and lodging; if invited, he enjoys a plentiful supply of requisites and medicines for use in sickness, but he gets little if uninvited.   With whatsoever fellows in the holy life he dwells, their behaviour (towards him) in action of body, speech and thought is generally pleasing, rarely displeasing; moreover their presents to him are generally pleasing, rarely displeasing.

Again, as to those afflictions which originate from bile,[3] phlegm, wind, from the union of bodily humours, from changes of seasons, from stress of circumstances,[4] from personal assaults,[5] or from the ripeness of one's karma,—such do not trouble him much.   He is free from sickness.   As to the four musings which belong to the higher thought and lead to happy

---

[1] *Cf. Dial.* iii, 242, *kāyena phassitvā=nāma-kāyena* (*Comy.*) as below at § 113.   *Cf. K.S.* v, 202 *n.*   Some MSS. *passitvā*, others *phusitvā*.

[2] As at *A.* iii, 33.

[3] *Cf. S.* iv, 230=*K.S.* iv, 155, 161 *n.*; *MP.* 134.

[4] *Visama-pariharajani*, at *S.* iv. expl. as ' untoward happenings,' but here ' from sitting or standing too long.'

[5] *Opakkamikāni*, such as imprisonment, flogging or (as at *S.* iv) arrest for robbery or adultery or assault.   *Comy.*

living in this very life, he is a winner of them at will, without difficulty and without trouble.[1]   By destroying the āsavas he reaches the heart's release, the release by wisdom, himself comprehending it in this very life, and having attained it he abides therein.   Thus, monks, is a person a recluse exquisite among recluses.

Now, monks, if rightly speaking one would speak of the recluse exquisite among recluses, it is just of me that he would rightly use the words.   For I, monks, when invited enjoy a plentiful supply of robes, but get little if uninvited: likewise as regards alms-food and the rest.   With whatsoever fellows in the holy life I dwell, their behaviour (towards me) in action of body, speech and thought is generally pleasing, rarely displeasing.   Again, as to those afflictions which originate from bile and the rest . . . such do not trouble me much.   I am free from sickness.   As to the four musings, which belong to the higher thought . . . I am a winner of them at will.   By destroying the āsavas I reach the heart's release . . . and abide therein.   So monks, if rightly speaking one would speak about the recluse exquisite among recluses, it is just of me that he would rightly use the words.

These, monks, are the four persons found existing in the world.'

§ viii (88). *Kinds of recluses (b).*[2]

' Monks, these four persons are found existing in the world.   What four ?

The unshaken recluse, the blue-lotus recluse, the white-lotus recluse and the recluse exquisite among recluses.

And how, monks, is a person an unshaken recluse ?

Herein a monk, by the wearing out of three fetters is a stream-winner, of a nature not to go to the downfall, one assured, bound for enlightenment.   Thus, monks, is a person an unshaken recluse.

And how, monks, is a person a blue-lotus recluse ?

---

[1] *Cf. K.S.* v, 280; *Buddh. Psych.* 114 *ff.*

[2] These next three suttas seem added afterwards to support the usual definitions of those on the Four Paths. *Cf.* § 7 *n.*

Herein a monk, by utterly wearing out three fetters and by weakening lust, anger and delusion, is a once-returner. Coming back just once more to this world he makes an end of Ill. Thus, monks, is a person a blue-lotus recluse.

And how, monks, is a person a white-lotus recluse ?

Herein a monk, by utterly wearing out the five fetters which cause rebirth here, is apparitionally born, destined there to pass utterly away, of a nature not to return from that world. Thus, monks, is a person a white-lotus recluse.

And how, monks, is a person a recluse exquisite among recluses ?

Herein a monk by the destruction of the āsavas reaches the heart's release, the release by wisdom, that is free from the āsavas . . . and abides therein. Thus is a person a recluse exquisite among recluses.

These, monks, are the four persons found existing in the world.'

§ ix (89). *Kinds of recluses* (c).

' Monks, these four persons are found existing in the world. What four ?   (*The same as before.*)

And how, monks, is a person an unshaken recluse ?

Herein a monk is one of right view, right aim, right speech, right action, right way of living, right effort, right mindfulness and right concentration. Thus a person is an unshaken recluse.

And how, monks, is a person a blue-lotus recluse ?

Herein a monk is one of right view and the rest . . . he is one of right knowledge, of right release. Yet does he not abide experiencing with his own person the eight deliverances. Thus a person is a blue-lotus recluse.

And how, monks, is a person a white-lotus recluse ?

Herein a monk is one of right view and the rest . . . he is one of right knowledge, of right release, and he abides experiencing with his own person the eight deliverances. Thus a person is a white-lotus recluse.

And how is a person a recluse exquisite among recluses ?

Herein a monk, if invited, enjoys a plentiful supply of robes, but gets little if uninvited (*as in* § 7). Now, monks, if rightly

speaking one would speak about the recluse exquisite among
recluses, it is just of me that he would rightly use the words.

Thus, monks, these four persons are found existing in the
world.'

§ x (90). *Kinds of recluses (d)*.

'Monks, these four persons . . . the exquisite among
recluses.

And how, monks, is a person an unshaken recluse ?

Herein, monks, one is a pupil, who has not made up his mind,[1]
but lives aspiring for the unsurpassed rest from the toil.   Thus
a person is . . .

And how, monks, is a person a blue-lotus recluse ?

Herein a monk dwells in the contemplation of the rise and
fall of the five-grasping-groups, thus: Such is form, such is the
arising of form, such is the passing away of form.   Such is
feeling . . . such is perception . . . such are the activities . . .
such is consciousness, such the arising, such the passing away
thereof.   But he does not abide experiencing with his own
person the eight deliverances.   Thus a person is . . .

And how, monks, is a person a white-lotus recluse ?

Herein a monk dwells in the contemplation of the rise and
fall of the five-grasping-groups, thus: Such is form . . . such
the passing away thereof.   But he does abide experiencing
with his own person the eight deliverances.   Thus a person
is . . .

And how, monks, is a person a recluse exquisite among
recluses ?

Herein a monk if invited (*as in* § 7).   Now, monks, if rightly
speaking one would speak about the recluse exquisite among
recluses, it is just of me that he would rightly use the words.

Thus, monks, these four persons are found existing in the
world.'

---

[1] *Appatta-mānaso.*   See *n.* above to VII, § i (*patta-kammāni*).   Here
Comy. says *arahatt' atthāya payogaŋ anārabhitvā ṭhito pamāda-vihārī.*
He is not yet in earnest about the goal.   Perhaps it means 'has not
mastered his mind.'

CHAPTER X.—ASURAS.

§ i (91). *Asuras.*[1]

' Monks, these four persons are found existing in the world. What four ?

The asura with a retinue of asuras, the asura with a retinue of devas, the deva with a retinue of asuras, and the deva with a retinue of devas.

And how, monks, is a person an asura with a retinue of asuras ?

In this case, monks, a certain person is immoral, of a wicked nature, and his company is like unto him. Thus a person is . . .

And how, monks, is a person an asura with a retinue of devas ?

In this case, monks, a person is immoral, of a wicked nature, but his company is virtuous, of a lovely nature. Thus a person is . . .

And how, monks, is a person a deva with a retinue of asuras ?

In this case, monks, a person is virtuous, of a lovely nature, but his company is immoral, of a wicked nature. Thus a person is . . .

And how, monks, is a person a deva with a retinue of devas ?

In this case, monks, a person is virtuous, of a lovely nature, and his company is like unto him. Thus a person is . . .

So these are the four persons found existing in the world.'

§ ii (92). *Concentration (a).*[2]

' Monks, these four persons are found existing in the world. What four ?

Herein, monks, a certain person is one who gains mental calm of the self, but does not gain the higher wisdom of insight into things.[3]

---

[1] This sutta may be compared with Ch. VI, § 3. *Comy.* def. *asura* as ' *bībhaccho,* awful, vile.'

[2] The title for these three suttas is that of the *uddāna.*

[3] *Adhipaññā-dhamma-vipassanā. Cf. Dial.* i, 237 *n.* Here *dhamma* = *dhammā,* viz. *sankhārā,* etc. (*Comy.*), as shown in § 4.

Herein again, monks, a certain person is one who gains the higher wisdom of insight into things, but does not gain mental calm of the self.

Herein again, monks, a certain person is one who gains neither of these things. Yet again a certain person is one who gains both.

These four persons are found existing in the world.'

§ iii (93). *Concentration* (b).

' Monks, these four persons are found existing in the world. (*The previous sutta is repeated.*)

Then, monks, he who gained mental calm in himself, but not the higher wisdom of insight into things, should make an effort to establish the one and attain the other. Then at some future time he is one who has gained both of these things.

Then, monks, he who has gained the higher wisdom of insight into things, but not mental calm in himself, should make an effort to establish the one and attain the other. Then at some future time he is one who has gained both.

Then, monks, he who has gained neither mental calm in himself nor the higher wisdom of insight into things should put forth intense desire, effort, exertion, impulse, unobstruction, mindfulness and attention for the attainment of those profitable states.

Just as, monks, when one's turban or head is ablaze,[1] for the extinguishing thereof one must put forth intense desire, effort, exertion, impulse, unobstruction, mindfulness and attention, even so must that person put forth intense desire, and the rest, for the attainment of those profitable states. Then at some future time he is one who has gained both mental calm in himself and the higher wisdom of insight into things.

So, monks, he who has gained both these things should make an effort to establish just those profitable states and further to destroy the āsavas.

These, monks, are the four persons found existing in the world.'

---

[1] For this and the favourite simile of the blazing turban *cf. S.* i, 108, iii, 143, v, 440; *Sisters*, p. 172; *A.* iii, 308, iv, 320, v, 93 *ff.*

§ iv (94). *Concentration* (c).

' Monks, these four persons are found existing in the world. What four ?

(*The second sutta is repeated.*)

Now, monks, this person who has gained mental calm in himself, but not the higher wisdom of insight into things, might approach one who has done so and address him thus:

" Pray, your reverence, how are the activities to be regarded ? How are the activities to be understood ? How are the activities to be seen into ?"

Then the other expounds to him according as he himself has seen and known: " Thus and thus, your reverence, should the activities be regarded, understood, seen into."

Then at some later time he is one who has gained both mental calm in himself and the higher wisdom of insight into things.

Now, monks, this person who has gained the higher wisdom of insight into things, but not mental calm in himself, might approach one who has done so, and address him thus:

" Pray, your reverence, how should the mind be steadied ? How should the mind be made to settle down ? How should the mind be made one-pointed ? How should the mind be concentrated ?"

Then that other expounds to him according as he himself has seen and known: " Thus and thus, your reverence, should the mind be steadied, made to settle down, made one-pointed, concentrated."

Then at some later time he is one who has gained both the higher wisdom of insight into things and mental calm in himself.

Then, monks, he who has gained neither condition might approach one who has gained both and address him thus:

" Pray, your reverence, how should the mind be steadied . . . concentrated ? How should the activities be regarded, understood, seen into ?"

Then that other expounds to him . . . Then at some later time he is one who has gained both of these things.

Then, monks, this person who has gained both mental calm in himself and the higher wisdom of insight into things should make an effort to establish just those profitable states and further to destroy the āsavas.

These, monks, are the four persons found existing in the world.'

§ v (95). *The firebrand.*

'Monks, these four persons are found existing in the world. What four ?

He who is bent neither on his own profit nor on the profit of another; he who is bent on another's profit, but not on his own; he who is bent on his own profit, not another's, and he who is bent[1] on the profit both of himself and of another.

Just as, monks, a firebrand from a funeral pyre, blazing at both ends and in the middle smeared with dung,[2] serves no purpose[3] as fuel in village or as timber in forest,—using such a figure do I speak of this person who is bent neither on his own profit nor on another's.

Then, monks, this person who is bent on another's profit but not his own is more excellent and exalted than these two persons.

Again, monks, this person who is bent on his own profit, not another's, is more excellent and exalted than these three persons. Whereas he who is bent on the profit both of self and of another is of these four persons chief and best, topmost,[4] highest and supreme.

Just as, monks, from a cow comes milk, from milk cream, from cream butter, from butter ghee, from ghee the skimmings of ghee, and that is reckoned[5] the best,—even so this person,

---

[1] *Paṭipanno*=our phrase, 'is out for'; *cf. SnA.* ii, 486; *Pts. of Contr.* 16. But *cf.* above II, 5 and 6.

[2] *Gūthâgata*; so *Comy.*, but *P. Dict.* 'turned to dung (?).' It refers to the smearing of torches with the (sacred) cowdung at the cremation. *Cf. S.* iii, 93; *K.S.* iii, 79 (where my trans. is not quite correct); *SA.* ii, 303 *n.*; *Itv.* 90; *JA.* i, 482 (said of Devadatta, who is called in the gāthas *ubhato paduṭṭho*).

[3] *Pharati*=*sādheti. Comy.*   [4] *Mokkho (mukha).*

[5] *Cf. S.* iii, 264=*A.* iii, 219, v, 182.

who is bent on his own profit as well as on the profit of another, is of these four persons chief and best, topmost, highest and supreme.

These four persons, monks, are found existing in the world.'

§ vi (96). *Profit of self (a)*.[1]

' Monks, these four persons are found existing in the world. What four ?

He who is bent on his own profit, not another's; he who is bent on another's profit, not his own; he who is bent on the profit of both; he who is bent on the profit of neither.

And how, monks, is a person bent on his own profit, not another's ?

Herein, monks, a certain person is bent on the restraint of lust in self, but does not incite another to the restraint of lust. He is bent on the restraint of hatred in self, but does nct incite another to such restraint . . . on the restraint of delusion in self, but does not incite another to such restraint. Thus, monks, a person is bent on his own profit, not on another's.

And how, monks, is a person bent on another's profit, not on his own ?

Herein, monks, a certain person who is not bent on the restraint of lust in self incites another to such restraint . . . who is not bent on the restraint of hatred in self incites another to such restraint . . . who is not bent on the restraint of delusion in self incites another thereto. Thus, monks, a person is bent on another's profit, not on his own.

And how, monks, is a person bent neither on his own nor on another's profit ?

Herein, monks, a certain person is not bent on the restraint of lust . . . hatred . . . delusion in self, nor does he incite another to such restraint.

And how, monks, is a person bent on the profit both of self and another ?

---

[1] At *Pugg.*, p. 54; *cf. K.S.* v, 55. The *uddāna* calls these next three suttas *Santi, Attahita*. As the latter title only is relevant, I give it to all three.

Herein a person is both bent on the restraint of lust . . .
hatred . . . delusion in self and incites another to such
restraint. Thus, monks, a person . . .

So these four persons are found existing in the world.

§ vii (97). *Profit of self (b).*

(*The first paragraph of* § 6 *is repeated.*)

' And how, monks, is a person bent on the profit of self, not
of another ?

Herein, monks, a certain person is quick to observe[1] in
teachings that are profitable, has naturally a good memory
for teachings he has heard, examines the meaning of teachings
he has learned by heart, and by understanding both the
meaning and the letter thereof, walks in accordance with
Dhamma.

Yet is he not possessed of a charming voice or delivery, not
possessed of urbane speech, distinctly and clearly enunciated,
so as to make his meaning clear.[2] Nor is he one to teach, urge,
incite and gladden his fellows in the holy life. Thus, monks,
a person is bent on the profit of self, not of another.

And how, monks, is a person bent on the profit of another,
not of self ?

Herein, monks, a certain person is not possessed of a charming voice . . . so as to make his meaning clear, but he is one
to teach, urge, incite and gladden his fellows in the holy life.
Thus a person is bent . . .

And how, monks, is a person bent on neither his own nor
another's profit ?

Herein, monks, a certain person is neither possessed of a
charming voice . . . nor is he one to teach . . . his fellows
in the holy life. Thus a person . . .

And how, monks, is a person bent on the profit both of self
and of another ?

Herein, monks, a certain person is possessed of a charming

---

[1] *Khippa-nisanti. Cf. A.* iii, 201, iv, 296, *sīghaŋ jānituŋ samattho.*
Comy.

[2] *S.* i, 240, ii, 280; *Ud.* 59; *supra*, text 51.

voice . . . and he is one to teach . . . his fellows in **the holy** life. Thus a person . . .

So these, monks, are the four persons found existing in the world.'

§ viii (98). *Profit of self (c).*

(*This sutta simply repeats the four persons of the first paragraph of each sutta, with the two negative ones last.*)

§ ix (99). *Precepts.*

(*The first paragraph as in* § 7.)

' And how, monks, is a person bent on his own profit, not another's ?

Herein a certain person, as regards himself, abstains from killing, but does not incite another to do so; abstains from stealing . . . wrong conduct in sense-desires . . . from lying . . . from liquor fermented and distilled, but does not incite another so to abstain. Thus a person . . .

And how, monks, is a person bent on another's profit, **not his own** ?

Herein a certain person does not himself abstain from killing and the rest, but incites another to do so. Thus a person . . .

And how, monks, is a person bent neither on his own nor on another's profit ?

Herein a certain person neither himself abstains nor incites another to abstain from killing and the rest. Thus a person . . .

And how, monks, is a person bent both on his own profit and another's ?

Herein a certain person both himself abstains from killing and the rest and incites another to do so. Thus a person . . .

So these, monks, are the four persons found existing in the world.'

§ x (100). *Potaliya.*[1]

Now Potaliya the Wanderer came to visit the Exalted One, and on coming to him greeted him courteously. . . . As he

---

[1] *Cf. Pugg* 50; *supra*, § 83.

sat at one side the Exalted One said this to Potaliya the Wanderer:[1]

'Potaliya, these four persons are found existing in the world. What four ?

Herein, Potaliya, a certain person speaks in dispraise of what deserves not praise, seasonably saying what is a fact and true; but does not speak in praise of what deserves praise in like manner.

Then again, Potaliya, a certain person speaks in praise of what deserves it, but not in dispraise of what deserves it not, saying seasonably what is a fact and true.

Yet again, Potaliya, a certain person speaks neither in dispraise of what deserves it not, nor in praise of the praiseworthy, saying seasonably what is a fact and true.

Once more, Potaliya, a certain person speaks both in dispraise of what deserves it not and in praise of what is praiseworthy, saying seasonably what is a fact and true.

These, Potaliya, are the four persons found existing in the world. Now, Potaliya, of these four, which person in your view is to be accounted[2] most admirable and rare ?'

(*Potaliya repeats the four classes.*)

'Of these four persons, master Gotama, he who speaks neither in dispraise of what deserves not praise nor in praise of the praiseworthy, saying seasonably what is a fact and true, —this person in my view is to be accounted most admirable and rare of these four. Why so ? Because, master Gotama, his indifference[3] is admirable.'

'Now, Potaliya, there are these four persons found existing in the world (*he repeats* § i). Of these four persons, Potaliya, (I maintain that) he who speaks in dispraise of what deserves not praise and in praise of what is praiseworthy, saying seasonably what is a fact and true,—he is the most admirable and

---

[1] *Cf. M.* i, 359 (*Potaliya-sutta*), where the householder P., evidently of a disputatious character, is indignant at being called 'householder' by the B., claiming to have given up all. At *M.* iii, 207 he is called *Potali-putta*, the Wanderer, having been such three years.

[2] *Khamati = vuccati. Comy.*   [3] Or impartiality, *upekhā.*

rare. Why so ? Because, Potaliya, his discrimination of proper occasions[1] is admirable.'

'Well, master Gotama, these four persons are found . . . (*he repeats the B.'s words*). Of these four, master Gotama, he who speaks in dispraise of what deserves not praise and in praise of the praiseworthy, saying seasonably what is a fact and true,—he (as you say) is the most admirable and rare. Why so ? Because, master Gotama, his discrimination of proper occasions is admirable.

It is excellent, master Gotama ! It is wonderful, master Gotama ! Just as if, master Gotama, one should raise the fallen or show forth the hidden, cr point the way to him that wanders astray, or hold up a light in the darkness so that they who have eyes may behold objects,—even so in divers ways has dhamma been set forth by the worthy Gotama. I do go for refuge to the worthy Gotama ! May the worthy Gotama accept me as a lay-disciple from this time forth, as long as life may last, as one who has gone to him for refuge.'

(THE THIRD FIFTY SUTTAS)

CHAPTER XI.—RAIN-CLOUD.[2]

§ i (101). *Rain-cloud* (a).

Thus have I heard: On a certain occasion the Exalted One was staying near Sāvatthī at Jeta Grove in Anāthapiṇḍika's Park. Then the Exalted One addressed the monks, saying, 'Monks.'

'Yes, lord,' replied those monks to the Exalted One. The Exalted One said this:

'Monks, there are these four rain-clouds. What four ?

The thunderer not the rainer. The rainer not the thunderer. The neither thunderer nor rainer. The both thunderer and rainer. These are the four.

---

[1] *Kālaññutā.*

[2] This chapter may be compared with *K.S.* iii, pp. 192, 200 for subject. The sutta also occurs at *Pugg.* 42.

In like manner, monks, these four persons resembling rain-clouds are to be found existing in the world. What four? (*The names are repeated.*)

Now, monks, how is a person a thunderer but no rainer?

In this case, monks, a person speaks but acts not. Thus he is one who thunders but rains not. Just as that cloud thunders but rains not, so using this figure do I speak of this person.

And how, monks, is a person a rainer but no thunderer?

In this case, monks, a person is one who acts but speaks not. Thus he is one who rains but thunders not. Just as that cloud . . . using this figure do I speak of this person.

And how, monks, is a person one who is neither thunderer nor rainer?

In this case a person neither speaks nor acts. Thus he is . . .

And how, monks, is a person both thunderer and rainer?

In this case a person both speaks and acts. Thus he is . . .

So these are the four persons found existing in the world.

§ ii (102). *Rain-cloud* (b).

' Monks, there are these four rain-clouds. What four? (*As above.*)

In like manner, monks, these four persons resembling rain-clouds are found existing in the world. . . .

And how, monks, is a person a thunderer but not a rainer?

In this case, monks, a certain person masters Dhamma, to wit: *Sutta, Geyya, Veyyākaraṇa, Gāthā, Udāna, Itivuttaka, Jātaka, Abbhutadhamma* and *Vedalla*.[1] Yet he understands not, as it really is, the meaning of: This is Ill, and the rest. He understands not, as it really is, the meaning of: This is the practice going to the ending of Ill. Thus, monks, a person is one who thunders but rains not. Just as that rain-cloud thunders but rains not, even so using this figure do I speak of this person.

And how, monks, is a person one who rains but thunders not?

---

[1] *Cf. Pugg.* 43.

In this case a certain person does not master Dhamma . . .
yet he does understand, as it really is, the meaning of: This
is Ill . . . . This is the practice going to the ending of Ill.
Thus, monks, a person is one who rains but thunders not. . . .

And how, monks, is a person neither thunderer nor rainer ?

In this case a certain person neither masters Dhamma . . .
nor understands, as it really is, the meaning of: This is Ill . . .
This is the practice going to the ending of Ill. Thus is a
person who neither thunders nor rains. . . .

And how, monks, is a person both thunderer and rainer ?

In this case a certain person both masters Dhamma, to wit:
Sutta, Geyya, and the rest, and understands, as it really is,
the meaning of: This is Ill . . . This is the practice going
to the ending of Ill. . Thus, monks, is a person who both
thunders and rains. Just as this rain-cloud both thunders
and rains, even so using this figure do I speak of this person.

So these, monks, are the four persons found existing in the
world.'

§ iii (103). *The pot.*[1]

' Monks, there are these four pots. What four ?

The empty and closed, the full and open, the empty and
open, and the full and closed pot.

In like manner, monks, there are these four persons resembling pots to be found existing in the world. What four ?
The empty . . . the full and closed.

Now, monks, how is a person empty and closed ?

In this case the mien[2] of a certain person is charming,
whether he be departing or approaching, looking forward or
backward, bending or unbending (his arm), or bearing outer
robe, bowl and (ordinary) robe.. But he understands not,
as it really is, the meaning of: This is Ill . . . This is the
practice going to the ending of Ill. Thus, monks, a person
is empty and closed. As is that pot which is empty and closed,
even so using this figure do I speak of this person.

And how, monks, is a person full and open ?

---

[1] *Cf. Pugg.* 44, 45.   [2] *Cf. infra,* § 122.

In this case the mien of a certain person is not charming . . .
but he does understand, as it really is, the meaning of: This
is Ill . . . This is the practice going to the ending of Ill.
Thus a person is full and open. . . .

And how, monks, is a person empty and open ?

In this case neither is the mien of a certain person charming . . . nor does he understand . . . the meaning of: This
is Ill . . . Thus is a person empty and open. . . .

And how, monks, is a person full and closed ?

In this case the mien of a certain person is charming . . .
and he does understand, as it really is, the meaning of: This
is Ill; This is the arising of Ill; This is the ending of Ill; This
is the practice going to the ending of Ill. Thus, monks, is a
person full and closed. Just as that pot is full and closed,
even so using this figure do I speak of this person.

So these, monks, are the four persons found existing in the
world.'

§ iv (104). *Pools of water*[1] *(a)*.

' Monks, there are these four pools of water. What four ?

The shallow which looks deep, the deep which looks shallow,
the shallow which looks shallow, and the deep which looks
deep.[2] These are the four . . .'

§ v (105). *Pools of water (b)*.

' Monks, there are these four pools of water. What four ?
(*As above.*)

In like manner, monks, there are these four persons resembling pools of water found existing in the world. What
four ? (*As in previous sutta.*)

Now, monks, how is a person shallow but seemingly deep ?'
(*The same qualities for all four as in sutta* § 3.)

§ vi (106). *Mangoes.*[3]

' Monks, there are these four mangoes. What four ?

The unripe which looks ripe, the ripe which looks unripe,

---

[1] *Cf. Pugg.* 46.

[2] *Cf. Dialogues*, ii, p. 50, ' deep it is and it looks deep.'

[3] *Cf. Pugg.* 44.

the unripe which looks unripe, and the ripe which looks ripe. These are the four . . .

In like manner, monks, there are these four persons resembling mangoes found existing in the world. What four ? (*As above.*)

And how, monks, is a person ripe and ripe-looking ?' (*The same qualities as in* § 3.)

§ vii (107). *Mice.*[1]

' Monks, there are these four mice. What four ? The one that digs a hole[2] but does not live in it, the one that lives in a hole it has not dug, the one that neither digs a hole nor lives in a hole, and the one that both digs a hole and lives in it. These are the . . .

In like manner, monks, there are these four persons resembling mice found existing in the world. . . . What four ? (*As above.*)

And how, monks, is a person one who digs a hole but lives not in it ?

Herein a certain person masters Dhamma (*as at* § 2 *above*) . . . But he does not understand, as it really is, the meaning of: This is Ill . . . This is the practice going to the ending of Ill. Thus he is one who digs a hole but lives not in it. As is the mouse that digs a hole but lives not in it, even so using this figure do I speak of this person.' (*The other persons as at* § 2.)

§ viii (108). *Oxen.*[3]

' Monks, there are these four oxen. What four ? The one that is fierce to the cows of its own herd, but not to the cows of another herd, the one that is fierce to the cows of another herd but not to those of its own herd, the one that is fierce to both sorts alike, and the one that is fierce to neither sort. These are the four . . .

---

[1] *Cf. Pugg.* 43.

[2] Text and *Pugg. khattā; Comy. kattā,* so also *Sinh.* text with *v.l. khantā* (*khanati*).

[3] *Cf. Pugg.* 47.

In like manner, monks, these four persons resembling oxen are to be found existing in the world. What four ? (*As above.*)

And how, monks, is a person (like) an ox fierce to the cows of its own herd ?

In this case a certain person is a terror to his own company,[1] but not to another's company. Thus a person is . . . Just as, monks, an ox is fierce to the cows of its own herd, so using this figure do I speak of this person.

And how, monks, is a person (like) an ox that is fierce to the cows of another herd but not to those of its own ?

In this case a certain person is a terror to another's company, not to his own. Thus a person is . . . Just as an ox is fierce . . . so do I speak of this person.

And how, monks, is a person (like) an ox fierce to the cows both of its own herd and another's ?

In this case a certain person is a terror both to his own company and another's. Thus a person is . . . Just as an ox is fierce to . . . even so do I speak of this person.

And how, monks, is a person (like) an ox fierce neither to the cows of its own herd nor to those of another herd ?

In this case a certain person is a terror neither to his own company nor to another's company. Thus a person is . . . Just as an ox is fierce neither to . . . So do I speak of this person.

These four persons, monks, resembling oxen, are found existing in the world.'

§ ix (109). *Trees.*[2]

' Monks, there are these four trees. What four ?

Sapwood trees surrounded by sapwood, sapwood surrounded by heartwood, heartwood surrounded by sapwood, and heartwood surrounded by heartwood. These are the four.

In like manner, monks, these four persons resembling trees are found existing in the world. What four ? (*As above.*)

---

[1] *Parisā* is the retinue of a wandering teacher or a monk's fellow-residents.

[2] *Cf. Pugg.* 52.

And how, monks, is a person like sapwood surrounded by sapwood ?

In this case a certain person is immoral, of a wicked nature, and his company is like unto him.   Thus a person . . .

And how, monks, is a person like sapwood surrounded by heartwood ?

In this case a certain person is immoral, of a wicked nature, but his company is virtuous, of a lovely nature.   Thus a person . . .

And how, monks, is a person like heartwood surrounded by sapwood ?

In this case a certain person is virtuous, of a lovely nature, but his company is immoral, of a wicked nature.   Thus a person is . . .

And how, monks, is a person like heartwood surrounded by heartwood ?

In this case a certain person is virtuous, of a lovely nature, and his company is like unto him.   Thus a person is . . . Just as that tree of heartwood is surrounded by heartwood trees, even so using this figure do I speak of this person.

These, monks, are the four persons found existing in the world.'

§ x (110).   *Snakes.*[1]

' Monks, there are these four snakes.   What four ?

The venomous but not fierce,[2] the fierce but not venomous, the one that is both, the one that is neither.

Just in the same way, monks, these four persons resembling snakes are found existing in the world.   What four ?   (*As above.*)

And how is a person venomous but not fierce ?

In this case, monks, a certain person is quick to anger, but his anger lasts not long.   Thus a person is . . .

And how, monks, is a person fierce but not venomous ?

In this case a certain person is not quick to anger, but his anger lasts long.   Thus a person is . . .

---

[1] *Cf. Pugg.* 48; *K.S.* iv, 107 *n.*; *SnA.* 458; *Expos.* ii, 395.

[2] Lit. ' possessed of poison but not fiercely poisonous.'

And how, monks, is a person both fierce and venomous ?

In this case a certain person is quick to anger and his anger lasts long.   Thus a person is . . .

And how, monks, is a person neither fierce nor venomous ?

In this case a certain person is neither quick to anger nor does his anger- last long.   Thus a person is . . .   Just as is that snake that is neither fierce nor venomous, so using this figure do I speak of this person.

So these, monks, are the four persons resembling snake that are found existing in the world.'

CHAPTER XII.—KESI.

§ i (111). *Kesi.*[1]

Now Kesi the horse-trainer came to visit the Exalted One, and on coming to him he saluted the Exalted One and sat down at one side.   As he sat thus the Exalted One said this to Kesi the horse-trainer:

' You yourself, Kesi, are a trained man,[2] a trainer of horses for driving.   Now, Kesi, pray how do you train a tameable horse ?'

' As for me, your honour, I train a tameable horse by mildness, also by harshness, also by both mildness and harshness.'[3]

' But suppose, Kesi, a tameable horse does not submit to your training by mildness nor to the training by harshness nor yet to the training by both methods, what do you do ?'

' In such a case, your honour, I destroy him.   Why so ? With the idea: Let him not be a discredit to my teacher's clan.   However, your honour, the Exalted One is unsurpassed as a trainer of men for driving.   Pray, your honour, how does the Exalted One train a tameable man ?'

' For my part, Kesi, I too train a tameable man by mild-

---

[1] The word means ' with a mane.'   *Cf. K.S.* iv, 216-18.   *Assa-damma-sārathi* =' a driver of trainable horses.'

[2] Text *saŋyato; A. sa-saññato.*

[3] *Comy.* gives as examples of the one: ' proper regard, good food, sweet water, gentle speech '; of the other, ' hobbling, bridling, goading, whipping, harsh speech.'

ness, also by harshness, also by both together. This, Kesi,
is the way by mildness:—Thus is good conduct in body; thus
is the result of good conduct in body. Thus is good conduct
in speech; thus is the result of good conduct in speech. Thus
is good conduct in thought; thus is the result of good conduct
in thought. Thus are devas and thus are men.

And this, Kesi, is the way by harshness:—Thus is bad
conduct in body; thus is the result of bad conduct in body.
Thus is bad conduct in speech; thus is the result of bad
conduct in speech. Thus is bad conduct in thought; thus is
the result of bad conduct in thought. Thus is rebirth as an
animal; thus is the realm of petas.

And this, Kesi, is the way by both mildness and harshness:—
Thus is good conduct in body . . . in thought; thus is the
result thereof. Thus is bad conduct in body . . . in thought;
thus is the result thereof. Thus are devas and men; thus is
rebirth as an animal;[1] thus the realm of petas.'

'But, your honour, if the man for training won't submit
to the training by mildness, by harshness, nor to the two
together, pray what does the Exalted One do ?'

'In such case, Kesi, I destroy him.'

'But surely the Exalted One does not take life ! And yet
the Exalted One spoke thus: " I destroy him, Kesi !" '

'True it is, Kesi, that taking life does not become a Tathāgata. Yet if the man to be trained submits not to the training
by mildness, by harshness or both together, then the Tathāgata
thinks it not worth while to admonish that man, nor do his
wise fellows in the God-life think it worth while to admonish
that man. This, Kesi, is destruction for a man in the discipline
of the Ariyan,[2]—when both the Tathāgata and his fellows
in the God-life think it not worth while to admonish him.'

'Destroyed indeed,[3] your honour, is a man by the Wellfarer,

---

[1] *Tiracchāna (gāmin)*.   *S.A.* i, 221 on the idea, says: ' merely illus-
trative=*vinipāta*.'

[2] Whereas growth (*vuḍḍhi*) is willingness to attend to *dhamma*.
Cf. K.S. v, 97.

[3] Text *so hi nūna yo* (?) *sugatāhato* (*v.l. suhato*); *Sinh.* text *so hi
nuna suvadho*. *Comy.* has nothing to say.

when both the Tathāgata and his fellows in the God-life think it not worth while to admonish him ! It is wonderful, your honour ! It is marvellous ! May the Exalted One accept me as a follower from this time forth, so long as life lasts, as one who has taken refuge with him.'

§ ii (112). *Speed.*[1]

' Monks, possessed of four qualities a rājah's goodly thoroughbred steed is worthy of a rājah, and is reckoned an attribute of a rājah. What are the four qualities ?

Straightness,[2] speed, patience and docility. Possessed of these four qualities a rājah's goodly steed is reckoned an attribute of a rājah.

In like manner, monks, possessed of four qualities a monk is worshipful, worthy of gifts and offerings, of salutations with clasped hands, a field of merit unsurpassed for the world. What four ?

Straightness, speed, patience and docility. Possessed of these four . . . a field of merit unsurpassed for the world.'

§ iii (113). *The goad.*

' Monks, these four goodly thoroughbred steeds are found existing in the world. What four ?

In this case, monks, we may have a certain goodly thoroughbred steed which at the very sight of the shadow of the goad-stick is stirred,[3] feels agitation (thinking): What[4] task, I wonder, will the trainer set me today ? What return[5] can I make him ? Here, monks, we may have such a steed, and this is the first sort of goodly thoroughbred steed found existing in the world.

Then again, monks, we may have a certain goodly thoroughbred steed which is not stirred at the mere sight of the goad-stick, feels no agitation, but when his coat is pricked with

---

[1] *Cf. A.* iii, 94.   [2] *Ajjava* = *uju-bhāva. Comy.*

[3] *Cf. K.S.* i, 13; *Dhammapada*, ver. 143.

[4] Text *kathaṃ*; Sinh. text and *Comy. kiṃ.*

[5] *Kiṃ paṭikaromi* seems to mean that the horse intends to do his best in return for the training.

the goad he is stirred, feels agitation (thinking): What task,
I wonder . . . This is the second sort. . . .

Then again, monks, we may have a certain goodly thoroughbred steed which is not stirred . . . at sight of the goad-
stick, nor yet when his coat is pricked with the goad, but when
his flesh is pierced he is stirred, he feels agitation (thinking):
What task, I wonder . . . This is the third sort. . . .

Once more, monks, we may have a goodly thoroughbred
steed, which is stirred, feels agitation neither at sight of the
goad-stick nor when his coat is pricked, nor yet when his
flesh is pierced with the goad-stick; but when he is pierced
to the very bone he is stirred, feels agitation (thinking):
What task, I wonder, will the trainer set me today ? What
return can I make him ? Here we have such a goodly
thoroughbred steed . . . This is the fourth sort. . . .

Thus, monks, these four goodly thoroughbred steeds are
found existing in the world.

Just in the same way, monks, these four goodly thoroughbred men are found existing in the world. What four ?

In this case, monks, here we may have a certain goodly
thoroughbred man who hears it said that in such and such a
village or township is a woman or a man afflicted or dead.
Thereat he is stirred, he feels agitation. Thus agitated he
strictly applies himself. Thus applied he both realizes in
his own person[1] the supreme truth,[2] and sees it by penetrating
it with wisdom. Just as, monks, that goodly thoroughbred
steed on seeing the shadow of the goad-stick is stirred, feels
agitation, even so using this figure do I speak of this goodly
thoroughbred man. Such in this case is the goodly thoroughbred man. This is the first sort. . . .

Again, monks, here we may have a goodly thoroughbred
man who does not hear it said that in such and such a village or
township is a woman or a man afflicted or dead, but with his
own eyes beholds such. Thereupon he is stirred, he feels
agitation (*as above*) . . . Just as, monks, that goodly

---

[1] *Kāyena* (as at § 87 above)=*nāma-kāyena. Comy.*
[2] *Nibbāna. Comy.*

thoroughbred steed on having his coat pricked (with the goad-stick) is stirred . . . even so using this figure do I speak of this goodly thoroughbred man . . . Such in this case is . . . This is the second sort. . . .

Then again, monks, here we may have a certain goodly thoroughbred man who does not hear it said . . . nor yet with his own eyes beholds a woman or a man afflicted or dead, but his own kinsman or blood-relation is afflicted or dead. Thereupon he is stirred . . . Just as, monks, that goodly thoroughbred steed on having his flesh pierced is stirred . . . even so using this figure do I speak of this goodly thoroughbred man . . . Such in this case is . . . This is the third sort. . . .

Once more, monks, here we may have a goodly thoroughbred man who neither hears it said . . . nor yet with his own eyes beholds . . . nor is his own kinsman or blood-relation afflicted or dead, but he himself is stricken with painful bodily feelings, grievous, sharp, racking, distracting, discomforting, that drain the life away. Thereat he is stirred, he feels agitation. Being so stirred he strictly applies himself. Thus applied he both realizes with his own person the supreme truth and sees it by penetrating it with wisdom. Just as, monks, that goodly thoroughbred steed on being pierced to the very bone is stirred, feels agitation, even so using this figure do I speak of this goodly thoroughbred man. Of such a sort, monks, is the goodly thoroughbred man in this case. This is the fourth sort.

These, monks, are the four sorts of thoroughbreds among men found existing in the world.'

§ iv (114). *The elephant.*[1]

' Monks, possessed of four qualities a rājah's elephant is worthy of the rājah, a possession of the rājah, is reckoned an attribute of a rājah. What are the four qualities ?

Herein, monks, a rājah's elephant is a listener, a destroyer, a bearer, a goer. And how, monks, is a rājah's elephant a listener ?.

---

[1] At *A.* iii, 161 (in the Fives, with *rakkhitā* added).

In this case, monks, whatever task the trainer of elephants to be driven imposes on him, whether he has performed it before or not, the rājah's elephant makes that his object,[1] gives attention to it, considers it with all his mind, with ready ear listens thereto. Thus, monks, is a rājah's elephant a listener.

And how, monks, is a rājah's elephant a destroyer ?

In this case, monks, a rājah's elephant entering battle destroys elephant and mahout, horse and rider, chariot and driver and footman. Thus is he a destroyer.

And how, monks, is a rājah's elephant a bearer ?

In this case, monks, a rājah's elephant entering battle bears the blows of spear, sword, arrow and axe, also the din of drum and kettledrum, of conch, tam-tam and other noise. Thus he is a bearer.

And how, monks, is a rājah's elephant a goer ?

In this case, monks, a rājah's elephant, in whatever direction the trainer of elephants to be driven turns him, whether he has gone there before or not, thither he quickly goes. Thus he is a goer.

So possessed of these four qualities, monks, a rājah's elephant is worthy of the rājah . . . an attribute of a rājah.

In like manner, monks, possessed of four qualities a monk is worshipful . . . a field of merit unsurpassed for the world. What four ?

Herein, monks, a monk is a listener, a destroyer, a bearer and a goer.

And how is a monk a listener ?

In this case, when Dhamma-discipline is set forth by a Tathāgata, a monk makes that his object, gives attention to it, considers it with all his mind, with ready ear listens to Dhamma. Thus is a monk a listener.

And how is a monk a destroyer ?

In this case a monk does not admit sensual thinking that has arisen, he abandons, restrains, makes an end of it, forces it not to recur. So also with regard to malicious thinking . . .

---

[1] *Aṭṭhikatvā. Cf. D.* ii, 204; *S.* i, 141, v, 95. *Comy. aṭṭhiko hutvā.*

harmful thinking . . . he does not admit evil, unprofitable states that occur from time to time; he abandons them, restrains, makes an end of them, forces them not to recur. Thus he is a destroyer.

And how is a monk a bearer ?

In this case a monk bears heat, cold, hunger, thirst, contact of flies, mosquitoes, wind and sun and creeping things. He bears abusive, pain-causing ways[1] of speech. He submits to painful bodily feelings, grievous, sharp, racking, distracting and discomforting, that drain the life away. Thus a monk is a bearer.

And how is a monk a goer ?

In this case a monk quickly goes thither, whither in this long journey he has never gone before, to wit: to the calming of all the activities, to the forsaking of every basis of rebirth, to the destruction of craving, to passionlessness, to ending, to Nibbāna. Thus a monk is a goer.

Possessed of these four qualities a monk is worshipful . . . a field of merit unsurpassed for the world.'[2]

§ v (115). *Occasions.*

' Monks, there are these four occasions. What four ?

There is, monks, the occasion when action is unpleasant and unprofitable to the doer; that when action is unpleasant but profitable to the doer; that when action is pleasant but unprofitable to the doer; and the occasion when action is both pleasant and profitable to the doer.

Now, monks (in the first instance), in a case when action is both unpleasant and unprofitable to the doer, one deems action inadvisable for both reasons, for it is both unpleasant and unprofitable.

Then again, in the second instance, that is, when action is unpleasant but profitable, one may know who is a fool and

---

[1] *Duruttānaŋ* (*du-v-utta*). *Comy.* has no remark here, but on *A.* iii, 163 says: *duṭṭhu vuttānaŋ, dosa-vasena pavattitānaŋ, pharusa-vacanānaŋ;* and for *durāgatānaŋ* says: *dukkh' uppādākārena sotadvāraŋ āgatānaŋ.* See *Dhp.* ch. xxiii (*Nāga*).

[2] *I.e.*, for others to make meritorious gifts.

who a wise man in the matter of manly strength, manly vigour
and energy.   For, monks, the fool has no such consideration as
this: Though this is an occasion when action is unpleasant,
yet it is one which brings profit.   Accordingly he does not
act, and his inaction brings him loss.   But the wise man thus
considers: Though this is an occasion when action is unpleasant,
yet it brings profit to the doer.   Accordingly he acts, and
profit results.

Now in the third case when action is pleasant but unprofitable,—in this case also one may know who is a fool and
who a wise man in the matter of manly strength, manly vigour
and energy.   For, monks, the fool does not thus consider:
Though this act is pleasant, yet it brings loss.   Accordingly
he acts and the result is loss.   Whereas the wise man thus
reflects: Though this act is pleasant, yet its results bring loss.
So he acts not and the result is to his profit.

Lastly, monks, in the case where action is both pleasant
and profitable, one deems action advisable for both reasons,
for it is both pleasant and profitable; that is why one deems
action advisable.

So these are the four occasions (of action).'

§ vi (116). *Earnestness.*

'On four occasions, monks, earnestness should be applied.
What four ?

Monks, do ye abandon evil practice in body.   Do ye develop
good practice in body.   Therein be ye not remiss.   Monks,
do ye abandon evil practice in speech . . . in thought.
Therein be ye not remiss.   Monks, do ye abandon wrong
view.   Develop right view.   Be ye not remiss therein.

Monks, when in a monk evil practice in body is abandoned
and good practice in body developed; when evil practice in
speech . . . in thought is abandoned and good practice in
speech and thought developed, and when right view is developed, that monk has no fears about the life to come, about
death.'[1]

---

[1] *Comy.* takes this to mean that he is *khiṇāsava*, but says others
regard it as referring to the Stream-winner (who is assured of safety).

§ vii (117). *On guard.*

'Monks, on four occasions should earnestness, mindfulness and guard of one's thoughts be exerted by one's own person.[1] On what four occasions ?

With the thought: Let not my mind run riot amid things passionate, by one's own person should earnestness, mindfulness and guard of one's thoughts be exerted.[2]

With the thought: Let not my mind be malicious amid things malicious, by one's own person should earnestness . . . be exerted.

With the thought: Let not my mind be deluded amid things delusive, by one's own person should earnestness, mindfulness and guard of one's thoughts be exerted.

When a monk's mind, by abandoning passion, does not run riot amid things passionate; when his mind, by abandoning malice, is not malicious amid things malicious; when his mind, by abandoning delusion, is not deluded among things delusive, then he fears not, trembles not, is not shaken, falls not into fearfulness, he goes not according to what Wanderers may say.'[3]

§ viii (118). *Stirring emotion.*[4]

'Monks, these four places are to be looked upon by a believing clansman with feelings of emotion. What four ?

At the thought: Here the Tathāgata was born, the believing clansman should look with feelings of emotion. At the thought: Here the Tathāgata was enlightened with supreme enlightenment, the believing clansman should look with feelings of emotion. At the thought: Here the Tathāgata set rolling the supreme Dhamma-wheel, the believing clansman should look with feelings of emotion. At the thought: Here the Tathagata was utterly released in the Nibbāna-state

---

[1] *Atta-rūpena,* but *Comy.* (followed at *K.S.* iv, 60) takes it as meaning *attha-*, 'for one's own profit.' *Cf. supra,* §§ 87, 113 (*kāyena*).

[2] *Cf. S.* iv, 307.

[3] *Na samaṇa-vacana-hetu gacchati. Cf. A.* i, 174, *samaṇa-vādo.*

[4] *D.* ii, 140 (said to Ananda).

wherein nought remains behind, the believing clansman should look with feelings of emotion.

These are the four places . . .'

· § ix (119). *Fears* (a).[1]

' Monks, there are these four fears. What four?

Fear of birth, fear of old age, fear of disease and fear of death.

These are the four fears.'

§ x (120). *Fears* (b).

' Monks, there are these four fears. What four?

Fear of fire, fear of water, fear of the rājah, fear of the bandit. These four . . .'

CHAPTER XIII.—FEARS.

§ i (121). *Self-reproach.*

' Monks, there are these four fears. What four?

Fear of self-reproach, fear of others' reproach,[2] fear of punishment and fear of the way of woe.

And what, monks, is fear of self-reproach?

Herein, monks, a certain one thus reflects: Were I to practise evil conduct in body, speech and thought, would not the self reproach me[3] as to virtue therein? Accordingly, scared by the fear of self-reproach, he abandons the practice of evil conduct in body, speech and thought, and makes-to-grow the practice of good conduct therein, and carries about[4] a pure self. This, monks, is called " fear of self-reproach."

And what, monks, is fear of others' reproach?

Herein, monks, a certain one thus reflects: Were I to practise evil conduct in body, speech and thought, would not others

---

[1] These two suttas should belong to the next chapter in context.

[2] This is *hiri-ottappaŋ*.

[3] Text *kiñ ca taŋ kammaŋ attā*, but *Sinh.* text *kiñ ca taŋ maŋ attā*, which I follow. Others, apparently to get rid of this *attā* and *maŋ* difficulty, read *kiñci taŋ kammaŋ ; kiñci kammaŋ ; kiñ ca taŋ ; kiñ ca taŋ dhammaŋ*, etc. *Cf. G.S.* i, 52, 130, 133.

[4] *Cf.* ch. I, §§ 3, 4.

reproach[1] me as to virtue therein ?   Accordingly, scared by the
fear of others' reproach, he abandons the practice of evil
conduct in body, speech and thought, and makes-to-grow the
practice of good conduct therein and carries about a pure
self.   This, monks, is called " the fear of others' reproach."

And what, monks, is fear of punishment ?

In this case a certain one beholds the rājahs seizing a bandit,
a miscreant, and subjecting him to divers forms of punishment;
flogging him with whips, with canes or cudgels; cutting off
his head, his foot, hand and foot, his ear, nose, ear and nose;
torturing him with the " gruel-pot," with the " chank-shave ";
torturing him with " Rāhu's mouth," with the " fire-garland,"
with the " flaming hand," with the " hay-twist," the " bark-
dress," with the " antelope," with " flesh-hooking," with the
"disc-slice," with the " pickling process," with "circling the
pin," torturing him with the " straw-mattress."   Then they
spray him with boiling oil, give him as food to dogs, spit him
alive on a stake and chop his head off.[2]

Then he thinks thus: If I were to do such deeds as those
for which the rājahs seize a bandit, a miscreant, and so treat
him . . . they would surely treat me in like manner.   Thus
scared by the fear of punishment he goes not about plundering
others' property.   This, monks, is called " fear of punishment."

And what, monks, is the fear of the way of woe ?

In this case a certain one thus reflects : For one who
practises evil conduct in body, speech and thought there is a
bad result in the life to come.   Now if I were to practise evil
conduct in body, speech and thought, when body breaks up,
should not I be reborn after death in the waste, the way of
woe, the downfall, in purgatory ?   Accordingly, scared by the
fear of the way of woe he abandons the practice of evil conduct
in body, speech and thought, and makes-to-grow the practice
of good conduct therein, and carries about a pure self.
This, monks, is called the " fear of the way of woe."

So these, monks, are the four fears.'

---

[1] Text should read *upavadeyyuy*.
[2] For these tortures see *D.* i, 276; *Mil.P.* 197; *G.S.* i (*The Twos*),
p. 42 *n.*

§ ii (122). *The wave.*[1]

' Monks, there are these four perils to be looked for in him who goes down to the water. What four ?

Peril of waves, peril of crocodiles, peril of whirlpools, and peril of sea-monsters.[2] These are the four perils.

In like manner, monks, in some clansman here who has gone forth from the home to the homeless life under this Dhamma-discipline these four perils may be looked for. What four ?

Peril of waves, peril of crocodiles, peril of whirlpools and peril of sea-monsters. And of what sort, monks, is peril of waves ?

In this case a certain clansman who has in faith gone forth from home to the homeless life, thinks thus: Here am I, launched upon birth, old age and death, on sorrow and grief, woe, lamentation and despair, launched upon Ill, overwhelmed by Ill. Maybe of all this mass of Ill some ending may be shown. To such an one who has thus[3] gone forth his fellows in the God-life preach, and admonish him, saying: " Thus should you retreat, thus advance; thus should you look forward and backward, bend or unbend (your arm); thus should you bear outer robe and bowl and inner robe."

Then it occurs to him: I who aforetime lived at home was wont to preach to and admonish others. Yet these people, who are to my thinking no more than sons or grandsons,— these people think that I am one to be preached to and admonished. Thus he, angered and offended,[4] abandons the training and turns back to the low life. This one, monks, is called " a monk who abandons the training and turns back to the low life, scared by the peril of waves." " Peril of the waves," monks, is a term for wrath and resentment.[5] This is called " peril of waves."

---

[1] At *M.* i, 460 (*Cātuma*); *Sisters,* 174.

[2] *Susukā. Cf. SA.* i, 211. It is a big fish (*Comy. caṇḍa-maccha*) which makes a hissing sound (? sea-cow), not an alligator (as *P. Dict.*), which has already been mentioned. *Cf. K.S.* iv, 97 (*The Ocean*).

[3] Text should read *tathā* as on next page.

[4] Text should read *anattamano.*

[5] *Sa-ummī. Cf. M.* i, 360; *It.* 114, where the idea is that of swelling up.

And of what sort, monks, is peril of crocodiles ?

In this case a certain clansman has in faith gone forth from the home to the homeless life. He thinks thus: Here am I, launched upon birth, old age and death . . . maybe of all this mass of Ill some ending may be shown. To such an one who has thus gone forth his fellows in the God-life preach and admonish him thus: " You should eat this, not that. You should swallow[1] this, not that. You should taste this, not that. You should drink this, not that. You should eat, swallow, taste and drink what is fitting, not what is unfitting. You should eat, swallow, taste and drink at the proper, not at the improper time."

Then he thinks thus: I who aforetime lived at home used to eat, swallow, taste and drink just what I liked, and refused to eat; swallow, taste and drink what I did not like. I used to eat, and so forth, both what was fitting and unfitting, and that too whether the time was proper or improper.

But now when believing householders offer me choice food both hard and soft at an improper time, methinks they are putting a bridle[2] on my mouth. Thus he abandons the training and turns back to the low life. This one, monks, is called " a monk who abandons the training and turns back to the low life because he is scared by the peril of crocodiles." " Peril of crocodiles," monks, is a term for gluttony. This is called " peril of crocodiles."

And of what sort, monks, is peril of whirlpools ?

In this case a certain clansman[3] has in faith gone forth from home to the homeless life. He thinks thus: Here am I launched upon birth, old age . . . maybe of all this mass of Ill some ending may be shown. He having thus gone forth, robing himself in the forenoon and taking bowl and robe, sets out for village or township to beg an alms, with body unguarded, with speech unguarded, with thoughts unguarded, with mind-

---

[1] The difference between *khādati* and *bhuñjati* seems to be that between chewing, biting hard food and swallowing soft food. Just below our text reads *khāyitaŋ* for *khāditaŋ* (of M.).

[2] *Mukhâvaraṇaŋ*, lit. ' locking or bolting.'

[3] Text should read *kulaputto*.

fulness not established, with faculties uncontrolled. Then he sees a housefather or son of a housefather indulging in, provided with and practising the five sense-pleasures. Then he thinks thus: I too aforetime when living at home indulged in, was provided with and practised the five sense-pleasures. Moreover since wealth exists in my family, I could enjoy it and do good works therewith. How now if I were to abandon the training, turn back to the low life, enjoy my wealth and do good deeds therewith ?

Accordingly he does so. This one, monks, is called "a monk who abandons the training and turns back to the low life because he is scared by the peril of whirlpools." "Peril of whirlpools," monks, is a term for the five sense-pleasures. This, monks, is called "peril of whirlpools."

And what, monks, is the peril of sea-monsters ?

In this case, monks, a certain clansman who has in faith gone forth from the home to the homeless life . . . thinks thus: Here am I launched upon birth, old age . . . maybe of all this mass of Ill some ending may be shown. He, having thus gone forth, robes himself in the forenoon . . . and sets out for some village or township to beg an alms, with body un-guarded, with speech unguarded, with thoughts unguarded, with mindfulness not established, with faculties uncontrolled. Then he sees womenfolk partly clothed, partly attired. On seeing that sight passion assails[1] his heart. With heart assailed by passion he abandons the training and turns back to the low life. This one, monks, is called "a monk who, scared by the peril of sea-monsters, abandons the training and turns back to the low life." "Peril of sea-monsters," monks, is a term for womenfolk. This, monks, is called "peril of sea-monsters."

So these, monks, are the four perils to be looked for in some clansman here who has rightly gone forth from home to the homeless life under this Dhamma-discipline.'

§ iii (123). *Different persons (a).*

' Monks, these four persons are found existing in the world. What four ?

---

[1] *Anuddhaṃseti*, at *A.* i, 266. *Comy.* expl. as *paribhāsati, codeti.*

Now, monks, a certain person here, aloof from sense-desires, aloof from evil conditions, enters upon the first musing, which is accompanied by thought directed and sustained, born of seclusion, zestful and easeful, and abides therein. He enjoys[1] its sweetness, longs for it and finds happiness therein. Established therein, given thereto, generally spending his time therein and not falling away therefrom, when he makes an end he is reborn in the company of devas of the Brahmā-group. A kalpa, monks, is the life-span of the devas of the Brahmā-group. Therein the ordinary man stays and spends his time according to the life-span of those devas; then he goes to purgatory or the womb of an animal, he goes to the peta-realm. But a disciple of the Exalted One, after staying there and spending his time according to the life-span of those devas, finally passes away in that same state. Such, monks, is the distinction, such the specific feature, the difference between the learned Ariyan disciple and the unlearned ordinary man in the matter of bourn and rebirth.

Again, monks, a certain person here, by the calming down of thought directed and sustained, enters upon the second musing, that calming of the inner self, that one-pointedness of mind apart from thought directed and sustained, that is born of mental balance, zestful and easeful, and having attained it abides therein. He enjoys its sweetness, longs for it and finds happiness therein. Established therein, given thereto, generally spending his time therein and not falling away therefrom, when he makes an end he is reborn in the company of the Radiant devas. Now, monks, the life-span of those devas is two kalpas. Therein the ordinary man stays and spends his time according to the life-span of those devas. Then he goes to purgatory . . . (*as above*). Such is the distinction . . . in the matter of bourn and rebirth.

Again, monks, a certain person here, by the fading out of zest, disinterested, mindful and composed, experiences in his

---

[1] *Assādeti. Comy.* der. from *sādu* (sweet); *sukha-sādena assādeti. Cf. Pts. of Contr.* 258 (for the *kappa*), 278 (for the objection that such pleasure is disputable). At *G.S.* i, 245 in three instances he is reborn with devas having other qualities than these.

own person[1] that ease of which the Ariyans declare: " He
who is disinterested and alert dwells at ease,"—thus he attains
and abides in the third musing. He enjoys its sweetness, longs
for it and finds happiness therein. Established therein . . .
when he makes an end he is reborn in the company of the
Ever-radiant[2] devas. Now, monks, the life-span of those
devas is four kalpas. Therein the ordinary man stays . . .
then he goes to purgatory . . . Such is the distinction . . .
in the matter of bourn and rebirth.

Once more, monks, a certain person here, by abandoning
both ease and discomfort, by the ending of both happiness
and unhappiness felt before, attains the fourth musing, a state
of neither ease nor discomfort, an equanimity of utter purity,
and having attained it abides therein. He enjoys its sweetness,
longs for it and finds happiness therein.[3] Established therein . . . when he makes an end he is reborn in the company
of the Vehapphala devas.[4] Now, monks, the life-span of the
Vehapphala devas is five hundred kalpas. Therein the
ordinary man stays and spends his time according to the life-
span of those devas . . . then goes to purgatory . . . Such,
monks, is the distinction, such the specific feature, the difference between the learned Ariyan disciple and the unlearned
ordinary man in the matter of bourn and rebirth.

These, then, monks, are the four persons found existing
in the world.'

§ iv (124). *Different persons* (b).

' Monks, these four persons are found existing in the world.
What four ?

Now, monks, a certain person here, aloof from sense-
desires . . . enters upon the first musing . . . and having

---

[1] *Kāyena*, as at § 87, 113; *Cf. K.S.* v, 190.

[2] *Subhakiṇṇa* or *-kiṇha*. Expl. as different in this respect from the
Radiant (Ābhassara) above; *cf.* § 232.

[3] The question arises, as in note above, ' How can he enjoy or desire
it, if he has become disinterested ?'

[4] *Cf. M*. i, 329, iii, 103; *JA*. iii, 358. Commentaries do not explain
the name (? air-fruit), which possibly means a refined form of ether
of the 10th Brahmaloka.

---

attained it abides therein. There, whatsoever conditions arise by way of form,[1] feeling, perception, the activities, consciousness, those conditions he comes to regard as impermanent, as Ill, as a disease, as an imposthume, as a barb, as pain, ill-health, alien, transitory, as empty and not of the self.[2] When body breaks up after death he is reborn in the company of the devas of the Pure Abodes.[3] Monks, this rebirth is not partaken of by ordinary men.

Then again, monks, a certain person here, by the calming down of thought directed and sustained . . . attains to and abides in the second musing . . . the third musing . . . the fourth musing. There, whatsoever conditions arise by way of form, feeling, perception, the activities, consciousness, he regards them as impermanent . . . as empty and not of the self. When body breaks up . . . he is reborn in the company of the devas of the Pure Abodes. . . . Monks, this rebirth is not partaken of by ordinary men.

So these four persons are found existing in the world.'

§ v (125). *Amity* (a).[4]

Monks, these four persons are found existing in the world. What four?

Herein, monks, a certain person lives irradiating one quarter (of the world) with a heart possessed of amity; so also as to the second, third and fourth quarter of the world; and in like manner above, below, across, everywhere, for all sorts and conditions, he lives irradiating the whole world with a heart

---

[1] *Rūpa-gataŋ. Comy.* 'just rūpa.'

[2] The body-grasping group. *Cf.* K.S. iii, 103 *n.*, 155, iv, 50, 135.

[3] *Suddhāvāsa. Cf. S.* i, 26 (*S.A.* i, 75); *G.S.* i, 213; *K.S.* v, 58, 180 (where I wrongly trans. *Akaniṭṭha* by 'Pure Abodes'); *Dial.* ii, 39 *n.* ('Peerless Ones'): 'The five rūpa-lokas which are the abode of the non-returning *khīṇāsava.*' Such an one is called 'one who goes upstream (*uddhaŋsota*).' *Comy.* on text below states that by developing the fourth *jhāna* he is reborn there. Ordinary men fall back to rebirth in a good family. Apparently this development by musing is necessary to lift one out of the 'downward' stream.

[4] For these Sublime or God-moods *cf. K.S.* v, 98 *n.*; *Gotama the Man*, 180, and *Sakya*, 216 *f.*, 392, by Mrs. Rhys Davids.

possessed of amity that is widespread, grown great and boundless, free from enmity and untroubled. He enjoys the sweetness of it, longs for it and finds happiness therein. Established therein, given thereto, generally spending his time therein and not falling away therefrom, when he makes an end he is reborn in the company of devas of the Brahmā-group. A kalpa, monks, is the life-span of those devas (*as in* § 3). Therein the ordinary man stays . . . but a disciple of the Exalted One finally passes away in that same state. Such, monks, is the distinction . . . between the learned Ariyan disciple and the unlearned ordinary man in the matter of bourn and rebirth.

Then again, monks, a certain person 'here lives irradiating one quarter of the world with a heart possessed of compassion . . . possessed of sympathy . . . possessed of equanimity; so also as to the second, third, and fourth quarters of the world . . . free from enmity and untroubled. He enjoys the sweetness of it . . . established therein . . . he is reborn in the company of the Radiant devas . . . of the Ever-radiant devas . . . of the Vehapphala devas (*the whole as in* § 3). Such, monks, is the distinction . . . between the learned Ariyan disciple and the unlearned ordinary man in the matter of bourn and rebirth.

So these four persons are found existing in the world.'

§ vi (126). *Amity* (*b*).

' Monks, these four persons are found existing in the world. What four ?

Herein, monks, a certain person lives irradiating one quarter (of the world) with a heart possessed of amity . . . that is widespread, grown great and boundless, free from enmity and untroubled.

Therein whatsoever conditions arise by way of form . . . those conditions he comes to regard as impermanent . . . not of the self (*as in previous* §). When body breaks up after death he is reborn in the company of the devas of the Pure Abodes. . . . Monks, this rebirth is not partaken of by ordinary men.' (*The same for the other three Moods.*)

§ vii (127). *Marvels* (a).[1]

'Monks, on the manifestation of a Tathāgata, Arahant, a Fully Enlightened One, four wonderful, marvellous things are manifested. What four?

When a Bodhisattva, deceasing from the Tusita-deva-group, mindful and composed descends into his mother's womb, then in the world, together with its devas, its Māras, its Brahmās, with its host of recluses and brāhmins, of devas and mankind, then an infinite, glorious radiance is manifested, surpassing the deva-majesty of the devas. Even the gloom of space between the worlds, the fathomless[2] darkness, the murk of darkness, where even the radiance of our moon and sun, though of such wondrous power and majesty, cannot be manifested,—even there an infinite, glorious radiance is spread abroad, surpassing the deva-majesty of the devas. Likewise those creatures that have come into being there, becoming aware of each other through that radiance, exclaim: "It seems, friends, that there be other creatures also that have come into being here." Monks, on the manifestation of a Tathāgata, Arahant, a Fully Enlightened One, this is the first wonderful, marvellous thing manifested.

Then again, monks, when a Bodhisattva, mindful and composed, comes forth from his mother's womb, then in the world ... an infinite, glorious radiance is manifested. . . . Even the gloom of space between the worlds . . . even there an infinite, glorious radiance is spread abroad. . . . Likewise those creatures . . . Monks, on the manifestation of a Tathāgata . . . this is the second wonderful, marvellous thing manifested.

Then again, monks, when a Tathāgata is enlightened with the unsurpassed perfect enlightenment, then in the world . . . (*the same as before*) . . . Monks, on the manifestation of a Tathāgata . . . this is the third wonderful, marvellous thing manifested.

---

[1] The first two sections are at *D.* ii, 13, 15; *Dial.* ii, 8 *n.*; *cf. M.* iii, 118; *JA.* i, 51. This sort of sutta, acc. to *Expos.* i, 33, is to be reckoned as belonging to the *Abbhuta-dhamma* of the nine well-known sections.

[2] *Asaṃvuta=heṭṭhâpi appatiṭṭhā. Comy.*

Yet again, monks, when a Tathāgata sets rolling the un-surpassed Dhamma-wheel, then in the world . . . this is the fourth wonderful, marvellous thing manifested.

These, monks, are the four wonderful, marvellous things manifested on the manifestation of a Tathāgata, Arahant, a Fully Enlightened One.'

§ viii (128). *Marvels (b).*

' Monks, on the manifestation of a Tathāgata . . . four wonderful, marvellous things are manifested. What four ?

Monks, folk take pleasure in the habitual,[1] delight in the habitual, are excited thereby. But when Dhamma contrary to such is taught by a Tathāgata, folk are ready to hear it, they lend an ear, they apply their minds thereto. This is the first wonderful, marvellous thing manifested. . . . Monks, folk take pleasure in pride, delight in pride, are excited by pride. But when Dhamma for controlling pride is taught by a Tathā-gata, folk are ready to hear it, they lend an ear, they apply their minds thereto. This is the second wonderful, marvellous thing manifested. . . .

Monks, folk take pleasure in excitement, delight in it, are excited thereby. But when Dhamma that allays excitement is taught by a Tathāgata, folk are ready to hear it. . . . This is the third wonderful, marvellous thing manifested.

Monks, folk are come to ignorance, are become blinded, over-cast by ignorance. But when Dhamma controlling ignorance is taught by a Tathāgata, they are ready to hear it, they lend an ear to it, they apply their minds thereto. This, monks, is the fourth wonderful, marvellous thing manifested when a Tathāgata, Arahant, a Fully Enlightened One is manifested.

So these are the four wonderful, marvellous things mani-fested. . . .'

§ ix (129). *Marvels (c).*[2]

' Monks, there are these four wonderful, marvellous things about Ānanda. What are the four ?

---

[1] *Ālayārāma. Cf. Vin.* i, 4; *S.* i, 136. 'The five sense-pleasures.' *Comy.* This misses the point in a new gospel. *Cf. Sakya,* pp. 39, 117.

[2] *D.* ii, 145.

If a company of monks comes to visit Ānanda, they are delighted at the sight of him. Then if Ānanda speaks Dhamma,[1] they are delighted with what he says. Dissatisfied is the company of monks when Ānanda becomes silent.

If a company of nuns comes to visit Ānanda . . . If a company of disciples who are laymen comes to visit Ānanda . . . If a company of disciples who are laywomen comes to visit Ānanda, they are delighted at the sight of him. Then if Ānanda speaks Dhamma they are delighted with what he says. Dissatisfied is the company of disciples that are laywomen when Ānanda becomes silent.

These, monks, are the four wonderful, marvellous things about Ānanda.'

§ x (130). *Marvels (d)*.[2]

'Monks, there are these four wonderful, marvellous things about a wheel-turning ruler. What four ?

If a company of noblemen comes to visit a wheel-turning ruler, they are delighted at the sight of him. Then if the ruler speaks they are delighted with what he says. Dissatisfied, monks, is a company of noblemen when the wheel-turning ruler becomes silent.

(*The same for a company of brāhmins, of householders, of recluses.*)

These then, monks, are the four wonderful, marvellous things about a wheel-turning ruler.

Just in the same way, monks, there are four wonderful, marvellous things about Ānanda.' (*The previous sutta is repeated.*)

---

[1] *Comy.* here does not allow that A. preached Dhamma (as doctrine) to these people, but suggests that he 'asked about their health, whether they were attending to their exercises, and were dutiful to their superiors. Speaking to women, he asks whether they are observing the eight ordinances for behaviour towards monks. To layfolk, *not* 'Does your head ache ? Are your children and wives well ?' but, 'Do you keep the precepts ? Do you feed holy men ?' But see § 159 below, where he is found teaching Dhamma, and again §§ 170, 204.

[2] *Cf. D.* ii, 145. Here *Comy.* gives us some imaginary conversations with the rājah.

CHAPTER XIV.—ON PERSONS.

§ i (131). *Fetters.*

' Monks, there are these four persons found existing in the world. What four ?

Herein, monks, in a certain person the fetters that pertain to this world are not got rid of, those that give rise to rebirth are not got rid of, those that give rise to becoming are not got rid of.

Herein again in a certain person the fetters that pertain to this world are got rid of, but not the others . . .

Herein again in a certain person the first two sets of fetters are got rid of, but not those that give rise to becoming.

Herein again in a certain person all three (sets of) fetters are got rid of.

Now, monks, in what sort of person are none of the three (sets of) fetters got rid of ?

In the Once-returner. In this person none of the (sets of) fetters are got rid of.

Again, in what sort of person is the first got rid of but not the other two ?

In the one who goes upstream,[1] who goes to the Elder Devas . . .[2]

Again, monks, in what sort of person are the first two (sets of fetters) but not the third got rid of ?

In him who passes finally away in mid-term[3] (of deva-life).

Again, monks, in what sort of person are all three sets of fetters got rid of ?

In the Arahant. In this person, monks, the fetters pertaining to this world are got rid of, likewise those that give rise to rebirth, likewise those that give rise to becoming.

So these are the four sorts of persons found existing in the world.'

---

[1] *Uddhaṃsoto.* *Cf. G.S.* i, 213 ; *S.* v, 237, etc.; *S.B.B.* vii, p. 75.

[2] *Akaniṭṭha.* *Comy.* def. thus: ' No youngsters there.'

[3] *Antarā-parinibbāya.*

§ ii (132). *Reply.*[1]

' Monks, these four persons are found existing in the world. What four ?

He who replies to the point, not diffusely: he who replies diffusely, not to the point: he who does both: he who does neither. These are the four.'

§ iii (133). *Quick-witted.*[2]

' Monks, these four persons are found existing in the world. What four ?

He who learns by taking hints:[3] he who learns by full details:[4] he who has to be led on (by instruction):[5] he who has just the word (of the text)[6] at most. These are the four.'

§ iv (134). *Effort.*[7]

' Monks, these four persons are found existing in the world. What four ?

He who lives on the fruit of his effort, not of his deed: he who lives on the fruit of his deed, not of his effort: he who does both: he who does neither. These are the four.'

---

[1] *Pugg.*, p. 42. *Yutta-paṭibhāno : Comy.*, ' When asked a question he makes a fit reply, does not answer hastily but at leisure.' *Pugg.A.* 223 gives instances of each quality. (*Yutta* = succinct; *mutta* = loose, rambling.) *Paṭibhāno* also seems to mean ' of ready wit ' and ' with repartee.'

[2] *Pugg.*, p. 41; *Netti*, 211; *SA.* i, 202, ii, 4; *Pugg.A.* 222; *SnA*, ii, 163.

[3] *Ugghaṭitaññu* = (brief-learner) = *saṅkhepaññu*.

[4] *Vipañcitaññu* (diffuse-learner) = *vitthāritaññu*. The usual spelling is *vipacita.*

[5] *Neyyo* = *netabba* (*Netti*, 211). One text has *ñeyya.*

[6] *Padaparamo* = *vyañjana-padam eva paramaɳ assa*, one who learns by heart, is word-perfect but without understanding it.

[7] *Pugg.*, p. 51. *Comy.* distinguishes the two as *vāyāma-phala* and *puñña-phala*, and gives as instances:—The four firmament kings and all devas without effort live on merit. Rājahs and royal ministers live on both. Beings in purgatory form the fourth class.

§ v (135). *Blameworthy.*[1]

' Monks, these four persons . . .   What four ?

The blameworthy, the very blameworthy, the slightly blameworthy, the blameless.   These are the four.

And how, monks, is a person blameworthy ?

In this case a certain person is liable to blame for his deeds in body, speech and thought.   Thus he is blameworthy.

And how, monks, is a person very blameworthy ?

In this case a certain person is liable to much blame for his deeds in body, speech and thought, and to slight blame for deeds that are blameless.   Thus he is more to be blamed than praised.

And how, monks, is a person only slightly blameworthy ?

In this case a certain person is liable to little blame for his deeds in body, speech and thought, and to little blame for deeds that are blameworthy.   Thus he is only slightly blameworthy.

And how is a person blameless ?

In this case a certain person is not to be blamed at all for his deeds in body, speech and thought.   Thus he is blameless.

These are the four persons . . .'

§ vi (136). *Virtue (a).*[2]

' Monks, these four persons . . .   What four ?

Herein, monks, a certain person is complete neither in virtue nor in concentration, nor in wisdom.

Herein again a certain person is complete in virtue, but not in the other two.

Herein again a certain person is complete in virtue and concentration but not in wisdom.

Herein again a certain person is complete in all three things.

These are the four persons . . .'

---

[1] *Pugg.*, p. 41.

[2] This sutta, with the first quality omitted, comes in the Threes at *Pugg.*, p. 37, where the second quality is that of Stream-winner *and* Once-returner; the third, of Non-returner; the fourth, of Arahant. Acc. to *Comy.*, here the first is the ' ordinary blind person '; the second, the virtuous worldling ; the third, the Stream-winner, Once-returner and Non-returner; the fourth, the *khīnāsava.*

§ vii (137). *Virtue (b).*

' Monks, these four persons . . . What four ?

Herein, monks, a certain person respects not virtue, puts not virtue first; respects not concentration, puts not concentration first; respects not wisdom, puts not wisdom first.[1]

Herein again a certain person respects virtue and puts it first; but respects not concentration and wisdom nor puts them first.

Yet again a certain person respects and puts first virtue and concentration, but not wisdom.

Yet again a certain person respects virtue, concentration and wisdom and puts them first.

So these are the four persons found existing in the world.'

§ viii (138). *Subdued.*

' Monks, these four persons are found . . . What four ?

The subdued[2] in body but not in mind; the unsubdued in body but subdued in mind; he who is subdued in neither; he who is subdued in both.

And how, monks, is a person subdued in body but not in mind ?

In this case a certain person makes his bed and lodging in the lonely glades and solitude of a forest, but meanwhile thinks sensual thoughts, malicious thoughts and harmful thoughts. Thus, monks, a person is subdued in body but not in mind.

And how is a person unsubdued in body but subdued in mind ?

In this case a certain person makes not his bed and lodging in . . . a forest, yet meanwhile he thinks unworldly thoughts, thoughts not malicious, not harmful. Thus a person is unsubdued in body but subdued in mind.

---

[1] *Ādhipateyya* or *Ādhipateyya* (*cf. G.S.* i, 130 *n.*): ' regard or predominance.' *Comy.* is silent here. On *A.* i, 147 (*ādhip.*) it has *jeṭṭhaka-kāraṇato*, ' putting in first place.'

[2] *Nikaṭṭha* seems to occur here only in the Nikāyas. It is equal to *niggata. Anikaṭṭha-citta=anupaviṭṭha. Comy.*

And how is a person subdued neither in body nor in mind ?

In this case a certain person makes not his bed and lodging
. . . in a forest, yet meanwhile he thinks sensual, malicious
and harmful thoughts.

And how is a person subdued both in body and in mind ?

In this case a certain person makes his bed and lodging in
the lonely glades and solitude of a forest, and at the same time
thinks unworldly thoughts, thoughts not malicious, not harmful.   Thus a person is subdued both in body and in mind.

So these four persons are found existing in the world.'

§ ix (139). *Dhamma-talk.*[1]

' Monks, there are these four talkers of Dhamma.   What
four ?

Herein, monks, a certain person talking Dhamma says little
and that not to the point; while his company is unskilled to
judge what is to the point or otherwise.   Such, monks, is
the Dhamma-talker, and he is reckoned to talk to a company
of like nature.[2]

Then again, monks, a certain person talking Dhamma says
little and that to the point, while his company is skilled to
judge what is to the point or otherwise.   Such, monks, is
the Dhamma-talker, and he is reckoned to talk to a company
of like nature.

Herein again, monks, a certain person talking Dhamma
says much and what is off the point, while his company is
unskilled to judge what is to the point or otherwise.   Such,
monks, is the Dhamma-talker, and he is reckoned to talk to
a company of like nature.

Herein again, monks, a certain person talking Dhamma says
much and what is to the point, while his company is skilled
to judge what is to the point or otherwise.   Such, monks, is
the Dhamma-talker, and he is reckoned to talk to a company
of like nature.

So these are the four Dhamma-talkers.'

---

[1] *Pugg.*, p. 42
[2] Text should read *evarūpāya parisāya* (as *Sinh.* text) throughout.

§ x (140). *Expounder.*

' Monks, there are these four expounders. What four ?

There is the expounder who is at a loss[1] as regards the meaning but not the letter (of a passage). Also the one who is at a loss as regards the letter but not the meaning. Also the one who is at a loss in both cases. And there is the expounder who is not at a loss either as regards the meaning or as regards the letter (of a passage). These are the four.

Monks, it is unlikely, it is impossible that one possessed of the four analytical powers[2] should be at a loss both in the meaning and in the letter.'

CHAPTER XV.—SPLENDOUR.

§ i (141). *Splendours.*

' Monks, there are these four splendours. What four ?

The splendour of the moon, of the sun, of fire and of wisdom. These are the four. Of these four, monks, the splendour of wisdom is the chief.'

§ ii (142). *Radiances.*

' Monks, there are these four radiances. What four ?

The radiance of the moon, of the sun, of fire and of wisdom. These are the four. Of these four, monks, the radiance of wisdom is the chief.'

§ iii (143). *Lights.*

' Monks, there are these four lights. What four ?

The light of the moon, of the sun, of fire and of wisdom. These are the four. Of these four, monks, the light of wisdom is the chief.'

---

[1] *Pariyādānaŋ gacchati,* ' when asked for exegesis he comes to a stand. *Cf. Pugg.* 13.

[2] The four *paṭisambhidā* are: analysis of meaning (*attha*), of reasons (*dhamma*), of definitions (*nirutti*), of wisdom (*paṭibhāna*). *Cf.* § 173.

§ iv (144). *Brilliance.*

' Monks, there are these four brilliances. What four ?
The brilliance of the moon, of the sun, of fire and of wisdom.
These are the four. Of these four, monks, the brilliance of
wisdom is the chief.'

§ v (145). *Lamps.*

' Monks, there are these four lamps. What four ?
The lamp of the moon, of the sun, of fire and of wisdom.
These are the four. Of these four, monks, the lamp of wisdom
is the chief.'

§ vi (146). *Seasons (a).*

' Monks, there are these four seasons. What four ?
Hearing Dhamma in due season, discussion[1] of Dhamma
in due season, calming in due season, insight in due season.
These are the four . . .'

§ vii (147). *Seasons (b).*

' Monks, there are these four seasons which, if rightly
developed, rightly revolved, gradually bring about the destruction of the āsavas. What four ?
Hearing Dhamma in due season, discussion of Dhamma in
due season, calming in due season, insight in due season.
These are the four.
Just as, monks, on a hilltop[2] when the sky-deva rains thick
drops, that water, pouring down according to the slope of
the ground, fills up the clefts, chasms and gullies of the hill-
side; when these are filled, they fill the pools; when these
are filled, they fill the lakes; when these are filled, they fill
the rivulets; these being filled fill up the great rivers; the great
rivers being filled fill the sea, the ocean;—just so, monks,
these four seasons, if rightly developed, rightly revolved,
gradually bring about the destruction of the āsavas.'

---

[1] *Sākaccha. Cf. infra,* § 187; iii, 81.
[2] *Cf. S.* ii, 32.

§ viii (148). *Wrong practice.*

' Monks, there are these four wrong practices. What four ?
Lying speech, spiteful speech, bitter speech and idle babble.
These four.'

§ ix (149). *Right practice.*

' Monks, there are these four right practices. What four ?
Truthful speech, speech not spiteful, mild speech and mantra
speech . . .'[1]

§ x (150). *Essences.*

' Monks, there are these four essences. What four ?
The essence of virtue, the essence of concentration, the
essence of wisdom, the essence of release. These are the four
essences.'

(THE FOURTH OR GREAT FIFTY SUTTAS)

CHAPTER XVI.—CONTROLLING POWERS.

§ i (151). *Controlling powers (a).*[2]

' Monks, there are these four controlling powers. What
four ?
The controlling power of faith, of energy, of mindfulness,
and the controlling power of concentration. These are the
four . . .'

§ ii (152). *(Controlling) powers (b).*

' Monks, there are these four powers.[3] What four ?
The power of faith, of energy, of mindfulness, of concentration.'

---

[1] *Mantā-bhāsā: cf. infra, § 221. Comy. mantā-sankhātāya paññāya
paricchinditvā kathitakā.* For similar expl. *cf. SnA.* 204, etc., and *P.
Dict. s.v.; Nidd.* 497 (=*paññā*); *SA.* i, 273 (*mantā-vacanaŋ*=*subhā-
sitaŋ*); *D.* ii, 246, *mantāya bodhabbaŋ.*

[2] *Indriyāni. Cf. K.S.* v, 168, 179 (Six faculties). I have kept
'faculties' for those that are physical. That of insight is added to our
four. They are much the same as *balāni*, ' strong things ' (below).

[3] *Cf. K.S.* v, 223.

§ iii (153). *Powers (a)*.

' Monks, there are these four powers.   What four ?
The power of faith, of energy, of innocence,[1] of collect-edness.'[2]

§ iv (154). *Powers (b)*.

' Monks, there are these four powers.   What four ?
The power of mindfulness, of concentration, of innocence, of collectedness.'

§ v (155). *Computation*.

' Monks, there are these four powers.   What four ?
The power of computation,[3] of cultivation, of innocence, of collectedness.'

§ vi (156). *The æon*.

' Monks, there are these four incalculable periods of the æon.[4]   What four ?
When the æon rolls up, it is no easy thing to reckon: So many years, so many hundred years, so many thousand years, so many hundred thousands of years.
When the æon being rolled up stands still, it is no easy thing to reckon: So many years . . . so many hundred thousands of years.
When the æon rolls out it is no easy thing to reckon: So many years.
When the æon being rolled out stands still, it is no easy thing to reckon: So many years . . . so many hundred thousands of years.
These, monks, are the four incalculable periods of the æon.'

---

[1] *Anavajja=niddosa.   Comy.*

[2] *Sangāha.   Comy.*, however, appears to take it as from *sangaṇhana* (showing kindness).

[3] *Paṭisankhāna.*   The first two at *G.S.* i, 47 *n*.

[4] *Cf. D.* i, 14, iii, 109; *Mil. Pañh.* 232; *Pts. of Contr.* 258.   Our *Comy.* on the passage=*VM.*, p. 414, but the ref. there given to this passage is wrong.   ' Rolls up and out' approaches our in- and e-volution.

§ vii (157). *Disease.*

'Monks, there are these two diseases. What two ?
Disease of body and disease of mind.

Monks, there are to be seen beings who can admit freedom
from suffering from bodily disease for one year, for two
years, for three, four, five, ten, twenty, thirty, forty, fifty
years; who can admit freedom from bodily disease for even a
hundred years. But, monks, those beings are hard to find
in the world who can admit freedom from mental disease even
for one moment,[1] save only those in whom the āsavas are
destroyed.

Monks, there are these four diseases of one who has gone
forth (from the worldly life). What four ?

Here, monks, we may have a greedy one, full of vexation,
discontented with this or that supply of robe and alms-food,
lodging, seat, medicines and requisites for sickness. He,
being greedy and so forth, conceived[2] an evil longing for consideration, for gain, honours and fame. He rouses himself,
exerts himself, makes an effort to get these things. Of set
purpose[3] he visits families, of set purpose he takes a seat, of
set purpose he speaks Dhamma, of set purpose he restrains
the calls of nature. These, monks, are the four diseases of
him who has gone forth.

Therefore, monks, thus must ye train yourselves: We will
not become greedy, full of vexation, discontented with this
or that supply of robe and alms-food, lodging, seat, medicines
and requisites for sickness. We will not conceive an evil
longing for consideration, for gain, honours and fame. We
will not rouse ourselves, exert ourselves, make an effort to
get these things. We will become enduring of cold, hunger,
thirst, contact of flies and mosquitoes, of wind and rain and
creeping things.[4] We will become bearers of abusive, pain-
causing ways of speech. We will submit to painful bodily

---

[1] *Cf. K.S.* iii, 2.   [2] *Panidahati.*
[3] *Cf. A.* i, 133. *Sankhāya,* gerund. He undergoes privations of
routine, etc., with this aim.
[4] *Cf. supra,* § 114.

feelings, grievous, sharp, racking, distracting and discomforting, that drain the life away. Thus, monks, must ye train yourselves.'

§ viii (158). *Falling away.*

Then the venerable Sariputta addressed the monks, saying, ' Monks.'

' Yes, sir,' replied those monks to the venerable Sariputta. The venerable Sariputta said this:

' Whosoever, your reverences, be it monk or nun, has observed in himself four qualities, needs must come to this conclusion:[1] I am falling away in good qualities. This was called " falling away " by the Exalted One.

What are the four ? Abundance of lust, abundance of hatred, abundance of delusion. Moreover, into profound matters, into conclusions right or wrong, the eye of wisdom in him does not penetrate.[2]

Whosoever, your reverences, be it monk or nun, has observed in himself these four qualities must needs come to this conclusion . . .

But, your reverences, whosoever, be it monk or nun, has observed in himself four qualities, needs must come to this conclusion: I am not falling away in good qualities. This was called " Not falling away " by the Exalted One. What are the four ? Gradual decrease in lust, hatred and delusion. Moreover, into profound matters, into conclusions right or wrong, the eye of wisdom in him does penetrate.

Whosoever, your reverences, has observed . . . must so conclude.'

§ ix (159). *The nun.*[3]

On a certain occasion the venerable Ānanda was staying at Kosambī, in Ghosita Park. Now on that occasion a certain nun addressed a certain man, saying:[4]

---

[1] *Niṭṭhaŋ gantabbaŋ. Cf. G.S.* i, 253.

[2] *Na kamati=na vahati, pavattati, SA.* on *S.* iv, 283=*na carati, pavisati, SnA.* on *Sn.* 177; here it=*nâvagāhati, nappavattati, paṭivedhati. Comy.*

[3] For visiting nuns *cf. K.S.* v, 134.

[4] *Comy.* asserts that she was enamoured of Ānanda.

'Come, thou good fellow! Go to master Ānanda, and on coming to him in my name worship with thy head the feet of the worthy Ānanda and say: " Sir, a nun named so and so is sick, in pain, stricken with a sore disease. She worships with her head the feet of the worthy Ānanda." And do you say this: " It would be a good thing, sir, if the worthy Ānanda would visit the nuns' lodging where that nun is, out of compassion for her." '

'Yes, lady,' replied that man, and went to the venerable Ānanda (and did as he was told).

Then the venerable Ānanda, robing himself and taking bowl and outer robe, went to visit that nun.

Now that nun saw the venerable Ānanda from afar as he was coming, and on seeing him she covered her head[1] and lay down on a couch. Then the venerable Ānanda came to where she was, and on reaching her sat down on a seat made ready. As he sat there the venerable Ānanda said this to that nun:[2]

'Sister, this body has come into being through food, is dependent on food. The food must be abandoned. Sister, this body has come into being through craving, is dependent on craving. Craving must be abandoned. Sister, this body has come into being through pride, is dependent on pride. Pride must be abandoned. Sister, this body has come into being through sexual intercourse. Sexual intercourse must be abandoned. The breaking down of the bridge[3] which is in sexual intercourse has been spoken of by the Exalted One.

---

[1] It is contrary to Vinaya rules for a nun or female devotee (*Pāṭi-mokkha, Sekhiya*) to hear dhamma with head covered or reclining or wearing sandals. Strangely *Comy.* does not notice it. But *cf. K.S.* iv, 78 f., where a brāhmin lady is rebuked by Udāyin for so doing.

[2] *Comy.* remarks that in order to disillusion her of her passion he spoke of the ' foul things ' (*asubha-kathaŋ*).

[3] *Setu-ghāto = pada-ghāto, paccaya-ghato. Camy. Cf. A.* i, 261; *Buddh. Psych. Eth.,* p. 87. Our text reads *methuno ca setughāto vutto* (which would mean ' sexual intercourse *and* bridge-breaking '); while the *Siamese* text reads *methune pahātabbo, methune setu-ghāto,* which is preferable. *Sinh.* text has *methune* only (the proper construction acc. to other passages where the phrase occurs). Here I follow the *Siamese* text. The saying is not recorded, as far as I know.

Sister, as to this saying: "This body has come into being through food, is dependent on food; the food must be abandoned,"—it was said in this connexion.

Herein, sister, a monk takes food with reflection and judgment,[1] not for sport, not for indulgence, not for personal charm, not for beautifying, but just enough for the support, for the upkeep of body, for its resting unharmed, for helping the living of the God-life. (He takes food with the thought:) Thus do I check my former feeling and set going no new feeling; thus maintenance shall be mine,[2] blamelessness and comfort in life. Then some time later, though dependent on food, he abandons food. As to the saying that body has come into being through food, whatever was thus said was said in this connexion.

Sister, as to the saying: "This body has come into being through craving, is dependent on craving; craving must be abandoned,"—it was said in this connexion.

Herein, sister, a monk hears it said: "They say that such and such a monk, by destroying the āsavas, himself in this very life thoroughly comprehending it, realizes the heart's release, the release by wisdom, that is free from the āsavas, and having attained it abides therein." To him it occurs: Surely[3] I too, by destroying the āsavas . . . having attained it shall abide therein. Then some time later, though dependent on craving, he abandons craving. As to the saying, sister, that body has come into being through craving, is dependent on craving, craving must be abandoned,—whatever was said thus was said in this connexion.

Sister, as to the saying: "This body has come into being through pride, is dependent on pride; pride must be abandoned,"—it was said in this connexion. In this case, sister, a monk hears it said: "They say that such and such a monk,

---

[1] *Cf. S.* ii, 98 (*Maṇsaputta*), iv, 104; *Expos.* ii, 511; *VM.* 31; *supra*, § 37. *Comy.* says nothing here nor at *S.* ii *loc. cit.*, but refers to *VM. loc. cit.*, which equals *Expositor loc. cit.*

[2] Text omits *me*.

[3] *Kudassa nāma. Cf. A.* i, 107. For another word, *kudāssu*, see *SA.* i, 124; *S.* ii, 5; *SA.* ii, 21 (*katarasmin nu kāle ?*).

by destroying the āsavas . . . having attained the release by
wisdom abides therein." To him it thus occurs: That one by
destroying the āsavas . . . can realize and attain and abide
in the release by wisdom. Then why not I ?[1] Then some time
later, though dependent on pride, he abandons pride. Sister,
as to the saying: "This body has come into being through
pride, is dependent on pride; pride must be abandoned,"—it
was said in this connexion.

Sister, as to the saying: "This body has come into being
through sexual intercourse, (is dependent on sexual intercourse; sexual intercourse must be abandoned);[2] the breaking
down of the bridge which is in sexual intercourse has been
spoken of by the Exalted One " . . .'

Thereupon the nun rose from the couch, put her upper
robe on one shoulder, fell with her head at the feet of the
venerable Ānanda and said:

' O, sir, my fault overcame me, who am so foolish, so stupid,
so wrong, that I acted thus ! O, sir, let master Ānanda
acknowledge my fault as such, for my restraint in future
time !'

' Verily, sister, your fault overcame you, thus foolish, thus
stupid, thus wrong, that you acted thus. But inasmuch as
you, sister, have seen your fault as such and have confessed
it as is right, we do acknowledge it of you. This indeed,
sister, is growth in the discipline of the Ariyan, when, seeing
his fault as such, one makes confession as is right and comes
to restraint in future time.'[3]

§ x (160). *The Wellfarer's Discipline.*[4]

' Monks, when a Wellfarer or a Wellfarer's Discipline abides
in the world, that is done for the profit of many, the happiness

---

[1] *Kimanga panāhaŋ.*
[2] Here out of delicacy, it seems, Ānanda does not expound further
as in the case of the other failings. I bracket the words.
[3] The usual formula of repentance. *Cf. Vin.* i, 315; *S.* ii, 127=*K.S.*
ii, 91; *Manual of a Mystic,* 7, etc. For *accaya* (fault) *cf. A.* i, 59, 103,
where he who refuses such an apology is reckoned a fool ; iv, 377.
[4] *Cf. S.* v, 14.

of many; it is out of compassion for the world, for the weal, for the profit, for the happiness of devas and mankind. And of what sort, monks, is a Wellfarer ?

Herein, monks, a Tathāgata arises in the world, an Arahant, a Fully Enlightened One, perfect in knowledge and conduct, a Wellfarer, a world-knower, unsurpassed driver of men to be driven, Teacher of devas and mankind, a Buddha, an Exalted One. This, monks, is a Wellfarer.

And of what sort, monks, is a Wellfarer's Discipline ?

He is one who teaches Dhamma, lovely in youth, lovely in middle age, lovely at the end of life,[1] both in the spirit and the letter. He makes plain the holy life, entirely complete and purified. This, monks, is the Discipline of a Wellfarer. Monks, when a Wellfarer or a Wellfarer's Discipline abides in the world, that is done for the profit of many, for the happiness of many; it is done out of compassion for the world, for the weal, for the profit, for the happiness of devas and mankind.

Monks, these four things conduce to the confusion, to the vanishing away of Saddhamma. What four ?

In this case, monks, the monks get by heart a text[2] that is wrongly taken,[3] with words and sense that are wrongly arranged. Now, monks, if words and sense are wrongly arranged, the meaning also is misleading. This is the first thing which conduces to the confusion, to the vanishing away of Saddhamma.

Then again the monks are difficult to speak to, possessed of qualities which make them difficult to speak to; they are intractable, incapable of being instructed.[4] This, monks, is the second thing. . . .

Then again those monks who are widely learned, versed in

---

[1] With *Sakya*, p. 73, I take these epithets to refer not to Dhamma itself but to the times of life. Elsewhere trans. ' Lovely in its middle,' etc.

[2] *Suttantaŋ pariyāpuṇanti=s. valañjenti. Comy. Cf. A.* i, 59; *M.* i, 133, where *Comy.* expl. by *ugganhanti.*

[3] *Duggahītaŋ* = ' in an impossible sense.' *Comy.*

[4] As at *S.* ii, 204 (a general complaint made to the Master by Kassapa). *A-ppadakkhiṇa-gāhin* =' a left-hander,' so ' clumsy.'

the doctrines,[1] who know Dhamma by heart, who know Vinaya by heart, who know the summaries[2] by heart,—these do not dutifully hand on a text to another; thus, when they pass away, the text is cut down at the root, it has nothing to stand on. This is the third thing. . . .

Yet again the elder monks live in abundance,[3] they are lax, taking the lead in backsliding (to the worldly life), shirking the burden of the secluded life, they set going no effort to reach the unattained, to win the goal not won, to realize the unrealized; so the generation that follows comes to depend upon their view. That generation also lives in abundance, is lax, takes the lead in backsliding (to the worldly life) . . . sets going no effort to reach the unattained, to win the goal not won, to realize the unrealized. This, monks, is the fourth thing which conduces to the confusion, to the vanishing away of Saddhamma.

Now, monks, these four things conduce to the support, to the non-confusion, to the not vanishing away of Saddhamma. What four ?

Herein the monks get by heart a text that is rightly taken, with words and sense that are rightly arranged. Now if words and sense are rightly arranged the meaning also is easy to follow. This is the first thing. . . .

Then again the monks are easy to speak to, possessed of qualities which make them easy to speak to; they are tractable, capable of being instructed. This, monks, is the second thing. . . .

Yet again those monks who are of wide knowledge, versed in the doctrines, who know Dhamma by heart, who know Vinaya by heart, who know the summaries by heart,—these dutifully hand on a text to another; thus, when they pass away,

---

[1] *Cf. A.* i, 117; *infra,* 169; iii, 360. *Āgat' āgamā.* The *āgama* (what one goes by) is canonical ' scripture.' In Ceylon the word is used today for the ' Buddhist religion.'

[2] *Mātikā*='leads, lodes ' (like *netti*) or mnemonics.

[3] *Cf. M.* i, 14, 32, etc.; *G.S.* i, 66. *Bāhulikā* (generally spelt *bāhullikā*). *Comy.* expl. as ' getting plenty of necessaries.' Such are called in *A.* i 'the ignoble company of monks.'

the text is not cut down at the root, it has something to stand on. This, monks, is the third thing. . . .

Yet again the elder monks live not in abundance, they are not lax, they take not the lead in backsliding (to the worldly life), they shirk not the burden of the secluded life, they set going an effort to reach the unattained, to win the goal not won, to realize the unrealized. So the generation that follows comes to depend upon their view. That generation also lives not in abundance . . . but makes an effort to realize the unrealized. This, monks, is the fourth thing that conduces to the support, to the non-confusion, to the not vanishing away of Saddhamma.

So these, monks, are the four things. . . .'

Chapter XVII.—Modes of Progress.[1]

§ i (161). *In brief.*

' Monks, there are these four modes of progress. What four ?
The painful mode of progress with sluggish intuition,[2] the painful mode with swift intuition, the pleasant mode of progress with sluggish intuition, the pleasant mode with swift intuition. These are the four. . . .'

§ ii (162). *In detail.*

' Monks, there are these four modes of progress (*as above*).

And of what sort, monks, is the mode of progress that is painful with sluggish intuition ?

In this case a certain one is by nature passionately lustful; he experiences the perpetual pain and dejection that are born of lust. Likewise he is by nature passionately malicious; he experiences the perpetual pain and dejection that are born of malice. Likewise he is by nature passionately infatuated; he experiences the perpetual pain and dejection that are born of delusion.

In such an one these five controlling faculties are dully

---

[1] *Cf. Dial.* iii, 101; *Buddh. Psych. Eth.* 53, 54; *Expos.* i, 243 *f.*

[2] *Abhiññā*='more-knowledge' or 'psychic power.'

manifested, to wit: the controlling faculty of faith, that of energy, that of mindfulness, that of concentration, and the controlling faculty of wisdom. Thus, owing to the dullness of these five faculties, sluggish is his attainment of the concentration that follows on[1] for the destruction of the āsavas.

This, monks, is called "the progress that is painful with sluggish intuition."

And of what sort, monks, is the mode of progress that is painful but with swift intuition ?

In this case a certain one is by nature passionately lustful . . . he experiences the perpetual pain and dejection that are born of lust, malice and delusion.

In such an one these five controlling faculties are manifested in abundance, to wit: the controlling faculty of faith . . . of wisdom. Thus, owing to the preponderance of these five faculties, swift is his attainment of the concentration that follows on for the destruction of the āsavas. This, monks, is called "the progress that is painful but with swift intuition."

And of what sort, monks, is the mode of progress that is pleasant, but with sluggish intuition ?

In this case a certain one is not by nature passionately lustful; he does not experience the perpetual pain and dejection that are born of lust. Nor is he by nature passionately malicious; he does not experience the perpetual pain and dejection that are born of malice. Nor is he by nature passionately infatuated. He does not experience the perpetual pain and dejection that are born of delusion. But in such an one these five controlling faculties are dully manifested, to wit: the controlling faculty of faith . . . of wisdom. Thus, owing to the dullness of the five faculties, sluggish is his attainment of the concentration that follows on for the destruction of the āsavas. This, monks,

---

[1] *Ānantariyaŋ* (sc. *samādhiŋ*). *Cf. VM.* ii, 675, which quotes our sutta, and *Sn.* 226:

> Yaŋ Buddha-seṭṭho parivaṇṇayi suciŋ
> Samādhiŋ ānantarikaŋ nam āhu.

This failure to attain is due to the hindrances (*cf. Expos.* i, 244)— *i.e.*, it is difficult for him to give up the lower nature without a great struggle. This painful progress is described in § 163.

is called "the mode of progress that is pleasant, but with sluggish intuition."

And of what sort, monks, is the mode of progress that is both pleasant and accompanied by swift intuition ?

In this case a certain one is not by nature passionately lustful (*as in previous* §§) . . . born of delusion. And in such an one these five controlling faculties are manifested in abundance, to wit: the controlling faculty of faith, that of energy, that of mindfulness, that of concentration, that of wisdom. Thus, owing to the preponderance of the five faculties, swift is his attainment of the concentration that follows on for the destruction of the āsavas. This, monks, is called "the mode of progress that is both pleasant and accompanied by swift intuition."

So these are the four modes of progress.'

§ iii (163). *The unlovely.*

' Monks, there are these four modes of progress. What four ? (*as in* § 161).

And of what sort, monks, is the painful mode of progress with sluggish intuition ?

In this case a monk[1] lives contemplating the unloveliness in body, aware of the repulsiveness of food, aware of his distaste for all the world, aware of impermanence in all the activities. Thus awareness of death is implanted in the very self. He lives dependent on these five powers of a pupil: the power of faith, the power of modesty, that of self-restraint, that of energy, and the power of wisdom. But in him these five controlling faculties are dully manifested, to wit: the controlling faculty of faith, that of energy, that of mindfulness, that of concentration, and the controlling faculty of wisdom. Thus, owing to the dullness of these five controlling faculties, sluggish is his attainment of the concentration that follows on for the destruction of the āsavas. This, monks, is called "the mode of progress that is painful with sluggish intuition."

---

[1] In previous suttas any person, not necessarily a monk, is spoken of. *Cf. Dhp. v.* 8; *Itiv.* 80. For the ' foul things ' see *K.S.* v, 111, 112, 300.

And of what sort, monks, is the mode of progress that is painful, but with swift intuition ?

In this case a monk lives contemplating the unloveliness in body . . . (*as above*). Thus the awareness of death is well implanted in the very self. He lives dependent on these five powers of a pupil: the power of faith . . . of wisdom. But in him these five controlling faculties are manifested in abundance, to wit: the controlling faculty of faith . . . of wisdom. Thus, owing to the preponderance of these five controlling faculties, swift is his attainment of the concentration that follows on for the destruction of the āsavas. This, monks, is called "the mode of progress that is painful but with swift intuition."

And of what sort, monks, is the mode of progress that is pleasant but with sluggish intuition ?

In this case a monk, aloof from sense-desires, aloof from evil conditions . . . enters upon the first musing, which is accompanied by thought directed and sustained, born of seclusion, zestful and easeful, and abides therein. Then by the calming down of thought directed and sustained, he enters upon the second musing, that calming of the inner self, that one-pointedness of mind, apart from thought directed and sustained, that is born of mental balance, zestful and easeful, and having attained it abides therein. Then by the fading out of zest, disinterested, mindful and composed, he experiences in his own person that ease of which the Ariyans declare: " He who is disinterested and alert dwells at ease." So he attains and abides in the third musing. Then by abandoning both ease and discomfort, by the ending of both the happiness and the unhappiness felt before, he attains the fourth musing, a state of neither ease nor discomfort, an equanimity of utter purity, and having attained it abides therein. He lives dependent on these five powers of a pupil: the power of faith, . . . the power of wisdom. But in him these five controlling faculties are dully manifested, to wit: the controlling faculty of faith ... of wisdom. Thus, owing to the dullness of these five, sluggish is his attainment of the concentration that follows on for the destruction of the āsavas. This, monks, is called "the mode of progress that is pleasant, but with sluggish intuition."

And of what sort, monks, is the mode of progress that is both pleasant and accompanied by swift intuition ?

In this case a monk, aloof from sense-desires . . . (*the whole as above down to*) . . . He lives dependent on the five powers of a pupil . . . But in him these five controlling faculties are manifested in abundance, to wit: the controlling faculty of faith . . . of wisdom. Thus, owing to the preponderance of these five controlling faculties, swift is his attainment of the concentration that follows on for the destruction of the āsavas. This, monks, is called "the mode of progress that is both pleasant and is accompanied by swift intuition."

So these are the four modes of progress.'

§ iv (164). *Patient* (a).

' Monks, there are these four modes of progress. What four ?

The mode of progress that is impatient, that which is patient, that which tames, and the mode of progress that calms.

And of what sort, monks, is the mode of progress that is impatient ?

In this case a certain one reviles again him that reviles, insults again him that insults, abuses again him that abuses. This is called "the impatient mode of progress."

And of what sort, monks, is the patient mode of progress ?

In this case a certain one reviles not, insults not, abuses not again him that reviles, insults and abuses. This is called "the patient mode of progress."

And of what sort, monks, is the mode of progress that tames ?

In this case a monk,[1] seeing an object with the eye, is not misled by its outer view nor by its lesser details. Since coveting and dejection, evil, unprofitable states, might flow in upon one who lives with the faculty of the eye uncontrolled, he applies himself to such control, sets a guard over the faculty of eye, attains control thereof. When he hears a sound with the ear, or with the nose smells a scent, or with the tongue

---

[1] *Cf. K.S.* iv, 63.

tastes a savour, or with body contacts tangibles, when with mind he cognizes mental states, he is not misled by their outer view nor by their lesser details. But since coveting and dejection, evil, unprofitable states, might flow in upon one who . . . he sets a guard over the faculty of mind, attains control thereof. This is called "the mode of progress that tames."

And of what sort, monks, is the mode of progress that calms?

In this case a monk admits not sensual thinking that has arisen. He abandons, restrains, calms it down, makes an end of it, forces it not to recur.[1] So also with regard to malicious thinking . . . harmful thinking. He does not admit evil, unprofitable states that occur from time to time; he abandons them, restrains, calms them down, makes an end of them, forces them not to recur. This, monks, is called "the mode of progress that calms."

So these are the four modes of progress.'

§ v (165). *Patient (b)*.

'Monks, there are these four modes of progress. What four? (*as above*).

And of what sort, monks, is the mode of progress that is impatient?

In this case a certain one is impatient of cold, heat, hunger, thirst, the contact of flies, mosquitoes, of wind and sun and creeping things. He is impatient of abusive, pain-causing ways of speech. He is impatient of painful bodily feelings, grievous, sharp, racking, distracting and discomforting, that drain the life away. This, monks, is called "the impatient mode of progress."

And of what sort, monks, is the patient mode of progress?

In this case a certain one is patient of cold and the rest. . . .

And of what sort, monks, is the mode of progress that tames?

In this case a certain one, seeing an object with the eye, is not misled by its outer view. . . .

And of what sort, monks, is the mode of progress that calms?

---

[1] *Cf.* § 114 above.

In this case a monk admits not sensual thinking (*as in* §164). This is called "the mode of progress that calms."

So these are the four modes of progress.'

§ vi (166). *In further detail.*[1]

' Monks, there are these four modes of progress.   What four ?

The mode of progress that is painful with sluggish intuition, that which is painful with swift intuition, that which is pleasant with sluggish intuition, and the mode of progress that is pleasant and accompanied with swift intuition.

Now here, monks, the mode of progress that is painful with sluggish intuition is reckoned low[2] in both respects, both as regards its pain and its sluggishness.   That is how it is reckoned low in both respects.

Then again, monks, that which is painful with swift intuition is reckoned low in respect of its being painful.

Then again, monks, that which is pleasant with sluggish intuition is reckoned low in respect of its being sluggish.

Yet again, monks, the mode of progress that is pleasant with swift intuition is reckoned excellent in both respects, both as regards its pleasantness and its swiftness.   Thus it is reckoned excellent in both respects.

So these are the four modes. . . .'

§ vii (167). *Sāriputta and Moggallāna (a).*

Now the venerable Sāriputta went to visit the venerable Moggallāna the Great, and on coming to him greeted him courteously, and after the exchange of greetings and courtesies, sat down at one side.   So seated the venerable Sāriputta said this to the venerable Moggallāna the Great:

' Moggallāna, your reverence, there are these four modes of progress. What four ? The mode of progress that is painful with sluggish intuition . . . (*as before*). These are the four.   Now, your reverence, by way of which of these four modes of progress was your heart released from the āsavas without grasping ?'

---

[1] Ref. to § 162.   [2] *Hīna.*

'Sāriputta, your reverence, there are (as you say) these four modes of progress. . . . Now of these four the one I followed was the mode of progress that is painful, but with swift intuition. By way of this mode of progress was my heart released from the āsavas without grasping.'

§ viii (168). *Sāriputta and Moggallāna (b).*

Now the venerable Moggallāna the Great went to visit the venerable Sāriputta . . . and said this to him:

'Sāriputta, your reverence, there are four modes of progress. . . . Now, your reverence, by way of which of these four was your heart released from the āsavas without grasping ?'

'Moggallāna, your reverence, there are (as you say) these four modes. . . .

Now of these four the one I followed was the mode of progress that is pleasant with swift intuition. By way of this mode of progress was my heart released from the āsavas without grasping.'

§ ix (169). *With some effort.*

'Monks, these four persons are found existing in the world. What four ?

Herein, monks, a certain person in this very life is set free, but with some effort.[1] Again a certain person is set free when body breaks up, but with some effort. Herein again, monks,

---

[1] *Sa-sankhāra-parinibbāyī.* At *Dial.* iii, 227, 'with some toil.' At *PuggA.* on *Pugg.* 17 expl. as *dukkhena, kasirena, adhimatta-payogaŋ katvā* (with considerable effort). But at *Buddh. Psych. Ethics,* § 146, *n.* 1, explained as instigated. Generally, we may see that mediacy, absence of immediacy is meant. *Cf. K.S.* v, 57; *Expos.* i, 207: 'the import is *with external plan, effort, instigation, expedient, totality of causes.*' *Comy.* on *S.* v *loc. cit.* has *sappayogena* as at *VM.* ii, 710, where Prof. Maung Tin trans. (*Path of Purity,* iii, 874): 'Enters complete nirvāna with external instigation.'

As to *parinibbāyin, SA.* i, 20, 37 defs. 'gone out by the going out of the impurities.' *Comy.* on our text expands the textual explanation, saying that these grades are a matter of strength of the controlling faculties, but does not explain *parinibbāyin.*

a certain person is set free in this very life, but without effort. Yet again a certain person is set free when body breaks up, but without effort.

Now, monks, how is a person one who in this very life is set free, but with some effort ?

In this case a monk lives contemplating the unloveliness in body, aware of the repulsiveness of food, aware of his distaste for all the world, aware of impermanence in all the activities. Thus awareness of death is well implanted in the very self. He lives dependent on these five powers of a pupil, to wit: the power of faith, that of modesty, that of self-restraint, that of energy, and the power of wisdom. In him these five controlling faculties are manifested in abundance, to wit: the controlling faculty of faith, that of energy, that of mindfulness, that of concentration, and the controlling faculty of wisdom. Thus, by the preponderance of these five controlling faculties in this very life, he is set free, but with some effort.

And how, monks, is a person set free when body breaks up, but with some effort ?

In this case a monk lives contemplating the unloveliness in body (*as above* § 163) . . . but in him these five controlling faculties are dully manifested, to wit: the controlling faculty of faith . . . that of wisdom. Thus, by the dullness of these faculties, he is set free with some effort when body breaks up.

And how, monks, is a person set free in this very life, but without effort ?

In this case a monk, aloof from sense-desires . . . (*as in* § 3 *of* § 163) enters on and abides in the first . . . second . . . third . . . and fourth musing. He lives dependent on these five powers of a pupil. . . . In him these five controlling faculties are manifested in abundance. . . . Thus by the preponderance of these five controlling faculties he is set free in this very life without effort.

And how, monks, is a person one who is set free without effort when body breaks up ?

In this case a monk, aloof from sense-desires . . . enters on the four musings and abides therein. . . . He lives dependent on these five powers of a pupil . . . but in him these five controlling faculties are dully manifested. Owing to the dullness of these five faculties, it is not till body breaks up that he is set free without effort.

So these are the four persons found existing in the world.'

§ x (170). *Coupled.*[1]

On a certain occasion the venerable Ānanda was staying at Kosambī in Ghosita Park. Then the Venerable Ānanda addressed the monks, saying: ' Reverend sirs.'

' Your reverence,' replied those monks to the venerable Ānanda. The venerable Ānanda said:

' Reverend sirs, when anyone, be it monk or nun, proclaims in my presence that he has attained arahantship, all such do so by virtue of four factors or one of these four. What are they ?

Herein, your reverences, a monk develops insight preceded by calm. In him thus developing insight preceded by calm is born the Way.[2] He follows along that Way, makes it grow, makes much of it. In him following, developing, making much of that Way, the fetters are abandoned, the lurking tendencies[3] come to an end.

Or again, your reverences, a monk develops calm preceded by insight. In him developing calm preceded by insight is born the Way. He follows along that Way, makes it grow, makes much of it. In him following, developing, making much of that Way, the fetters are abandoned, the lurking tendencies come to an end.

Yet again, your reverences, a monk develops calm-and-

---

[1] *Yuga-naddha* (spelt also *-nandha*), ' bound in a pair.' This word is not listed in *A. index* or *P. Dict.* as occurring in the Nikāyas; but it occurs also at *M.* iii, 289 (*samatha-vipassanā*). I have not found it elsewhere except at *Pṭs.* ii, 98 (*Yuganandha-vagga*), which chapter is based on our sutta, there quoted and commented on. *Cf. Mil. P.* 117 (*yamaka-yamakā*); *VM.* 149 (*dhamma*); *UdA.* 153 (*yuga-nandha-samatha-vipassanā-balena*); 398 (*samathā-vipassanaɳ yuga-naddhaɳ yojetvā*); also 177.

[2] *Comy.* ' the first supramundane Path.'

[3] *Anusayā. Cf. K.S.* ii, 167 *n.* At *A.* iv, 9 seven are given. *Cf. A.* i, 44=*G.S.* i, 46.

insight coupled.[1] In him thus developing calm-and-insight coupled the Way is born. He follows along that Way. . . . As he does so the fetters are abandoned, the lurking tendencies come to an end.

Once more, your reverences, a monk's mind is utterly cleared of perplexities about Dhamma.[2] That is the time, your reverences, when his thought stands fixed in the very self, settles down, becomes one-pointed, is composed. In him the Way is born. He follows along that Way, makes it grow, makes much of it. In him following, developing, making much of that Way, the fetters are abandoned, the lurking tendencies come to an end.

Indeed, your reverences, when anyone, be it monk or nun, proclaims in my presence that he has attained arahantship, all such do so by virtue of four factors or one of these four.'

CHAPTER XVIII.—INTENTIONAL.

§ i (171). *Intention.*[3]

'Monks, where there is bodily action,[4] there arises to the self pleasure or pain caused by intention of bodily action.[5]

---

[1] See note above. Apparently to be taken in the sense of *samasisa* (synchronism). *Comy.* expl. ' at the moment of attainment he calms the activities; at the moment of calming the activities he makes the attainment. How ? He attains the first musing. Rising from that he calms the activities and attains the second musing. Rising from that, and so on. . . .'

[2] Here our text reads *dhamm' uddhacca-vigahītamanā* (?) *hoti. So* . . . But *Sinh.* text -*vigahitaŋ mānaŋ*; *Comy.* only *viggahītaŋ.* But the passage in *Pṭs.* ii, 93 (ref. to above) has -*viggahitaŋ mānasaŋ hoti* (which I follow). Apparently we should *begin* the next sentence with *Hoti so samayo* (as does *Comy.*) or repeat *hoti.* The process is explained at length *Pṭs.* ii, 100 *ff.*

[3] *Sañcetanā.* *Cf.* *M.* iii, 207; *K.S.* ii, 30, where Sāriputta instructs Ānanda in this subject, and *Expos.* i, 117 (*Discourse on Kamma*); *Pts. of Contr.* 225 (*The physical and moral*), both of which quote § 1.

[4] *Comy.* expl. *kāye* as *kāya-dvāre, kāya-viññattiyā* (by gesture). *Cf.* *Expos.* i, 109. The three doors of action are act of body, speech, thought. ' Acts pass through doors.'

[5] Or *kāya-sañcetanikā-hetu,* by reason of volition capable of causing an act.

. Or, monks, where there is action of speech, there arises pleasure or pain to the self caused by intentional action of speech. Or, monks, where there is thought, there arises pleasure or pain to the self caused by intentional action of thought. Or it is due to ignorance.[1]

Monks, it is due to ignorance that either of himself one plans planned bodily action, following on which arises to the self of him that pleasure or pain, or that others plan against him planned bodily action, following on which arises to the self of him that pleasure or pain. Either of set purpose, monks, one plans planned bodily action following on which arises to the self of him[2] that pleasure or pain, or not of set purpose does he plan such bodily action.

Again, either of himself, monks, one plans planned action of speech, following on which arises to the self of him that pleasure or pain, or others plan against him planned action of speech, following on which arises . . . Either of set purpose, monks, one plans planned action of speech . . . or not of set purpose does he plan such action.

Again, monks, either of himself one plans planned action of thought, following on which arises to the self of him that pleasure or pain, or others plan against him planned action of thought, following on which arises . . . Either of set purpose, monks, one plans planned action of thought . . . or not of set purpose does he plan such action of thought.

Monks, in these[3] instances ignorance is followed. But by the utter ceasing and ending of ignorance that bodily action exists not, following on which that pleasure or pain arises to the self of him; that action of speech . . . of thought exists not, following on which that pleasure or pain arises to the

---

[1] Here text adds *avijjā-paccayā vā*. This acc. to *S.* ii (which reads *va* and *Comy. ca*) belongs to next § in our text. *Comy.* has it both at the end of § 1 and at the beginning of § 2, acc. to which I trans. rather baldly to give the simple meaning.

[2] *Yaŋ assa ajjhattaŋ uppajjati* (subjective pleasure or pain).

[3] Here *S.* ii, 40 inserts *chasu*, but our texts and *Comy.* both at *S.* and here omit. As a matter of fact there are more than six. *SA.* has *catusu ṭhānesu*—i.e., the four alternatives in § 2, applied in a threefold way, make twelve.

self of him; there[1] is no field, no base, no sphere of action, no occasion, following on which that pleasure or pain arises to the self of him.'

§ ii (172). *Getting personality.*[2]

' Monks, there are these four ways of getting personality.[3] What four ?

There is, monks, the getting of personality in the getting of which one's own intention, not that of another person, has effect. . . . There is that in the getting of which another person's intention has effect, not one's own. There is that in which both one's own and another's intention have effect. There is that in which neither has effect. These make four.'

When this was said, the venerable Sāriputta said this to the Exalted One: ' Of this, lord, that has been uttered by the Exalted One in brief I understand the meaning in detail. In the case where there is getting of personality in which one's own intention, not another's, has effect, there is decease for those beings from that group[4] because of one's own intention. In the case where there is getting of personality in which another's intention, not one's own, has effect, there is decease for those beings from that group because of another's intention.[5] In the case where there is getting of personality in which both have effect, there is decease for those beings from that group[6] because of the intention both of oneself and of another.[7] But, lord, in the case where there is getting of personality in

---

[1] *Taŋ* may mean ' that field,' but its position seems to refer it to the state of end of ignorance.

[2] *Vibhatti* is the title in *uddāna*, but it should apply to the next sutta. Acc. to *Comy.* (but not *Sinh.* text) this section belongs to § 171. For the subject *cf. Dial.* iii, 222.

[3] *Attabhāva*, lit. self-state.

[4] *Comy.* states that this is the case with the devas called ' Pleasure-debauched ' (*khiddā-padosikā*). See *Dialog.* i, 32, ' for ages they pass their time in the pursuit of laughter and sport of sensual lusts; . . . through loss of self-control they fall from that state.'

[5] These are the ' debauched in mind devas ' (*mano-padosikā*) said to belong to the retinue of the Four Great Kings.

[6] *Kāya* here seems to have this meaning.

[7] Acc. to *Comy.* suicides and murdered people.

which neither has effect, what sort of devas are to be regarded therein ?'[1]

' In that case, Sāriputta, it is the devas who have attained the realm in which is neither-perception-nor-non-perception.'

' Pray, lord, what is the reason, what is the cause why certain beings deceasing from that group[2] are Returners, who come back to this state of things ?[3] Again, lord, what is the reason, what is the cause why certain beings deceasing from that group are Non-returners, who come not back to this state of things ?'

' In this (first) case, Sāriputta, in a certain person the fetters that bind to this world are not abandoned. Such an one in this very life attains the realm where there is neither-perception-nor-non-perception, and abides therein. He enjoys its sweetness, longs for it, finds happiness therein. Established therein, given thereto, generally spending his time therein, not falling away therefrom, when he makes an end he is reborn in that company. When he deceases thence he is a Returner, he comes back to this state of things.

In the other case, Sāriputta, in a certain person those fetters are abandoned. Such an one in this very life attains the realm where is neither-perception-nor-non-perception. He enjoys its sweetness . . . when he makes an end he is reborn[4] in that company, but deceasing thence he is a Non-returner, he comes not back to this state of things.

This is the reason, this is the cause, Sāriputta, why certain beings are Non-returners, who come not back to this state of things.'

§ iii (173). *Analysis.*[5]

Then the venerable Sāriputta addressed the monks, saying, ' Your reverences.'

---

[1] Here our text by error puts the question into next §.

[2] *Kāya* here seems to have this meaning.

[3] *Cf. G.S.* i, 58, ' because he is fettered as to the self,' while Non-returners are fettered only by externals.

[4] Text should read *uppajjati* for *āpajjati*.

[5] The four branches of analytical knowledge—viz., of meanings (*attha*), of conditions (*dhammā*), of definitions (*nirutti*), of intellect (*paṭibhāna*).

' Yes, your reverence,' replied those monks to the venerable Sāriputta. The venerable Sāriputta said this:

' Your reverences, when I had been six months ordained a monk, I grasped the analysis of meanings, specifically and according to the letter.[1] That I explain in various ways, I teach it, expound it, proclaim it, lay it down, open it up, analyse it and make it clear. If anyone has a doubt or perplexity, then what is the use of his questioning and my explaining,[2] when here is the Teacher face to face with us, he who is to us the well-skilled in things ?[3]

Your reverences, when I had been six months ordained a monk, I grasped the analysis of conditions, specifically and according to the letter. That I explain in various ways, I teach it, expound it, proclaim it, lay it down, open it up, analyse it and make it clear. If anyone has a doubt or perplexity, then what is the use of his questioning and my explaining, when here face to face with us is the Teacher, who is to us the well-skilled in things ?

Your reverences, when I had been six months ordained a monk I grasped the analysis of definitions . . . (*as before*) . . .

Your reverences, when I had been six months ordained a monk I grasped the analysis of intellect. . . . If anyone has a doubt or perplexity, then what is the use of his questioning and my explaining, when here face to face with us is the Teacher, who is to us the well-skilled in things ?'

---

[1] *Odhiso* (and *vyañjanaso*); the former word (limit) means ' within bounds,' 'limited to a particular sense.' *Anodhiso* = ' speaking generally.' *Cf. UdA.* 214 (*eka-vacanena*). Here *Comy.* expl. both as *kāranaso* and *akkharaso*.

[2] *So may paññena, ahay veyyākaranena.* (There is no verb here. *Comy.* supplies *upagacchatu* and *cittay ārādhessāmi.*) *Cf.* the similar forcible ellipse at *S.* iii, 108, *Ahay ovādena. Ahay anuggahena. Ahay anusāsaniyā*, said to Tissa. Here *Comy.* supplies a verb, *ugganhāmi.* I think it highly probable, as Mrs. Rhys Davids suggests (*Sakya*, 336-7), that this idiom has the meaning of ' What is the use of when . . . ?'

[3] *Dhammānay sukusalo.* This is like the often repeated phrase, *Bhagavammūlakā no dhammā. Cf. S.* ii, 24, 80, 198, etc. *Comy.* here supposes the Master to be present and to have requested *S.* to instruct the company.

§ iv (174). *Koṭṭhita.*

Then the venerable Koṭṭhita the Great[1] came to visit the venerable Sāriputta. On coming to him he greeted him courteously . . . and sat down at one side. So seated the venerable Koṭṭhita the Great said this to the venerable Sāriputta:

' Your reverence, does anything at all exist after the passionless ending, without remainder, of the six spheres of contact ?'

' Say not that, your reverence !'

' Then, your reverence, not anything exists after the ending . . . of the six spheres of contact.'[2]

' Say not that, your reverence !'

' Then there both is and is not anything existing after the passionless ending without remainder of the six spheres of contact.'

' Say not that, your reverence !'

' Your reverence, when questioned thus: " Is there . . . is there not . . . is there and is there not . . . neither is there nor is there not anything existing after the . . . ending . . . of the six spheres of contact ?" you reply: " Say not that, your reverence !" Pray, then, how is the meaning of what I said to be regarded ?'

' Your reverence, in saying that there is something left one makes difficulty where there is none. In saying that there neither is nor is not anything left one makes difficulty where there is none.[3]

---

[1] *Cf. A.* i, 24, ' chief of the masters of logical analysis.'

[2] *I.e.,* of sight, sound, smell, taste, touch and mental images. *Cf. K.S.* iii, 52.

[3] *Iti vadaŋ appapañcaŋ papañceti,* lit. ' obstructs the unobstructed.' *Papañca* is often taken to mean 'illusion.' It means ' prolixity, obstruction.' The taints of craving, view and pride are regarded as *papañca.* The Buddha is called *nippapañca.* Again *Papañca-sūdanī* (the destruction of difficulties) is the name of the *Commentary* on *Majjhima Nikāya. Cf. S.A.* ii, 32, *papañcaŋ katvā (idaŋ) kathitaŋ.*

Acc. to *Comy.* the first alternative is the eternalist heresy, the second is the annihilationist heresy. The other two will be the mystic ' unanswerables.'

So long, your reverence, as there is going to the six spheres
of contact, for just so long is there a going to difficulty. But,
your reverence, by the passionless ending without remainder
of the six spheres of contact there is calming down of difficulty.'

Now the venerable Ānanda came to visit the venerable
Koṭṭhita the Great, and on coming to him he greeted him
courteously and after the exchange of greetings and courtesies
sat down at one side. So seated the venerable Ānanda said
this to the venerable Koṭṭhita the Great :[1]

(*The question and answer are exactly as before.*)

§ v (175). *Upavāṇa.*[2]

Now the venerable Upavāṇa came to visit the venerable
Sāriputta . . . and said this to him:

' Pray, Sāriputta, your reverence, is there any end-maker[3]
by knowledge ?'

' Not in this case, your reverence.'

' Then, your reverence, is there any end-maker by conduct ?'

' Not in this case, your reverence.'

' Then is there any end-maker by knowledge-and-conduct ?'

' Not in this case, your reverence.'

' What, then, your reverence, is there any end-maker by
any other way than knowledge-and-conduct ?'

' Not in this case, your reverence.'

' Sāriputta, your reverence, when asked, "Is there any
end-maker by knowledge . . . by conduct . . . by knowledge-and-conduct ?" and "Is there any other way ?" you
reply, "Not in this case, your reverence." In what way then,
your reverence, is there an end-maker ?'

' Your reverence, if there were an end-maker by knowledge,
he would still be an end-maker with grasping (for another

---

[1] This is taken as a separate sutta by *Comy.* and *Sinh.* text.

[2] At *S.* i, 174 he waits on the Master and cures his sickness. At
S. ii, 41 he is taught about Ill; at *S.* iv, 41 about the practical use of
Dhamma. At *S.* v, 75 Sāriputta teaches him the Seven Limbs of
Wisdom as conducive to a happy life. At *A.* iii, 195 the Master
teaches him how the God-life may be attractive. *Cf. Pss. Br.* CLIII.

[3] Acc. to *Comy.* ' of the round of Ill.'

existence).¹ If there were one by conduct . . . by knowledge-and-conduct, he would still be an end-maker with
grasping. If, your reverence, there were an end-maker by
any other way than by knowledge-and-conduct, then the
ordinary man² would be an end-maker. Now, your reverence,
the ordinary man, living apart from knowledge-and-conduct,
being unversed in conduct, knows not, sees not things as they
really are. But if he be practised in conduct, he knows, he
sees things as they really are. So knowing, so seeing, he is an
end-maker.'

§ vi (176). *Aspiration.*

' Monks, the believing monk, if he would aspire³ perfectly,
should thus aspire: May I be like unto Sāriputta and Moggallāna !

Monks, these are a sort of scale and standard (whereby to
estimate) my disciples who are monks, namely Sāriputta
and Moggallāna.

Monks, the believing nun, if she would aspire perfectly,
should thus aspire: May I be like unto Khemā and Uppalavaṇṇā !

Monks, these are a sort of scale and standard (whereby
to estimate) my disciples who are nuns, namely Khemā
and Uppalavaṇṇā.'

(*The same is said of*) The housefather Citta and Hatthaka
of Āḷavī, and the women lay-disciples Khujjuttarā and Nanda's
mother Veḷukantakiyā.

§ vii (177). *Rāhula.*⁴

Now the venerable Rāhula came to visit the Exalted One,
and on coming to him saluted him and sat down at one side.
As he thus sat the Exalted One said this to the venerable
Rāhula:

---

¹ *Sa-upādāno=sa-gahaṇo hutvā. Comy.*

² *Puthujjano.*

³ As at *A.* i, 88; *G.S.* i, 79. *At K.S.* ii, 159 *āyācamāno,* translated
' admonishing,' should be ' praying, asking for a son, etc.'

⁴ The Buddha's only son.

'Rāhula, both the earth-element in the self[1] and that in external objects are just this earth-element. Thus should it be regarded, as it really is, by perfect wisdom: "This is not of me. Not this am I. Not to me is this the self." So seeing it, as it really is, by perfect wisdom, one has revulsion for the earth-element; by wisdom one cleanses the heart of passion.

Rāhula, both the water-element in oneself and that in external objects . . . the heat-element . . . the air-element . . . in the self and that in external objects are just this air-element. Thus should it be regarded, as it really is, by perfect wisdom: "This is not of me. Not this am I. Not for me is this the self." So seeing it, as it really is, by perfect wisdom, one has revulsion for the air-element; by wisdom one cleanses the heart of passion.

Now, Rāhula, when a monk beholds neither the self nor what pertains to the self in these four elements, this one is called " a monk who has cut off craving, has loosed the bond, and by perfectly understanding (this) vain conceit, has made an end of Ill." '[2]

§ viii (178). *The village pond.*

'Monks, these four persons are found existing in the world. What four ?

Herein, monks, a monk having attained to[3] some peaceful way of heart's release abides therein. He gives work of mind to the ending of the person-pack,[4] but as he does so his heart leaps not up, does not settle down, does not stay fixed in the

---

[1] *Comy.* refers to *Ambalaṭṭhika-sutta* (*M.* i, 414) and *Mahārāhulo-vāda-sutta* (*M.* i, 421), and *S.* ii, 140, 245, 252 equal to *S.* iii, 135; *S.* iv, 2, 3. In the first-mentioned greater detail will be found, and 'space' is included in the category. *Comy.* following *M. loc. cit.* takes this to mean 'in hair, bones, etc.,' as opposed to 'senseless things like rocks and solids.' *Cf. Buddh. Psych. Eth.* 207.

[2] *Cf. M.* i, 12.

[3] Text should read *upasampajja. Comy.* 'one of the eight attainments' (*i.e.*, the four musings and the four spheres of consciousness, etc.).

[4] *Sakkāya. Cf. K.S.* iii, 134 *n.*

ending of the person-pack; it is not released therefrom. For such a monk this ending of the person-pack is not to be looked for.

Just as if, monks, a man were to seize a branch with his hand smeared with resin;[1] that hand of his would cleave to[2] it, grip it, would be held fast;—even so, monks, when a monk has attained to some peaceful way of heart's release he abides therein. He gives work of mind to the ending of the person-pack, but as he does so his heart leaps not up, does not settle down, does not stay fixed in the ending of the person-pack; it is not released therefrom. For such a monk the ending of the person-pack is not to be looked for.

But in this case suppose a monk has attained to some peaceful way of heart's release and abides therein. He gives work of mind to the ending of the person-pack, his heart leaps up[3] thereto, settles down therein, stays fixed in the ending thereof; it is released therefrom. For such a monk as this the ending of the person-pack is to be looked for. Just as if, monks, a man were to seize a branch with a clean hand, that hand of his would not cleave to it, would not grip it, would not be held fast,—even so, monks, when a monk has attained to some peaceful way of heart's release and abides therein, he gives work of mind to the ending of the person-pack . . . for such a monk this ending of the person-pack is to be looked for.

Herein again, monks, suppose a monk attains to some peaceful way of the heart's release and abides therein. He gives work of mind to the breaking up of ignorance, but as he does so his heart leaps not up thereto, settles not down therein, stays not fixed therein, is not released therefrom. For such a monk this breaking up of ignorance is not to be looked for.

Suppose, monks, there is a village pond that has stood for

---

[1] *Lasa-gatena*, so texts and *Comy.* Cf. *K.S.* v, 127 (*lepa*).

[2] *Cf. Sn. v.* 791:

> *te uggahāyanti nirassajanti*
> *kapīva sākhaɱ pamuñcaɱ gahāya,*

and the simile of the monkey at *S.* v, 148.

[3] Text should read *pakkhandati.*

countless years, and a man blocks up all its inlets[1] and opens up all outlets, and the sky rains not down steadily,[2]—then for that village pond no breach of dyke[3] is to be looked for. Even so, monks, when a monk has attained to some peaceful way of heart's release . . . for such a monk this breaking up of ignorance is not to be looked for.

But in this case suppose a monk attains to some peaceful way of heart's release and abides therein. He gives work of mind to the breaking up of ignorance. His heart leaps up thereto, settles down therein, stays fixed in the ending thereof; it is released therefrom. For such a monk the breaking up of ignorance is to be looked for.

Suppose, monks, there is a village pond that has stood for countless years, and a man opens up all its inlets and blocks up all its outlets, and the sky rains down steadily. Thus for that village pond a breach of dyke is to be looked for. Even so, monks, when a monk attains to some peaceful way of heart's release, he abides therein; he gives work of mind to the breaking up of ignorance. As he does so his heart leaps up thereto, settles down therein, stays fixed therein, is released therefrom. For such a monk this breaking up of ignorance is to be looked for.

So these, monks, are the four persons to be found existing in the world.'

§ ix (179). *Nibbāna.*

Now the venerable Ānanda went to visit the venerable Sāriputta and on coming to him greeted him courteously. . . . As he sat at one side the venerable Ānanda said this to the venerable Sāriputta:

'Pray, Sāriputta, your reverence, what is the reason, what is the cause why certain beings in this world are not fully set free[4] in this very life ?'

---

[1] *Aya-mukhāni, cf. Dial.* 1, 125 *n.*

[2] *S.* v, 379.

[3] *Āli-=pāḷi* (*Comy.*); *cf. A.* iii, 28.

[4] *Parinibbāyanti,* lit. extinct. At *S.* iv, 102 Sakka asks the B. this same question. The answer is ' delight in sense-impressions.'

'In this matter, Ānanda, your reverence, beings do not understand, as it really is: This perception[1] partakes of worsening. They do not understand, as it really is: This perception partakes of stability. They do not understand, as it really is: This perception partakes of distinction. They do not understand, as it really is: This perception partakes of penetration.[2] This, your reverence, is the reason, this is the cause why some beings in this world are not fully set free in this very life.'

'But pray, Sāriputta, your reverence, what is the reason, what is the cause why certain beings in this world are fully set free in this very life ?'

'In this matter, your reverence, beings do understand, as it really is: This perception partakes of worsening . . . this perception partakes of penetration. This is the reason . . . why certain beings are fully set free in this very life.'

§ x (180). *Great authorities.*[3]

On a certain occasion the Exalted One was staying in Bhoganagara[4] at the Ānanda Shrine. Then the Exalted One addressed the monks, saying: 'Monks.'

'Yes, lord,' replied those monks to the Exalted One. The Exalted One said: 'Monks, I will teach you these four great authorities. Do you listen to it. Carefully give your minds to it and I will speak.' The Exalted One said this:

---

[1] *Saññā.* Cf. *D.* iii, 277=*Dial.* iii, 254; *VM.* i, 88=*Path of Purity*, ii, 103: 'Of these (forms of concentration) *the partaking of worsening* is due to the frequent arising of opposing states; *the partaking of stability* is due to the persistence of that mindfulness which is in conformity with concentration; *the partaking of distinction* is due to the attainment of a higher distinctive state; *the partaking of penetration* is due to the promptings of perception and attention associated with disgust (*cf.* *Pts.* i, 35).

[2] *Nibbedha.* At *Dial.* iii *loc. cit.* the trans. is 'leading to Nibbāna (?)'.

[3] As at *D.* ii, 123=*Dial.* ii; in both cases *Comy.* takes *mahāpadesa* as equal to *mahā-apadesa,* not *-padesa* (topic, place), so 'authority, reason, occasion.'

[4] *DA.* does not notice place or shrine. Our *Comy.* 'a vihāra built at the dwelling of the yakkha Ānanda.' The only other mention of Bh. is *Sn. v.* 1013 in a list of delightful spots.

' And what, monks, are the four great authorities ?

In this case, monks, a monk might say: " Face to face with the Exalted One, your reverence, did I hear it; face to face with him did I receive it.   This is Dhamma, this is Vinaya, this is the Master's teaching."

Now, monks, the words of that monk are neither to be welcomed nor scorned, but without welcoming, without scorning, the words and syllables thereof are to be closely scrutinized, laid beside Sutta and compared with Vinaya.[1] If, when thus laid beside Sutta and compared with Vinaya, they lie not along with Sutta and agree not with Vinaya, to this conclusion must ye come: Surely this is not the word of that Exalted One, Arahant, the Fully Enlightened One, and it was wrongly taken by that monk.   So reject it, monks.

Herein again a monk might say: " Face to face with the Exalted One, your reverence, did I hear it.   Face to face with him did I receive it.   This is Dhamma, this is Vinaya, this is the Master's teaching."

Now the words of that monk are neither to be welcomed nor scorned . . . but if, when laid beside Sutta and compared with Vinaya, they lie along with Sutta and agree with Vinaya, to this conclusion must ye come: Surely this is the word of that Exalted One . . . it was rightly taken by that monk. Then bear this in mind as the first great authority.

Then again a monk might say: " In such and such a dwelling-place resides an Order (of monks) together with an elder monk, a leader.   Face to face with that Order I heard it; face to face I received it.   This is Dhamma.   This is Vinaya.   This is the Master's teaching."

Now the words of that monk are neither to be welcomed nor scorned . . . but if, when laid beside Sutta and compared with Vinaya, they lie not along with Sutta and agree not with Vinaya, to this conclusion must ye come: Surely this is not

---

[1] There were evidently only two collections (baskets or pitakas). *Comy.* as at *DA.* ii, 566 attempts to prove that here *Sutta*=*Suttanta-Abhidhamma-Piṭakāni*. But *Abhidhamma* is obviously a much later collection.   Had there been any pitakas at the time of the composition of this sutta the word would surely have been used in it.

the word of that Exalted One . . . it was wrongly taken by
that Order (of monks). So do ye reject it, monks.

But, on the other hand, a monk might say: " In such and
such a dwelling-place resides . . . This is the Master's
teaching." Then, if, when laid beside Sutta and compared
with Vinaya, those words lie along with Sutta and agree
with Vinaya, to this conclusion must ye come: Surely this is
the word of that Exalted One . . . it was rightly taken by
that Order of monks. This, monks, is the second great
authority to bear in mind.

Yet again a monk might say: " In such and such a dwelling-
place resides a great number of elder monks, widely learned,[1]
versed in the doctrines, who know Dhamma by heart, who know
Vinaya by heart, who know the Summaries by heart. Face
to face with those elder monks I heard it; face to face did I
receive it. This is Dhamma. This is Vinaya. This is the
Master's teaching."

Now the words of that monk are neither to be welcomed nor
scorned . . . but if when laid beside Sutta and compared
with Vinaya, they lie not along with Sutta and agree not with
Vinaya, to this conclusion must ye come: Surely this is not
the word of that Exalted One . . . it was wrongly taken by
those elders. So do ye reject it, monks.

Herein again a monk might say: " In such and such a
dwelling-place resides a great number of elder monks. . . .
This is the Master's teaching." Now the words of that monk
. . . if, when laid beside Sutta and compared with Vinaya,
they lie along with Sutta and agree with Vinaya, then to this
conclusion must ye come: Surely this is the word of that
Exalted One and it was rightly taken by those elders. This,
monks, is the third great authority.

Herein again a monk might say: " In such and such a
dwelling-place resides a single elder monk, of wide learning,
versed in the doctrines, one who knows Dhamma by heart,
who knows Vinaya by heart, who knows the Summaries by
heart. Face to face with that elder monk I heard it, face

---

[1] *Cf. supra,* text 147.

to face did I receive it. This is Dhamma, this is Vīnaya, this is the Master's teaching.''

Now, monks, the words of that monk are neither to be welcomed nor scorned, but without welcoming, without scorning them, the words and syllables thereof are to be closely scrutinized, laid beside Sutta and compared with Vinaya. .If, when laid beside Sutta and compared with Vinaya, they lie not along with Sutta and agree not with Vinaya, to this conclusion must ye come: Surely this is not the word of that Exalted One, the Arahant, the Fully Enlightened One, and it was wrongly taken by that elder monk. So do ye reject it, monks.

If, however, a monk should say . . . (*as above*) . . . then, if when laid beside Sutta and compared with Vinaya, they lie along with Sutta and agree with Vinaya, then to this conclusion must ye come: Surely this is the word of that Exalted One, the Arahant, the Fully Enlightened One, and it was rightly taken by that elder monk. This, monks, is the fourth great authority.

So these, monks, are the four great authorities.'

Chapter XIX.—Fighting-Man.[1]

§ i (181). *Fighting-man.*

' Monks, possessed of four qualities a fighting-man is worthy of a rājah, is a possession of a rājah, is reckoned an attribute of a rājah. What are the four ?

Herein, monks, a fighting-man is skilled in points of vantage, he is a far-shooter, a shooter like lightning and a piercer[2] of a huge object.[3] Possessed of these four qualities . . . he is reckoned an attribute of a rājah.

In like manner, monks, possessed of four qualities a monk is worthy of respect, of offerings and gifts, of being saluted with clasped hands upraised, a field of merit unsurpassed for the world. What are the four ?

---

[1] *Cf. A.* i, 284=*G.S.* i, 263; *A.* iii, 84. *Comy.* calls this chapter *Brāhmaṇa-vagga.*

[2] *Padāletā,* or ' smasher.'   [3] See below, § 196.

In this case a monk is skilled in points of vantage, he is
a far-shooter, a shooter like lightning and a piercer of a huge
object.

Now in what way is a monk skilled in points of vantage ?

In this case a monk is virtuous, he dwells restrained with
the restraint of the Obligations; perfect in the practice of
right conduct he sees danger in the slightest faults; he takes
up and trains himself in the rules of morality.[1] Thus is a
monk skilled in points of vantage.

And how, monks, is a monk a far-shooter ?

Herein whatsoever object, be it past, future or present,
of the self or external to the self, gross or subtle, mean or
exalted, far or near,—every object in short that he beholds,
he looks upon it, as it really is, with right wisdom, thus:
This is not of me: Not this am I. Not for me is this the self.
Whatsoever feeling, be it past, future or present . . . he
feels, he looks upon it, as it really is, with right wisdom. . . .
Whatsoever perception . . . whatsoever activity . . . whatsoever consciousness he has, be it past, future or present,
of the self or external to the self, gross or subtle, mean or
exalted, far or near,—everything in short of which he is
conscious,—he looks upon it, as it really is, with right
wisdom, thus: This is not of me. Not this am I. Not
for me is this the self. That is how a monk is a far-
shooter.

And how is a monk a shooter like lightning ?

Herein a monk understands as it really is: This is Ill. This
is the arising of Ill. This is the ending of Ill. This is the
practice going to the ending of Ill. This is the ending of Ill.
Thus is he a shooter like lightning.

And how is a monk a piercer of a huge object ?

Herein a monk pierces through the huge mass of nescience.
That is how he is a piercer of a huge object.

Possessed of these four qualities a monk is worthy of offerings . . . a field of merit unsurpassed for the world.'

---

[1] See § 7 of Ch. IV.

§ ii (182). *Surety*.[1]

' Monks,[2] no recluse or brāhmin, no Deva, no Māra, no Brahmā can be surety against four things. What four ?

That what is of a nature to decay may not decay;[3] that what is of a nature to be diseased may not be diseased; that what is of a nature to die may not die; that the fruit of those evil deeds[4] that defile and lead to again-becoming, deeds unhappy whose fruit in future time is pain, rebirth, decay and death, may not come to pass,—no recluse, no brāhmin, no Deva, no Māra, no Brahmā can be surety against that.

Against these four things, monks, there can be no surety.'[5]

§ iii (183). *Hearsay*.

On a certain occasion the Exalted One was staying near Rājagaha, in Bamboo Grove at the Squirrels' Feeding-ground. Then the brāhmin Vassakāra,[6] a great official of Magadha, came to visit the Exalted One. On coming to him he greeted him courteously . . . and sat down at one side. So seated, the brāhmin Vassakāra, a great official of Magadha, said this to the Exalted One:

' For my part, master Gotama, I say this, I hold this view: If any man speaks of what he has seen, there is no harm in his saying " Thus I saw." If any man speaks of what he has heard, there is no harm in his saying " Thus I heard." If any man speaks of what he has sensed, of what he has understood, saying, " Thus I sensed, thus I understood," there is no harm resulting from that.'

' I, for my part, brāhmin, do not say that all that one has

---

[1] Quoted at *Kvu.* 457 = *Points of Contr.* 260 (where, as in our text, *jīri ti* is misprinted *jīvi ti*). It is expanded at *A.* iii, 54, where such wishes are termed *alabbhanīyāni*.

[2] Text misprints *bhikkhu*.

[3] Both text and *Kvu.* misprint *ma jīri ti* as *mā jīvi ti*.

[4] *Cf. S.* iv, 186.

[5] At *UdA.* 156, 178, where the B. guarantees a bevy of celestial nymphs to Nanda; it is equal to *paṭibhūto* (Skt. *pratibhū*, surety) and *paṭissava* (promise).

[6] See above, IV, § 5.

seen should be spoken of. Yet do I not say, brāhmin, that all
that one has seen should not be spóken of. And I say the
same of what is heard, sensed and understood. Not all that
one has heard, sensed or understood should be spoken of or
not spoken of.

Now, brāhmin, in so far as to him who speaks what he has
seen unprofitable states wax and profitable states wane, I
say that such a thing if seen should not be spoken of. In so far
as to him who speaks what he has heard, sensed and understood unprofitable states wax and profitable states wane, I
say that such a thing heard, sensed and understood should not
be spoken of. But in the case where unprofitable states wane
and profitable states wax, in one who speaks thereof I say that
such things should be spoken of.'

Thereupon the brāhmin Vassakāra, the great official of
Magadha, welcomed what was said by the Exalted One, and
returning thanks he rose from his seat and went away.

§ iv (184). *Fearless.*

Now the brāhmin Jāṇussoni[1] came to visit the Exalted One
and on coming to him greeted him courteously and . . . sat
down at one side. So seated the brāhmin Jāṇussoni said this
to the Exalted One:

'For my part, Master Gotama, I say this, I hold this view:
There is no one subject to death but fears, falls a-trembling
at the thought of death.'

'Well, brāhmin, there is such an one. But there is also
one subject to death who does not fear, who does not fall a-
trembling at the thought of death. And of what sort is that
one who being subject to death fears and falls a-trembling at
the thought of death ?

In this case, brāhmin, a certain oñe is not freed from passions,
not freed from lusts, not freed from -desire, affection, from
thirst and fever, not freed from craving. Then a grievous
sickness afflicts such an one. Thus afflicted by grievous
sickness it occurs to him: Alas ! the passions that I love will

---

[1] *Cf. S.* ii, 76, v, 4; *A.* i, 56, etc.

leave me, or I shall leave the passions that I love. Thereupon he grieves and wails, laments and beats the breast and falls into utter bewilderment. This one, brāhmin, being subject to death, is afraid, he falls a-trembling at the thought of death.

Again, brāhmin, here a certain one who as regards body is not freed from lusts . . . is not freed from craving. Then a grievous sickness afflicts him. Thus afflicted it occurs to him: Alas! the body that I love will leave me, or I shall leave the body that I love. Thereupon he grieves . . . and falls into utter bewilderment. This one, brāhmin, being subject to death, is afraid, he falls a-trembling at the thought of death.

Yet again, brāhmin, here a certain one has done no lovely deed, has done no profitable deed, has given no shelter to the timid;[1] he has done evil, cruel, wrongful deeds. Then a grievous sickness afflicts such an one. Thus afflicted by grievous sickness it occurs to him: Alas! I have done no lovely deed, I have done no profitable deed, I have given no shelter to the timid. I have done evil, cruel, wrongful deeds. To the doom of those who do such deeds hereafter I am going. Thereupon he grieves . . . and falls into utter bewilderment. This one, brāhmin, being subject to death is afraid, he falls a-trembling at the thought of death.

Yet again, brāhmin, here a certain one is doubtful, full of perplexity,[2] has come to no conclusion[3] as to true dhamma.[4] He grieves and wails, laments and beats the breast and falls into utter bewilderment. This one also, being subject to death, is afraid, he falls a-trembling at the thought of death. . . . Thus these four, being subject to death, are afraid. . . .

And of what sort, brāhmin, is he who, though subject to death, is not afraid, does not fall a-trembling at the thought of

---

[1] *Bhīruttāno* (*bhīru-tāṇa*). *Cf. Itv.* 25. *Comy.* expl. *bhītassa parittāya kattā.*

[2] Text *vicikicchī; Sinh.* text and *Comy. veci-. Cf. Expos.* ii, 491.

[3] *Aniṭṭhaŋ-gato.* [4] *Saddhamma.*

death ? (*exactly the same as before, but in the negative, for the first three*).

Once more, brāhmin, here a certain one is not doubtful, is not full of perplexity, has come to a conclusion[1] as to true dhamma. Then a grievous sickness afflicts him. Thus afflicted by grievous sickness it occurs to him: Surely I have no doubt, I have no worry, I have come to a conclusion as to true dhamma. Thus he grieves not, wails not, nor beats the breast, nor falls into utter bewilderment thereat.

This one, brāhmin, though subject to death, fears not, falls not a-trembling at the thought of death. So these are the four who . . . fear not.'

' It is wonderful, worthy Gotama ! It is marvellous, worthy Gotama ! May the worthy Gotama accept me as one who has gone to him for refuge from this day forth so long as life may last.'

§ v (185). *Brāhmin truths.*[2]

On a certain occasion the Exalted One was staying near Rājagaha on Vultures' Peak Hill. Now at that time a great number of notable Wanderers were abiding on the bank of Snake River[3] in the Wanderers' Park, to wit: Annabhāra, Varadhara, Sakuludāyin and other notable Wanderers.

Now at eventide the Exalted One, arising from his solitary musing, went towards the bank of Snake River, where was the Wanderers' Park.

On that occasion among those Wanderers holding other views, as they sat gathered together, this subject of talk chanced to arise: Such and such are the brāhmin truths. Such and such are the brāhmin truths.[4]

Now when the Exalted One reached those Wanderers, on

---

[1] Text should read *niṭṭhaŋ*.
[2] *Uddāna* calls it *Samaṇa-*.
[3] *Cf. supra*, text 29.
[4] *Five* are set forth at *M*. ii, 199—viz., truth, austerity, the good life, study and liberality. They admit that no one has realized all five for seven generations back. The Buddha then sets forth his own way to Brahmā--viz., the four Brahma-vihāras or God-moods.

coming to them he sat down on a seat made ready. When he
had sat down the Exalted One said this to those Wanderers:

' Pray, Wanderers, on what subject of talk were ye engaged
just now as ye sit here gathered together ? What was the
subject of talk ye have just now broken off ?'

' As to that, Master Gotama, as we sat here gathered together, the subject of talk that chanced to arise was this: Such
and such are the brāhmin truths. Such and such are the
brāhmin truths.'

' Well, Wanderers, these four brāhmin truths have been
set forth by myself after fully comprehending and realizing
them for myself. What four ?

In this case, Wanderers, the brāhmin[1] says thus: " All
living things are not to be harmed."[2] So saying, a brāhmin
speaks truth, not falsehood. Therein he has no conceit of
" recluse " or " brāhmin." He has no conceit of " better
am I," " equal am I," " inferior am I." Moreover by fully
comprehending the truth contained in that saying he is bent
on the practice of mercy and compassion for all living things.

Again, Wanderers, the brāhmin says thus: " All sense-
delights are impermanent, painful, of a nature to change."
So saying the brāhmin speaks truth, not falsehood. Therein
he has no conceit of " recluse " or " brāhmin " or " better am
I," or " equal am I," or " inferior am I." Moreover by fully
comprehending the truth contained in that saying he is bent
on the practice of distaste for sense-delights, for passionlessness, for making an end thereof.

Again, Wanderers, the brāhmin says thus: " All becomings
are impermanent, painful, of a nature to change." So saying
the brāhmin speaks truth, not falsehood. Therein he has no
conceit of " recluse " and the rest. . . . Moreover, by fully
comprehending the truth contained in that saying, he is bent
on the practice of distaste for becomings, for passionlessness,
for making an end thereof.

Yet again, Wanderers, the brāhmin says thus: " I have no

---

[1] =*khīnāsava.* *Comy.*
[2] *Avajjhā.* Text strangely reads *avijjā* (?).

part in anything anywhere, and herein for me there is no attachment to anything.''[1] So saying the brāhmin speaks truth, not falsehood. Therein he has no conceit of " recluse " or " brāhmin " or " better am I," or "equal am I," or " inferior am I." Moreover, by fully comprehending the truth contained in that saying he is bent on the practice of having nothing at all.[2]

So these, Wanderers, are the four brāhmin truths put forth by myself after fully comprehending and realizing them myself.'

§ vi (186). *Approach.*[3]

Now a certain monk came to visit the Exalted One, and on coming to him saluted the Exalted One and sat down at one side. As he sat thus that monk said this to the Exalted One:

'Pray, lord, by what is the world led ? By what is the world drawn along, under the sway of what that has arisen does it go ?'[4]

'Well, said ! Well said, monk ! Happy is your approach to a question,[5] happy is your ready wit and goodly is your

---

[1] *Nâhaŋ kvacani kassaci kiñcana ; tasmiŋ na ca mama kvacani katthaci kiñcanaŋ n' atthi* (as at *A.* i, 206 = *G.S.* i, 186). *Kiñcana* (hindrance or *palibodha*) is def. at *Netti*, 62 as *rāga-moha-dosa. Cf. UdA.* 119, 386; *VM.* ii, 654.

[2] *Ākiñcañña. Cf. K.S.* iv, 205 *n.*

[3] *Ummagga.* The *uddāna* calls it *ummanga*, as at *Vin.* v, 144. See *n.* below.

[4] The question is put in verse at *S.* i, 39:

Kenassu nīyati loko, kenassu parikassati ?
Kissassa ekadhammassa sabbe 'va vasam anvagu ?

Parikassati =ākaḍḍhīyati. Comy.

[5] *Bhaddaka te ummaggo. Cf. Vin.* v, 144; *S.* v, 16, where Bhadda (lucky) is the questioner. It may be a pun on his name, and the 'certain monk' here may be he. *Ummaggo* (tunnel or boring; in mining called 'upcast'); the *Ummagga-Jātaka* (the last but one in *JA.*):=*paññā-gamanaŋ. Comy.* But *cf. J.R.A.S.,* July, 1931, where Mr. E. H. Johnston discusses several Pāli words, this one amongst them, and points out that *Comy.* should probably read *pañha-ummaggo* here, which I think likely. I have previously trans. it 'penetration' (*K.S.* v, 16), but he thinks it means 'emergence of a desire for knowledge leading to questioning,' and refers to *ummujja-nimmujja*, con-

questioning. Your question is thus, is it not, monk? "Pray,
lord, by what is the world led? By what is the world drawn
along? Under the sway of what that has arisen does it
go?"'

'It is, lord.'

'Well, monk, the world is led by thought. By thought it
is drawn along. When thought has arisen, it goes under its
sway.'

'That is well said, lord,' replied that monk, welcoming what
was said by the Exalted One, and after thanking him asked
another question:

'As to the common saying: "Widely learned, one who
knows Dhamma by heart"—pray, lord, of what sort is one
widely learned, who knows Dhamma by heart?'

'Well said! Well said, monk! Happy is your approach
to a question, happy is your ready wit and goodly is your
questioning. You ask this, do you not? "Of what sort is
one widely learned, who knows Dhamma by heart?"'

'I do, lord.'

'Well, monk, I have taught Dhamma widely,—*Sutta,
Geyya, Veyyākarana, Gāthā, Udāna, Itivuttaka, Jātaka, Abbhutadhamma* and *Vedalla*.[1] Now if a monk understands the
meaning and (text of) Dhamma,—even if it be but a stanza
of four lines,—and be set on living in accordance with Dhamma,
he may well be called "one widely learned, who knows Dhamma
by heart."'

'It is well said, lord,' replied that monk, welcoming what

---

necting it with Skt. *unmiñjita-nimiñjita.* We have the word again
below, p. 189 of text. *Cf. S.* iv, 261 (*bhaddaka-magga*). My edition of
SA. iii on *S.* v, 16 has *paññā-ummagga paññā-vimaŋsana, paññā-gave-
sanaŋ* (my *Sinh.* MSS.), and Burmese *paññā-umango* (*sic*), which
Mr. Johnston quotes (probably from the Siamese ed.) as *pañhumango,
pañhāmaggo*, etc. *Comy.* on our passage (*Sinh.* printed ed., 1904,
p. 581, and my palm-leaf MS.) is: *ummaggo ti, ummujjanaŋ paññā-
gamanan ti attho; paññā eva vā ummujjan' atthena ummaggo ti vuccati*
(where again Mr. Johnston reads *ummango . . . ummujjanatthaŋ
ummango ti ?*). See my note below on p. 189 of text.

[1] *Cf. supra*, I, § 6 *n.*; 102. This list of works of a far later date is
obviously inserted by the compilers.

was said by the Exalted One, and after thanking him asked another question:

'As to the common saying, lord, "Learned, of penetrative wisdom "—pray, lord, of what sort is one learned, of penetrative wisdom ?'

'Well said ! Well said, monk ! Happy is your approach to a question . . . You ask this, do you not ? " Of what sort is one learned, of penetrative wisdom ?" '

'I do, lord.'

'In this case, monk, a monk hears it said: "This is Ill." By wisdom he penetrates the meaning of that saying and sees that it is so. He hears it said: "This is the arising of Ill . . . This is the ending of Ill . . . This is the practice going to the ending of Ill." By wisdom he penetrates the meaning of that saying and sees that it is so. Thus, monk, he is learned, of penetrative wisdom.'

'It is well said, lord,' replied that monk . . . and put yet another question:

'As to the common saying "Wise, of great wisdom," pray, lord, of what sort is one who is wise, of great wisdom ?'

'Well said ! Well said, monk ! . . . You ask this, do you not? " Who is wise, of great wisdom ?" '

'I do, lord.'

'Well, monk, in this case he who is wise, of great wisdom, thinks not with a view to harm either himself or another or both alike. So thinking he thinks with a view to the profit of self, of another, both of self and of another, to the profit of the whole world. Thus, monk, one is wise, of great wisdom.'

§ vii (187). *Vassakāra.*

On a certain occasion the Exalted One was staying near Rājagaha in Bamboo Grove, at the Squirrels' Feeding-ground. Then the brāhmin Vassakāra,[1] a great official of Magadha, came to visit the Exalted One, and on coming to him greeted him courteously. . . . As he sat at one side the

---

[1] *Cf. supra*, § 183.

brāhmin Vassakāra, a great official of Magadha. said this to
the Exalted One:

' Pray, master Gotama, could a bad man recognize a bad
man (so as to say): " This worthy is a bad man " ?'

' It is out of place, brāhmin; it is an impossibility for him to
do so.'

' Then pray, master Gotama, could a bad man recognize a
good man (so as to say): " This worthy is a good man " ?'

' It is out of place, brāhmin; it is an impossibility for him to
do so.'

' Then could a good man recognize a good man in like
manner ?'

' That, brāhmin, is a likely thing. It is possible for him to
do so.'

' Again, master Gotama, could a good man recognize a
bad man (so as to say): " This worthy is a bad man " ?'

' That again, brāhmin, is a likely thing. It is possible for
a good man to recognize a bad man (so as to say): " This
worthy is a bad man." '[1]

' Wonderful, master Gotama ! It is marvellous, master
Gotama, how well said is this by the worshipful Gotama,
thus: " It is out of place, it is an impossibility (in the case of
the first two)," and " It is a likely thing, it is possible (in the
case of the second two)."

Now, master Gotama, on a certain occasion the company of
the brāhmin Todeyya[2] were talking abusively, thus: " A
fool is the rājah Eḷeyya to be pleased with Rāma's son, the
recluse. Why ! he even went so far as to show the greatest
humility before him, such as saluting him, rising up in his
presence, putting his hands together and doing homage to
him. Moreover the retinue of the rājah Eḷeyya are fools,

---

[1] The four points are tersely stated in the couplet ascribed to Vappa,
one of the first disciples (*Pss. Brethren*, ver. 61). If we take the acts
of Eḷeyya as in the ' historic present,' and referring to a bygone
episode—as is very possible—we have here an allusion to Uddaka
Rāmaputta, one of the honoured teachers of Gotama.

[2] *Comy.*, *i.e. Tudigāma-vāsika*. At *S.* iv, 121 he is owner of the
mango-grove at Kāmaṇḍa. *Cf. M.* ii, 202.

such as Yamaka, Moggalla, Ugga, Nāvindaki, Gandhabba and
Aggivessa,[1] to be pleased with Rāma's son, the recluse. They
too went so far as to show the greatest humility before him . . .
doing homage to him."'

'Well, brāhmin, you see[2] that's just how the brāhmin
Todeyya leads them by the nose.[3] Now what think those
worthies: A wise man is the rājah Eḷeyya. Among those
superior in insight[4] in deciding matters of dispute and in the
interpretation of terms he is superior,—Do they think that ?'

'They do, sir. They think he is a wise man, as you say.
And it is just because the recluse, Rāma's son, is wiser than the
wise rājah Eḷeyya and superior to him in insight in deciding
matters of dispute and in the interpretation of terms in a still
higher degree,—it is for this reason that the rājah Eḷeyya is
pleased with him and shows the greatest humility before him,
such as saluting him, rising up in his presence, putting his
hands together and doing homage to him.'

'Now what think those worthies: Wise is the retinue of the
rājah Eḷeyya; namely, Yamaka and the others ? Among
those superior as to insight in deciding matters of dispute
and in the interpretation of terms they are superior,—Do
they think that ?'

'They do, sir. They think the retinue of the rājah Eḷeyya
to be wise. . . . And it is just because the recluse, Rāma's son,
is wiser than the wise retinue of the rājah Eḷeyya and superior
to them in insight . . . in a still higher degree,—it is for this
reason that the retinue of the rājah Eḷeyya are highly pleased
with the recluse, Rāma's son, and (in their turn) show the
greatest humility before him . . . and do homage to him.

It is wonderful, master Gotama ! It is marvellous how well
said was this by the worshipful Gotama, thus: " It is out of
place, brāhmin; it is an impossibility that a bad man should

---

[1] These names do not appear elsewhere.

[2] *Tyassudaŋ=te assudaŋ* (or ? *Assu idaŋ*). *Cf. S.* i, 195. Text
confuses the speakers in the arrangement of this and following §§.

[3] *Neti* acc. to *Comy.=anuneti, jānāpeti.* The idea is the same as
in § 6 (' by what is the world led along ').

[4] *Alam-attha-dasa.*

be able to recognize a bad man, that a bad man should be able to recognize a good man. But it is a likely thing, it is quite possible for a good man to recognize a good man, and for a good man to be able to recognize a bad man (so as to say): " This worthy is a bad man."

Well, master Gotama, I must be going. I am a busy man and have much to do.'

' Do as you think proper, brāhmin.'

So the brahmin Vassakāra, the great official of Magadha, being pleased with the words of the Exalted One, thanked him, rose from his seat and went away.

§ viii (188). *Upaka.*

On a certain occasion the Exalted One was staying near Rājagaha on Vultures' Peak Hill. Then Upaka, son of Maṇḍikā,[1] came to visit the Exalted One, and on coming to him saluted him and sat down at one side. So seated, Upaka, son of Maṇḍikā, said this to the Exalted One:

' As for me, sir, I say this, I hold this view: Whosoever starts abusive talk about another and carries it on, but cannot in every way make good his case, in failing to do so should be held blameworthy and guilty of offence.'

' Yes, Upaka, if he does so he is to be held blameworthy and guilty of offence. You yourself also,[2] Upaka, start abusive talk about another and carry it on. So doing and failing to make good your case, you are to be held blameworthy and guilty of offence.'

' There, sir ! Just like a man catching (his prey) with a big noose as soon as it puts its head out, even so am I caught by the Exalted One with the big noose of words as soon as I open my mouth !'[3]

---

[1] Is this the Upaka, *ājīvaka* or ascetic, who first heard Dhamma ? *Cf. Vin.* i, 8; *M.* 1, 170; *Gotama the Man*, 48. *Comy.* can only say, ' his name was Upaka, son of Maṇḍikā,' and that he was a supporter of Devadatta, and came to find out whether the Buddha would praise or blame him; but that others held that he came to abuse the Buddha on hearing that Devadatta had been ' consigned to hell' by him.

[2] Reading *pi* for *si* of text.

[3] Lit. ' just as I pop my head up,' used of a fish in water. *Comy.*

'Upaka, I have pointed out, "This thing is wrong," and that too in endless variation of word, syllable and Dhamma-teaching of a Tathāgata. So also, Upaka, have I pointed out, "This thing is right," and that too in endless variations of word, syllable[1] and Dhamma-teaching of a Tathāgata. Again, Upaka, I have pointed out, "This thing is right," and "This thing that is right must be made to grow." This thing that is right, Upaka, must be made to grow.'[2]

Thereupon Upaka, son of Maṇḍikā, was pleased with the words of the Exalted One, and after thanking him rose up from his seat and, saluting the Exalted One by keeping his right side towards him, went away to the rājah of Magadha, Ajātasattu, son of the Videhan.[3] On coming to him he related all the talk he had had with the Exalted One from beginning to end.

Thereupon the rājah of Magadha, Ajātasattu, son of the Videhan, was angry and in his displeasure exclaimed to Upaka, son of Maṇḍikā:

'What a pestilent fellow[4] is this salt-worker's boy! A scurrilous shameless rogue! To think that he should presume to revile that Exalted One, the Arahant, the Fully Enlightened One! Away with you, Upaka! Let me see you no more!'[5]

§ ix (189). *Realization.*

'Monks, there are these four things which are to be realized. What four?

There are things to be realized by one's own person,[6] by recollection, by sight, and there are things to be realized by wisdom.

---

[1] *Cf. S.* v, 430.

[2] Lit. 'made-to-become.'

[3] *Vedehi-putto. Cf. Dial.* ii, 78 *n. DA.* i, 139 has: 'This was the son of the daughter of the Kosalan rājah. *Vedehi* is a name for a wise man.' *SA.* i, 154 has 'son of the wise woman,' on *S.* i, 82.

[4] *Yāva dhaṁsī. Cf. M.* i, 236. Apparently he was of a low caste.

[5] 'And (adds *Comy.* delightedly) had him taken by the neck and dragged away.'

[6] *Kāyena* = *nāma-kāyena. Comy.*

And of what sort, monks, are the things to be realized by one's own person ?

The eight releases are so to be realized.

And of what sort, monks, are the things to be realized by recollection ?

One's former life is so to be realized.

And of what sort, monks, are the things to be realized by sight ?[1]

The decease and rebirth[2] of beings are so to be realized.

And of what sort, monks, are the things to be realized by wisdom ?

The destruction of the āsavas . . .

These are the four things to be realized.'

§ x (190). *The sabbath.*

On a certain occasion the Exalted One was staying near Sāvatthī, in East Park, at the storeyed house of Migāra's mother.[3] Now on that occasion the Exalted One was sitting surrounded by the Order of monks, that day being the sabbath.[4] Then the Exalted One, after scanning the Order of monks as they sat in perfect silence, addressed the monks, saying:

' Monks, this company is free from idle words and idle talk. It is pure and stablished in the essential.[5] Monks, such an Order of monks as this is a company such as it would be hard to find anywhere in the world. Such an Order of monks as this is worshipful, worthy of honour and gifts, worthy of worship with clasped hands upraised, a field of merit unsurpassed for the world. Monks, such an Order of monks as this is a company to which even a little being given is much, to

---

[1] Clairvoyance. ' The deva-sight.' *Comy.*

[2] Reading *cut' upapāto* for text's *cut' uppāto.*

[3] The lay-follower Visākhā, treated by her father-in-law, the wealthy Migāra, as ' mother.' For her sake he is said to have built this palace of 500 upper chambers and a thousand peaked roofs. *Cf. SnA.* ii, 502.

[4] *Tad-ahuposathe. Cf. UdA.* 296 (=*tasmiŋ uposatha-divasa-bhūte*), full-moon day.

[5] *Cf. Ud.* v, 5 for the driving out of an improper person from the assembly. *Sāre=sīlādi-sāre. Comy.*

which much being given is more. Such an Order of monks as this is a company worth going many a mile to see, even if one had to carry his food in a bag on his shoulder.[1] Of such a sort is this Order of monks.

Monks, there are abiding in this Order of monks those who have won access to devas.[2] There are those who have won access to Brahmā. There are those who have won access to the Imperturbable.[3] There are abiding in this Order of monks those who have won access to the Ariyan.[4]

And how has a monk won access to the devas ?

Herein a monk, aloof from sense-desires and so forth, having attained to the first musing abides therein . . . so with the second, third and fourth musings. That is how a monk has won access to the devas.

And how has a monk won access to Brahmā ?

Herein a monk with heart possessed of goodwill . . . of compassion . . . of sympathy . . . with heart possessed of equanimity abides suffusing one quarter of the world, also the second, third and fourth quarters, and in like manner above, below, across, everywhere, for all sorts and conditions; abides suffusing the whole world with a heart possessed of goodwill, compassion, sympathy, with equanimity that is widespread,

---

[1] *Puṭaŋsenāpi. Cf. D.* i, 117; *DA.* i, 288 (*puṭo aŋse assā ti*), and *infra*, § 242, *assa-* (read *aŋsa-*) *puŋaŋ khandhe āropetvā*, in both of which passages *Comy.* absurdly misunderstands the word and reads *assa-puṭa*, ' ash-bag ' (?), a mark of ignominy. *Comy.* reads *puṭosaŋ* (?)=*pātheyyaŋ*, and gives *v.l. puṭaŋsa* (as *Sinh.* text).

[2] *Cf. Gotama the Man*, 140; *Sakya*, 181, 227.

[3] *Anejja* (one who has reached the four formless worlds in musing). *Cf. D.* i, 76; *A.* iii, 93 etc.; *Pts. of Contr.*, 190 *n.*

[4] *Ariya-bhāvo. Comy.* ' having realized the Four Ariyan Truths they are no longer worldlings (ordinary men).' The word, often trans. ' worthy,' is applied to *Arahants*, but *cf. Expos.* i, 234, ' the Ariyans, that is, the Buddhas'; p. 452: ' Buddhas, lent (misprint for "silent ") Buddhas, Buddhas' disciples are (hence) called " Ariyans." Or, only the Buddhas herein are Ariyans. As has been said: " Bhikkhus, in the world of men and devas the Tathāgata is the Ariyan." ' *Cf. G.S.* i, 164 *ff.*, where the Buddha uses the term in several ways (*dibba-vihāra, Brahma-vihāra, Ariya-vihāra*), def. at *SnA.* ii, 136 as ' freedom from delusion.' Does the phrase occur elsewhere in the Canon ?

grown great and boundless, without enmity and untroubled.[1]
That is how a monk has won access to Brahmā.

And how has a monk won access to the Imperturbable ?

Herein a monk, passing utterly beyond all consciousness
of objects, by ending the consciousness of reaction, by dis-
regarding consciousness of diversity, thinking: Infinite is
space, attains and abides in the sphere of infinite space.
Passing utterly beyond the sphere of infinite space, reaching
the sphere of infinite consciousness, thinking: Infinite is
consciousness, he abides in the sphere of infinite consciousness.
Passing utterly beyond the sphere of infinite consciousness,
thinking: There is nothing at all, he attains and abides in the
sphere of nothingness.   Passing utterly beyond the sphere of
nothingness, he attains and abides in the sphere of neither-
consciousness-nor-unconsciousness.   Thus has a monk won
access to the Imperturbable.

And how has a monk won access to the Ariyan ?

Herein a monk understands, as it really is: This is Ill.
This is the arising of Ill.   This is the ending of Ill.   This is
the practice going to the ending of Ill.   Thus a monk has
won access to the Ariyan.'

CHAPTER XX.—THE GREAT CHAPTER.

§ i (191). *Heard with the ear.*

' Monks, four advantages are to be looked for from the
frequent verbal practice of teachings heard with the ear,[2]
from considering them in the mind, from thoroughly penetrating them by view.   What are the four ?

Herein a monk masters Dhamma, to wit: *Sutta, Geyya,
Veyyâkarana*[3] and the rest.   Those teachings heard with the
ear, often practised verbally, considered by the mind, are
thoroughly penetrated by view.   He making an end with

---

[1] For the *Brahma-vihāras*, or God-moods, see *Sakya*, 227; *K.S.* v,
98 *n.*

[2] *Sotânugatānaŋ.   Sinh.* text of *Comy.* reads *-dhatānaŋ* (?)

[3] See above, § 186 *n.*

memory confused is reborn in a certain company of devas.
There the happy ones recite to him Dhamma-verses.[1] Slow
to arise in him, monks, is memory, but that being very quickly
reaches excellence. This is the first advantage to be looked
for from the frequent verbal practice of teachings heard with
the ear, from considering them by the mind, from thoroughly
penetrating them by view.

Then again, a monk masters Dhamma (*as before*). He
making an end with memory confused is reborn in a certain
company of devas. There indeed the happy ones recite not
to him Dhamma-verses, but maybe some monk who has
more-power, one who has won mastery of mind,[2] is teaching
Dhamma to a company of devas. Then it occurs to him:
Why, this is just[3] the Dhamma-discipline according to which
formerly I practised the God-life! Slow to arise, monks, in him
is memory, but that being very quickly reaches excellence.[4]

It is just as if a man skilled in the sound of drums, while
going along the highroad,[5] should hear the sound of a drum.
He would have no doubt or uncertainty as to whether it was
the sound of a drum or not, but would just conclude that it
was so. In the same way, monks, a monk masters Dhamma,
to wit: *Sutta, Geyya* and the rest. Those teachings heard
with the ear . . . are thoroughly penetrated by view . . .
Slow to arise in him, monks, is memory, but that being very
quickly reaches excellence. This is the second advantage
to be looked for from the frequent verbal practice of teachings
heard with the ear, from considering them by the mind,
from thoroughly penetrating them by view.

Then again, monks, a monk masters Dhamma . . . and
is reborn in a certain company of devas. There indeed the
happy ones recite not to him Dhamma-verses, nor does some
monk who has more-power, one who has won mastery of

---

[1] Text *dhamma-padāni pi lapanti; Sinh.* text *-padāpi lapanti,* but
Comy. -padāpilapanti and *apilapanti* (? for *apilāpenti*).

[2] *Ceto-vasippatto. Cf. supra,* § 36.

[3] Here text has *vāso* (?). It is either *vā so* or more probably *va* for
eva. Comy. ettha vibhāvan' attho vā saddo.

[4] *Cf. K.S.* iv, 123.   [5] *Cf. DA.* i, 223.

mind, teach Dhamma to a company of devas; but maybe some one deva[1] is teaching Dhamma to a company of devas. Then it occurs to him: Why, this is just the Dhamma-discipline according to which formerly I practised the God-life! Slow to arise in him, monks, is memory, but that being very quickly reaches excellence.

It is just as if a man skilled in the sound of conches, while going along the highroad, should hear the sound of a conch. He would have no doubt or uncertainty as to whether it was the sound of a conch or not, but would just conclude that it was so. In the same way, monks, a monk masters Dhamma. . . . Slow to arise in him, monks, is memory, but that being very quickly reaches excellence. This is the third advantage to be looked for from the frequent verbal practice of teachings . . . from thoroughly penetrating them by view.

Yet again, monks, a monk masters Dhamma . . . and is reborn in a certain company of devas. There indeed the happy ones recite not to him Dhamma-verses, nor does some monk who has more-power, who has won mastery of mind, teach Dhamma to a company of devas, nor yet does some one deva teach Dhamma to a company of devas; but maybe someone apparitionally reborn (there) is reviving the memory of some other one apparitionally reborn. (He says) "Do you remember, good sir? Do you remember, good sir,[2] how formerly we used to practise the God-life?" Then the other says: "I do indeed remember, good sir! I do indeed remember!" Slow to arise, monks, in him is memory, but that being very quickly reaches excellence.

---

[1] *Comy.* instances *Pañcālacaṇḍa* (= *Kunāla* = *Bodhisattva*; *cf.* *JA.* v, 425), *Hatthaka Mahābrahmā, Sanay-kumāra Brahmā* (*cf.* *Dial.* i, 121, ii, 244, 292), the Virgin Youth who appears as 'Five-pointed Crest,' one of the five mind-born sons of Brahmā.

[2] *Opapātiko opapātikaŋ sāreti.* The word means 'one who just appears' in another plane of being, without anything corresponding to our physical rebirth. Here *Comy.* takes it to mean 'a *deva-putta* who had previously so become reminds a new-comer.'

[3] *Mārisa*, a term used by devas: *cf. K.S.* iv, 133, 186 *n.*

It is just as if two playmates[1] who used to play at mud-pies together were to meet some time or other. Then one of them says to the other: "Say, old man,[2] do you remember this? Do you remember that?" And the other replies: "I do indeed remember, old man! I do indeed remember!" Just in the same way, monks, a monk masters Dhamma . . . those teachings are thoroughly penetrated by view . . . that being very quickly reaches excellence. This, monks, is the fourth advantage to be looked for from the frequent verbal practice of teachings . . . from thoroughly penetrating them by view.

So, monks, these are the four advantages to be looked for . . .'

§ ii (192). *Conditions.*[3]

' Monks, these four conditions are to be understood by other four conditions. What are the four?

Monks, it is by association that one's virtue is to be understood,[4] and that too after a long time, not casually;[5] by close attention, not by inattention; by a wise man, not by one weak in wisdom.

Monks, it is by living with him[6] that a man's integrity is to be understood, and that too after a long time, not casually . . .

Monks, it is in time of distress that a man's courage is to be understood, and that too after a long time, not casually . . .

Monks, it is by converse with him[7] that a man's wisdom is to be understood, and that too after a long time, not casually; by close attention, not by inattention; by a wise man, not by one weak in wisdom.

Now I said: "It is by association that one's virtue is to be understood . . ." Owing to what did I say thus?

---

[1] Here *sahāyaka* is not quite the same as *sahāya*. The simile illustrates its use. *Sahāyako sahāyakam eva* (just below) has the significance of ' crony to crony.' *Cf.* the last words of the Buddha in addressing the monks.

[2] *Samma.*   [3] *Ṭhānāni*, lit. places.

[4] As at *S.* i, 78 and *Ud.* vi, 2; *UdA.* 332, where the rājah Pasenadi is instructed how to know an arahant.

[5] *Na ittaraṃ.*

[6] *Saṃvohārena. Ud.* has *sabbyohārena* (?).   [7] *Sākacchāya.*

In this case, monks, a person knows thus of another person by associating with him: For a long time this worthy has been one whose deeds are incongruous, inconsistent, shady and spotted.[1] His deeds are not consistent, his habits are not consistent with morals. This worthy is immoral, he is not virtuous.

Herein again, monks, by associating with him one knows thus of another person: For a long time this worthy has been one whose deeds are congruous, consistent, not shady, not spotted. His deeds are consistent, his habits are consistent with morals. This worthy is moral, he is virtuous.

Indeed, monks, it is by association that one's virtue is to be understood and that too after a long time . . . What is said thus was owing to this.

Now I said: " It is by living with him that a man's integrity[2] is to be understood." Owing to what did I say this ?

In this case, monks, a person knows thus of another person by living with him: This worthy, when with one person, behaves in one way; when with two persons, in another way; when with three, in yet another way; again otherwise when with many. In his former behaviour he departs from his latter behaviour. This worthy is not honest in his behaviour. This worthy is dishonest.

In this case again, monks, a person knows another by living with him. (So he concludes:) This worthy when with one person behaves just as he does with two, three or many. In his former behaviour he departs not from his latter behaviour. This worthy is honest, he is not dishonest.

Indeed, monks, it is by living with him that a man's integrity is to be understood . . . What I said was owing to this.

Now I said: " It is in time of distress that a man's courage[3] is to be understood." Owing to what did I say this ?

---

[1] *Khaṇḍa-kārī, chidda-kārī, sabala-kārī, kammasa-kārī*, referring to the oft-quoted words about *sīla*—*e.g., D.* ii, 80 (*sīlāni akhaṇḍāni, acchiddāni, asabalāni, akammasāni*); *cf. DA.* ii, 536 for defs. The metaphor is from first a garment torn all round, then perforated; next of cattle, variegated; lastly, dappled or blotched. *Comy., infra,* § 243.

[2] *Soceyyaŋ = suci-bhāva. Comy.*   [3] *Thāmo.*

In this case, monks, a certain one, afflicted by the loss of relatives or loss of wealth or by the misfortune of sickness, thus reflects:

Verily thus-come-to-be is this living in the world. Thus-come-to-be is the getting of a personality. According to this coming-to-be of living in the world and getting a personality eight world-conditions keep the world a-rolling and the world keeps a-rolling eight world-conditions, to wit:—gain and loss, disrepute and fame, blame and praise, happiness and unhappiness. So he, afflicted by loss of relatives, loss of wealth or the misfortune of sickness, sorrows, laments, is distressed and knocks the breast, wails and falls into utter bewilderment.

But in this case, monks, a certain one, afflicted by the loss of relatives . . . thus reflects: Verily thus-come-to-be is thus living in the world . . . and unhappiness. He, afflicted by the loss of relatives, loss of wealth or the misfortune of sickness, does not sorrow, does not falter, . . . nor falls into utter bewilderment. . . . Owing to that did I say this.

Now I said: " It is by converse with him that a man's wisdom is to be understood." Owing to what did I say this ?

In this case, monks, a person by conversing with another knows thus of him: Judging by this worthy's approach to a question,[1] judging by his intention, judging by his conversation,[2] he is weak in wisdom, he is not wise. What is the cause of that ?   In the case in question this worthy utters no profound profitable sentence[3] that calms, is sublime, is beyond the sphere of mere reasoning,[4] that is subtle and intelligible to the wise. As to Dhamma that this worthy talks, he is not

[1] *Ummaggo*, see *n.* above on § 186. Here the word has the double meaning of ' approach to a question ' and ' the rise ' of a fish. As quoted above, *SnA.* 50, the four bases of enlightenment are called *ussāha, ummagga, avatthānaŋ, hitacariyā.*

[2] Texts *samudācāro*, but *Comy.*, perhaps better, *samudāhāro* (=*pañha-pucchanaŋ*), acc. to which I translate.

[3] *Attha-padaŋ. Cf. A.* iii, 356. This seems to be the meaning at *Dhp. v.* 100, *ekaŋ atthapadaŋ seyyo, yaŋ sutvā upasammati.*

[4] *Atakkāvacaraŋ. Cf. S.* i, 136, *adhigato myāyaŋ dhammo gambhiro duddaso duranubodho santo paṇīto atakkāvacaro nipuṇo paṇḍita-vedaniyo.* (*Comy. yathā takkena nayaggāhena gahetuŋ,* but should prefix *na.*)

competent, either in brief or in detail, to explain its meaning, to show it forth, expound it, lay it down, open it up, analyse and make it plain. This worthy is weak in wisdom, he is not wise.

Just as if, monks, a man with good eyesight, standing on the bank of a pool of water, were to see a small fish rising, he would think: Judging by the uprise of this fish, judging by the size of the ripple it makes, judging by its speed, this is a small fish; this is not a big fish;—just in the same way, monks, a person by conversing with another knows thus of him: . . . This worthy is weak in wisdom, he is not wise.

Herein again, monks, a person by conversing with another knows thus of him: Judging by this worthy's approach to a question, judging by his intention, judging by his conversation, he is a wise man, he is not weak in wisdom.[1] What is the cause of that ?

In the case in question this worthy can utter a profound, profitable sentence, that calms, that is sublime, is beyond the sphere of mere reasoning, that is subtle and intelligible to the wise. As to Dhamma that this worthy talks, he is competent, both in brief and in detail, to explain its meaning, to show it forth, expound it, lay it down, open it up, analyse and make it plain. This worthy is a wise man, he is not weak in wisdom.

Just as if, monks, a man with good eyesight, standing on the bank of a pool of water, were to see a big fish rising, he would think: Judging by the uprise of this fish, judging by the size of the ripple it makes, judging by its speed, this is a big fish; this is not a small fish:—just in the same way, monks, a person, by conversing with another, knows thus of him: judging by this worthy's approach to a question, judging by his intention, judging by his conversation, he is a wise man, he is not weak in wisdom.

It is by converse with him, monks, that a man's wisdom is to be understood. So I said, and that is why I said it.

Thus, monks, these four conditions are to be understood by these other four conditions.'

---

[1] Here and below text gives the opposite meaning by transposing *paññavā* and *duppañño*.

§ iii (193). *Bhaddiya.*

On a certain occasion the Exalted One was staying near Vesālī, in Great Wood, at the Peaked-roof House. Then Bhaddiya the Licchavī came to visit the Exalted One, and on coming to him saluted him and sat down at one side. So seated Bhaddiya the Licchavī said this to the Exalted One: 'I have heard, sir, that Gotama the recluse is a juggler, that he knows a trick of glamour by which he entices away the followers of those holding other views.[1] Now, sir, as to those who say: "Gotama the recluse is a juggler who knows a trick of glamour by which he entices away the followers of those holding other views,"—pray, sir, do such express the views of the Exalted One and not misrepresent the Exalted One by what is not a fact? Do they speak in accordance with Dhamma? Does one who is of his Dhamma, who follows his views, fall into blame therefor? Sir, we would not misrepresent the Exalted One.'[2]

'Come now, Bhaddiya! Be not misled by report[3] or tradition or hearsay. Be not misled by proficiency in the Collections,[4] nor by mere logic or inference, nor after considering reasons, nor after reflection on and approval of some theory, nor because it fits becoming,[5] nor by the thought: The recluse is revered by us. But, Bhaddiya, when you know for yourselves: These things are unprofitable, these things are blameworthy, these things are censured by the intelligent, these things, when performed and undertaken, conduce to loss and sorrow,—then indeed, Bhaddiya, do you reject them.

Now what think you, Bhaddiya? When greed arises in a man's self, does it arise to his profit or to his loss?'

'To his loss, sir.'

---

[1] The same accusation is made at *M.* i, 375 by Upāli, the housefather.

[2] *Cf. S.* ii, 33, 41, etc.

[3] *Cf. A.* i, 190, advice to the Kālāmas; *G.S.* i, 171 *n.*

[4] *Piṭaka-sampādanena.* There were as yet no *written* pitakas, and it is doubtful whether the word was even used at the time.

[5] *Bhavya-rūpatāya*—i.e., not because you think it agrees with my (or a) doctrine of 'becoming.' 'Recluse' possibly refers to himself.

' Does not this man, thus become greedy, being overcome
by greed and losing control of his mind,—does he not kill a
living creature, steal, go after another's wife, tell lies and lead
another into such a state as[1] causes his loss and sorrow for a
long time ?'

' He does so, sir.'

' Now what think you, Bhaddiya ?   When malice arises . . .
when delusion arises . . . when violence[2] is added to these in
a man's self, do they arise to his profit or his loss ?'

' To his loss, sir.'

' And, Bhaddiya, does not this man, thus become violent,
being overcome by violence and losing control of his mind,—
does he not kill a living creature, steal, go after another's wife,
tell lies and lead another into such a state as causes his loss
and sorrow for a long time ?'

' He does so, sir.'

' Then what think you, Bhaddiya ?   Are these things
profitable or unprofitable ?'

' Unprofitable, sir.'

' Are they blameworthy or not ?'

' Blameworthy, sir.'

' Are they censured by the intelligent or not ?'

' They are censured, sir.'

' If performed and undertaken, do they conduce to loss and
sorrow, or how is it ?'

' They do conduce to loss and sorrow, sir.   It is just so,
methinks.'

' So then, Bhaddiya, as to my words to you just now:—
" Come now, Bhaddiya, be not misled by report or tradition
or hearsay.   Be not misled by proficiency in the Collections,
nor by mere logic or inference, nor after considering reasons,
nor after reflection on and approval of some theory, nor
because it fits becoming, nor by the thought: The recluse is

---

[1] *Yaŋ 'sa hoti* for *yaŋ assa hoti.   Comy.*

[2] *Sārambho* (not *saŋrambha* but *sa-ārambha*, 'accompanied by
violence ') is here added to the other three qualities at *A*. i. *Comy.*
def. as ' having the characteristics of going still further ' in any one of
these vices.

revered by us. But, Bhaddiya, when you know for yourselves: These things are unprofitable, these things are blameworthy, these things are censured by the intelligent; these
things, when performed and undertaken, conduce to loss and
sorrow—then indeed, Bhaddiya, do ye reject them,"—such
was my reason for uttering those words.

Come now, Bhaddiya! Be not . . . so misled. But if at
any time ye know of yourselves: These things are profitable,
these things are not blameworthy, these things are praised by
the intelligent, these things, when performed and undertaken,
conduce to profit and happiness,—then, Bhaddiya, undertake
them and remain doing them.

Now what think you, Bhaddiya ? When freedom from
greed arises in a man's self, does it arise to his profit or to his
loss ?'

' To his profit, sir.'

' Does not this man, not being greedy, not overcome by
greed, but having his mind under control,—does he not abstain
from killing and so forth, does he not abstain from leading
another into such a state as will be to his loss and sorrow for a
long time ?'

' He does, sir.'

' Now what think you, Bhaddiya ? When freedom from
malice . . . from delusion . . . from the violence that goes
with these arises in a man's self, does it arise to his profit or to
his loss ?'

' To his profit, sir.'

' Does not this man, being freed from the violence that goes
with these, not being overcome by that violence,[1] but having
his mind under control,—does he not abstain from killing and
so forth, does he not lead another into such a state as causes
his profit and happiness for a long time ?'

' He does, sir.'

' Now what think you, Bhaddiya ? Are these things
profitable or unprofitable ?'

---

[1] Text wrongly *asārambhena*; while just above *Sinh.* text has *asāraddho*
for *asārambho*.

' Profitable, sir.'

' Are they blameworthy cr blameless ?'

' Blameless, sir.'

' Are they censured or praised by the intelligent ?'

' They are praised, sir.'

' When performed and undertaken, do they conduce to profit and happiness or not, or how is it ?'

' They do conduce to profit and happiness, sir. It is just so, methinks.'

' So then, Bhaddiya, as to my words to you just now: " Come, Bhaddiya ! Be not misled. . . . But, Bhaddiya, when you know for yourselves: These things are profitable . . . undertake them and keep on doing so,"—such was my reason for uttering those words.

Now, Bhaddiya, all worthy[1] men in the world incite a follower thus: " Come, my good fellow! Restrain greed and keep on doing so. If you do that, you won't do a greedy deed with body, speech or thought. So with regard to malice . . . delusion . . . and the violence that goes with them. Keep on doing so, and you won't do a deed of violence with body, speech and thought." '

At these words Bhaddiya the Licchavī exclaimed to the Exalted One:

' It is wonderful, sir ! It is marvellous ! . . .[2] May the Exalted One accept me as his follower from this day forth so long as life may last, as one who has gone to him for refuge.'

' But, Bhaddiya, did I say to you " Come, Bhaddiya, be my follower. I will be your teacher " ?'

' No, sir.'

' Then, Bhaddiya, it seems that some recluse and brāhmins are vain and empty liars, and misrepresent me contrary to facts as being one who holds such a view, who proclaims such a view, in saying: " Gotama the recluse is a juggler. He knows

---

[1] *Sappurisā = Ariyā. Santo* may be participial or 'goodly.' Text should read *samādapenti*.

[2] *Pe* here in text means ' add the usual formula about showing a light,' etc.

a trick of glamour by which he entices away the followers of those holding other views." '

' A goodly thing, sir, is this enticing trick of glamour. A lovely thing, sir, is this enticing trick of glamour. I wish, sir, that my dear[1] kinsmen could be converted[2] by this enticement. Surely it would be to the profit and happiness of my dear kinsmen for a long time. Sir, if all the nobles . . . if all the brāhmins . . . the Vessā . . . if all the Sudras could be converted by this enticement, it would be to the profit and happiness of one and all of them.'

' So it would, Bhaddiya. So it would, Bhaddiya. If all the nobles . . . if all the brāhmins, Vessā and Sudras were to be converted to the abandoning of unprofitable things and to the undertaking of profitable things, it would be to their profit and happiness for a long time. If the world, with its devas, its Māras, its Brahmās, with its host of recluses and brāhmins, its devas and mankind, were to be converted to the abandoning of unprofitable things and to the undertaking of profitable things, it would be to their profit and happiness for a long time.

Why, Bhaddiya, if these great sāl-trees[3] could be converted by this enticement, it would be to their profit and happiness for a long time,—that is, if they could think,[4]—to say nothing of one who has become human.'

§ iv (194). *The Sāpūgyans.*

On a certain occasion the venerable Ānanda was staying among the Koliyans,—there is a place called Sāpūga,—in a township of the Koliyans. Then a great number of the Sāpū-. gyans of the Koliyan clan came to visit the venerable Ānanda, and on coming to him saluted him and sat down at one side.

---

[1] *Sinh.* text reads *māyāya me, bhante,* which seems a corruption of *piyā* of text, or perhaps we should add it after *āvaṭṭaniyā.*

[2] *Āvaṭṭeyyuŋ* (lit. ' would turn round '), perhaps a play on the word *āvaṭṭani.*

[3] Texts *ime ce pi; Comy. dve pi,* and adds that at the time of speaking two such trees stood by.

[4] The punctuation of text is misleading here.

As they sat thus the venerable Ānanda said this to the Koliyans of Sāpūga:

'Men of the Leopard's Path,[1] these four factors of exertion for utter purification have been fully proclaimed by that Exalted One who knows, who sees, that Arahant, the Fully Enlightened One, for the purification of beings, for the passing over grief and distress, for the making an end of sorrow and lamentation, for the winning of the Method, for the realization of Nibbāna. What are the four ?

The factor of exertion for the utter purification of morals, of thought, of view, and the factor of exertion for the utter purity of release.

And what, men of the Leopard's Path, is the factor of exertion for the utter purification of morals ?

In this case a monk[2] is virtuous, he undertakes and practises the precepts. This is called "utter purification of morals" (the resolve): I will bring to perfection such a purification of morals if it be incomplete, and if complete I will supplement it here and there by wisdom.[3] The desire to do, the effort, exertion, endeavour, persistence, mindfulness and attention applied thereto is called " a factor of exertion for the utter purification of morals."

And what, men of the Leopard's Path, is the factor of exertion for the utter purification of thought ?

In this case a monk, aloof from sense-desires, aloof from evil conditions, enters upon the first musing, which is accompanied by thought directed and sustained, born of seclusion, zestful and easeful, and abides therein.

---

[1] *Vyaggha-pajjā*. This particular tribal name acc. to *Comy.* (which also, at *DA.* i. 262 and *SnA.* 356, describes the origin of the Koliyans) arose from the fact that their chief town was built on the site of a *kola*-tree and on a track of leopards. There is a Burmese *v.l. -pathay*.

[2] It seems quite out of place to instance the conduct of monks on such an occasion, and in any case to treat a general audience of laymen to a discourse on the higher mental training. *Cf. Sakya*, 177, where Mrs. Rhys Davids points out that *jhāna* (musing) had come to be regarded purely as mind-practice.

[3] As at *A.* i, 125, *Tattha tattha paññāya anuggahissāmi*, and *infra*, § 243.

Then by the calming down of thought directed and sustained he attains and abides in the second musing, that inward calming, that single-mindedness apart from thought directed and sustained, that is born of mental balance, zestful and easeful.

Then by the fading out of zest, disinterested, mindful and composed, he experiences with body that ease of which the Ariyans declare: " He who is disinterested and alert, dwells at ease,". and he attains and abides in the third musing.

Then by abandoning both ease and discomfort, by the ending of both the happiness and unhappiness he had before, he attains and abides in the fourth musing, a state of neither ease nor discomfort, an equanimity of utter purity.

This is called " the utter purification of thought " (the resolve): I will bring to perfection such a purification of thought if it be incomplete, and if complete I will supplement it here and there by wisdom.   The desire, the effort . . . and attention applied thereto is called " a factor of exertion for the purification of thought."

And what, men of the Leopard's Path, is the factor of exertion for the utter purification of view ?

In this case a monk comes to understand, as it really is: This is Ill. This is the arising of Ill. This is the ending of Ill. This is the practice going to the ending of Ill. This is called "utter purification of view " (the resolve): I will bring to perfection such a purification of view if it be incomplete. . . . The desire to do, the effort . . . and attention applied thereto is called " a factor of exertion for the utter purification of view."

And what, men of the Leopard's Path, is the factor of exertion for the utter purification of release ? . . .

In this case the Ariyan disciple who is possessed of this factor of exertion for the utter purification of morals . . . of thought . . . of view, cleanses his heart of conditions that defile, he releases[1] his heart by means of conditions that release. So doing he attains perfection of release. This is called " the utter purification of release " (the resolve): I

---

[1] *Vimoceti*; *Sinh.* text *vimocayati*; *Comy. vimuccati.*

will bring to perfection such a purification of release if it be
incomplete, and if complete I will supplement it here and there
by wisdom. The desire, the effort, the exertion, endeavour,
persistence, mindfulness and attention applied thereto is
called " a factor of exertion for the utter purification of release."

So, men of the Leopard's Path, these are the four factors
of exertion for utter purification which were fully proclaimed
by that Exalted One who knows, who sees, the Arahant,
the Fully Enlightened One, for the purification of beings, for
the passing over grief and distress, for the making an end of
sorrow and lamentation, for the winning of the Method, for
the realization of Nibbāna.'

§ v (195). *Vappa.*[1]

On a certain occasion the Exalted One was staying among
the Sakyans at Kapilavatthu, in Banyan Park. At that time
Vappa the Sakyan, a disciple of the Unclothed,[2] went to visit
Moggallāna the Great, and on coming to him, saluted the
venerable Moggallāna the Great and sat down at one side.
As he sat thus, the venerable Moggallāna the Great was saying
this to Vappa the Sakyan, disciple of the Unclothed:

' There may be someone here, Vappa, restrained in body,
speech and thought owing to the waning of ignorance and the
arising of knowledge. Now, Vappa, do you see any cause
owing to which the āsavas causing pain would flow in upon[3]
the man at some future time ?'[4]

' Sir, I do see such a reason. There may be in this case a
certain previously done evil deed, whose fruit has not yet
ripened. Owing to that the āsavas causing pain might flow
in upon that man at some future time.'

---

[1] Gotama's uncle and a Sakyan rājah acc. to *Comy.* The Vappa
of the Pañca-Vaggiya. See Introduction, p. xiii.

[2] Nāta's son, the Jain.

[3] *Āsaveyyuṇ; v.l. anvāssaveyyuṇ.* Here we have the verb which
gives the real meaning of āsava, ' a flood which overwhelms.' Some
take it to mean a ' trickling,' or ' an open sore.'

[4] *Comy.* takes this ' future time ' to mean in his next birth, but this
would not necessarily be so.

At this juncture the conversation which the two were holding was broken off.

Then the Exalted One, at eventide rising from his solitary meditating, went towards the service-hall, and on reaching it sat down on a seat made ready. Having taken his seat the Exalted One said this to the venerable Moggallāna the Great:

'Pray, Moggallāna, on what subject are you talking as you sit here now, and what was the talk just interrupted ?'

' Lord, I was just saying to Vappa the Sakyan, disciple of the Unclothed, " There may be someone here, Vappa, restrained in body, speech and thought, owing to the waning of ignorance and the arising of knowledge. Now, Vappa, do you see any cause owing to which the āsavas causing pain would flow in upon the man at some future time ?" At these words, lord, Vappa was saying to me: " Sir, I do see such a reason. There may be in this case a certain previously done evil deed whose fruit has not yet ripened. Owing to that the āsavas causing pain might flow in upon that man at some future time." This was the subject we were engaged upon; then the talk was interrupted by the arrival of the Exalted One.'

Then said the Exalted One to Vappa the Sakyan, disciple of the Unclothed:

'If you, Vappa, would allow what you deem allowable, and reject what you deem should be rejected, and in case you should not understand the meaning of my words, if you would question me still further thus: " How is this, sir ? What is the meaning of that ?"—we might have a talk here.'

' I will indeed, lord, allow the Exalted One what I deem allowable and will reject what I deem should be rejected, and in case I do not understand the Exalted One's words I will question the Exalted One still further, thus: "What is this, lord ? What is the meaning of that ?" So be it. Let us have a talk here.'

' Now what think you, Vappa ? As to these āsavas which come about as a result of bodily activities,[1] in the case of one who abstains from bodily activities that cause vexation and

---

[1] *Kāya-samārambha-paccaya.*

distress, it follows that those āsavas causing pain do not exist
in him.[1] He does no fresh deed; as to his former deed, he
wears it out by constant contact with it,[2] by a wearing out[3]
that is plain to see, not just for a time; one that asks for
inspection, that leads onward, a wearing out that can be
understood by the intelligent, each for himself.[4] Now, Vappa,
do you see any reason why āsavas causing pain should flow
in upon him at some future time ?'

' No, lord, that cannot be.'

' Now again, Vappa, what think you ? As to those āsavas
that come about as the result of activities of speech . . . as a
result of activities of mind, in the case of one who abstains
from activities of speech and mind that cause vexation and
distress, it follows that those āsavas causing pain do not
exist in him. He does no fresh deed; as to his former deed,
he wears it out by constant contact . . . by a wearing out
that . . . can be understood by the intelligent each for himself. Now, Vappa, do you see any reason why āsavas causing
pain should flow in upon him at some future time ?'

' No, lord, that cannot be.'

' Again what think you, Vappa ? As to those āsavas
causing vexation and distress which result from ignorance,—
owing to the waning of ignorance and the arising of knowledge
it follows that those āsavas of vexation and distress do not
exist in him. He does no fresh deed; as to his former deed,
he wears it out by constant contact with it, by a wearing out
that is plain to see, not just for a time; one that asks for
inspection, that leads onward, a wearing out that can be
understood by the intelligent each for himself. Now, Vappa,
do you see any reason why āsavas causing pain should flow
in upon him at some future time ?'

' No, lord, that cannot be.'

' So then, Vappa, by the monk whose heart is perfectly

---

[1] *Evaŋ sa =evam assa.*

[2] *Phussa-phussa =phusitvā ; cf. K.S.* iv, 136 *n.*

[3] *Nijjarā =kilesa-jīraṇaka-paṭipadā. Cf. Furth. Dial.* i, 67.

[4] These epithets (*sandiṭṭhiko,* etc.) are usually applied to Dhamma.
Comy.

released six constant abiding-states[1] are attained. He, seeing
an object with the eye, is neither elated nor depressed, but
rests indifferent, mindful and comprehending. Hearing a
sound with the ear . . . smelling a scent with the nose . . .
tasting a savour with the tongue . . . with body contacting
tangibles . . . with mind cognizing mental states, he is neither
elated nor depressed, but rests indifferent, mindful and
comprehending.

When he feels a feeling limited by body,[2] he knows that he
so feels. He knows: When body breaks up, after life is used
up, all my experiences in this world will lose their lure and grow
cold.

Suppose, Vappa, that a shadow is cast by a stump.[3] Then
comes a man with axe and basket and cuts down that stump
by the root. So doing he digs all round it.[4] Having done so
he pulls up the roots, even the rootlets and root-fibres. He
chops that stump into logs, and having done so chops the
log into chips. The chips he dries in wind and sun, then
burns them with fire, then makes an ash-heap. The ash-heap
he winnows in a strong wind or lets the ash be carried away by
a swiftly flowing river. Verily, Vappa, that shadow cast
because of the stump is cut off at the root, made like a palm-
tree stump, made not to become again, of a nature not to
arise again in future time.

Just in the same way, Vappa, by a monk whose heart is
thus released six constant abiding-places are won. He, seeing
an object with the eye . . . with mind cognizing mental
states, is neither elated nor depressed, but abides indifferent,
mindful and comprehending. When he feels a feeling limited

---

[1] *Satata-vihāra. Cf. Dial.* iii, 234; *SnA.* 425; *VM.* i, 160; *Expos.*
i, 230; *Path of Purity,* ii, 442; *K.S.* iv (*Kindred Sayings on Sense*).

[2] *S.* ii, 83=*K.S.* ii, 57; *S.* v, 320=*K.S.* 283 (where I am not sure that
my trans. 'that his bodily endurance has reached its limit' is right).
Comy. explains *kāya-paricchinnaŋ . . . jīvita-paricchinnaŋ* as ' confined
to the limits of body and life.'

[3] This common simile, generally applied to a great tree, occurs at
S. ii, 88, 90, 91, 93, etc. Here the word *thūna* may mean 'stump'
or ' pillar ' (which, however, has no roots).

[4] *Palikhaṇeyya* I take to be equal to *parikhaṇeyya.*

by body . . . limited by life, he knows that he so feels.   He
knows: When body breaks up, after life is used up, all my
experiences in this world will lose their lure and grow cold.'

At these words Vappa, the Sakyan, disciple of the Unclothed,
said this to the Exalted One:

'Lord, just like a man desirous of wealth who tends his
property[1] but gets no increase therefrom, but instead gets
toil and trouble for his pains, even so, lord, did I, desirous
of profit, do service unto the Unclothed.   But I got no profit
thereby, but instead got toil and trouble for my pains.   I
myself, lord, from this day forth, whatever faith I had in
those fools the Unclothed,—I winnow it away in a strong
wind, or I let it be carried away by a swiftly flowing river.

It is wonderful, lord !   It is marvellous ! . . .   May the
Exalted One accept me as his follower from this time forth
so long as life shall last, as one who has gone to him for refuge.'

§ vi (196). *Sāḷha.*

On a certain occasion the Exalted One was staying near
Vesālī in Great Wood, at Peak-roofed House.   Now Sāḷha
the Licchavī and Abhaya the Licchavī[2] came to visit the
Exalted One, and on coming to him saluted him and sat down
at one side.   So seated Sāḷha the Licchavī said this to the
Exalted One:

'There are some recluses and brāhmins, lord, who proclaim
a twofold crossing of the flood, namely, the way made by
purity of morals and that made by self-mortification.[3]   What
says the Exalted One about this, lord ?'

'I do indeed say, Sāḷha, that purity of morals is a factor of
recluseship.   Those recluses and brāhmins who uphold self-
mortification, who make self-mortification essential, who
remain clinging to self-mortification,—they are incapable of
crossing the flood.   Moreover, Sāḷha, those recluses and

---

[1] *Assa paniyaŋ,* 'his wares.'   *Comy.* takes it as *assa-p.,* 'horse-
property.'

[2] For Abhaya see *M.* i, 392; *A.* i, 220; *K.S.* v, 107.   Sāḷha; for a monk
of this name see *D.* ii, 91; *K.S.* v, 312.

[3] *Tapo-jiguccha,* described in full at *Dial.* iii, 36, and below, § 198.

brāhmins who practise impurity of body, speech and thought,
who live in impurity,—they are incapable of knowledge and
insight, of the enlightenment that is unsurpassed.

Suppose a man, Sāḷha, desirous of crossing a river, takes a
sharp axe and enters the jungle. There he sees a mighty
sāl-tree, straight up, young, not of crooked growth.[1] He cuts
it down at the root. Having done so he lops it at the top, and
having lopped it at the top clears off branches and twigs and
makes it clean. Having done so he chips it roughly with
axes. Having chipped it with axes he does so with knives.
Having done that he smooths it with a scraper.[2] After that
he smooths it with rock-ball[3] and then brings it down to the
river. Now what think you, Sāḷha ? Is that man capable
of crossing the river ?'

' Not so, lord.'

' What is the cause of that ?'

' Why, lord, that sāl-tree log, though well worked outside,
is not cleaned out inside. This is to be expected of it,—the
log will sink, the man comes to misfortune and destruction.'

' Well, Sāḷha, just in the same way those recluses and
brāhmins who uphold self-mortification, who make self-
mortification essential, who cling to self-mortification, are
incapable of crossing the flood. Moreover, Sāḷha, those recluses and brāhmins who practise impurity of body, speech
and thought, who live in impurity,—they are incapable of
knowledge and insight, of the enlightenment which is unsurpassed. But on the other hand those recluses and brāhmins

---

[1] *Akukkucca-jātaŋ. Comy. Bhaveyya nu kho na bhaveyyā ti, ajā-
netabba-kukkuccaŋ,* ' not causing doubt or worry as to its suitability.'
But *Sinh.* text *akukkuka,* ' immeasurable by the *kukka.*' *Cf. M.* i, 233 =
S. iii, 141 (where *Comy.* has *akkusa-*). *Kukku* is a measure of length.
So I trans. ' of towering height ' at *K.S.* iii, 119, iv, 104 (with *Pāli Dict.*),
but Trenckner-Andersen (*P. D.*) has ' without fault or defect.' I now
trans. according to the idea of Mr. E. H. Johnston (*J.R.A.S.*, July, 1931),
who considers the word to be *akujjaka-,* a doublet of *uju,* or perhaps
' without bosses growing on it.'

[2] *Lekhanī* (not a pencil, as *P. Dict.*). *Comy. avalekhana-satthaka*
(a scraping-knife with handle, probably our ' spoke-shave ').

[3] This must be a sort of pumice-stone.

. . . who do not these things, but live purely, are capable
of knowledge and insight, of the enlightenment which is
unsurpassed.

But suppose a man, Sāḷha, desirous of crossing a river takes
a sharp axe and enters the jungle. There he sees a mighty
sāl-tree trunk, . . . after chipping it with knives he takes
a chisel and cleans out the inside till it is thoroughly hollowed
out. Then he takes a scraper and scrapes it and smooths
it with rock-ball. When he has done this he makes a boat of
it, fastens on oars and rudder and finally brings down the boat
to the river. Now what think you, Sāḷha? Is that man
capable of crossing the river?'

'Yes, he is, lord.'

'What is the cause of that?'

'Why, lord, that sāl-tree log is well worked outside and
thoroughly cleaned out inside, made into a boat and fitted
with oars and rudder. This is to be expected of it: the boat
will not sink and the man will reach the shore in safety.'[1]

'Well, Sāḷha, just in the same way those recluses and
brāhmins who are not upholders of self-mortification . . .
who live not clinging to self-mortification, are capable of
crossing the flood. And those recluses and brāhmins who
practise utter purity in body, speech and thought . . . who
live in utter purity are capable of knowledge and insight,
of the enlightenment which is unsurpassed.

Just as, Sāḷha, a fighting-man, though he knows many
cunning feats of archery,[2] is worthy of a rājah, is a pos-

---

[1] *Comy.* explains the parable thus: (a) The *log* is the personality;
the *river-stream*, the stream of *saṃsāra*; the *man* wishing to cross, one
who holds heretical views; the *outside* of the log is self-mortification
(*cf.* the Pharisees who clean the outside only); the *log* previous to being
hollowed out is the time of the man's immoral life; the *sinking* of the
log is his return to the round of rebirth. (b) The *man* wishing to cross
is the practiser of *yoga* (*yogāvacara*); the *outside* of the log is the time
of his self-restraint; the *hollowing* of it out is his purity of life; *oars and
rudder* are the energetic striving in body and mind; *crossing over* is
Nibbāna.

[2] *Kaṇḍa-cittakāni* (gen. 'varied, various, variegated,' but not
'wonderful arrows,' as *Pāli Dict.*). *Cittaka* or *citraka* is a mode of

session of a rājah, is reckoned an asset to a rājah in three ways.[1] What are the three ?

He is a far-shooter, a shooter like lightning, a piercer[2] of a huge object.

Just as, Sāḷha, a fighting-man is a far-shooter, even so is the Ariyan disciple possessed of right concentration. The Ariyan disciple, Sāḷha, who possesses right concentration, whatsoever object, be it past, future or present, personal or external to self, be it gross or subtle, mean or exalted, far or near; every object in short that he beholds—he looks upon it, as it really is, with right wisdom, thus: This is not of me. Not this am I. Not for me is this the self. Whatsoever perception, whatsoever activity . . . whatsoever consciousness he has . . . far or near . . . everything in short of which he is conscious—he looks upon it, as it really is, with right wisdom, thus: This is not of me. Not this am I. Not for me is this the self.

Just as, Sāḷha, a fighting-man is a shooter like lightning, even so is the Ariyan disciple possessed of right view. The Ariyan disciple, Sāḷha, who possesses right view understands, as it really is: This is Ill. This is the arising of Ill. This is the ending of Ill. This is the practice going to the ending of Ill.

Just as, Sāḷha, a fighting-man is a piercer of a huge object, even so the Ariyan disciple is possessed of right release. The Ariyan disciple who possesses right release pierces through the huge mass of nescience.'

§ vii‑(197). *Mallikā.*

On a certain occasion the Exalted One was staying near Sāvatthī, at Jeta Grove in Anāthapiṇḍika's Park. Now

---

fighting or manœuvres. (*Benfey, Skt. Dict.*, refers to *Harivaṃsa* 15, 979, and there are refs. in *Mahābharata* [*Adi Parva*]). *Comy.* gives a list of six—viz., *sara-laṭṭhi, -rajju-, -pāsāda, -sāni, -pokkharaṇī, -padumāni citrāni*, which I render tentatively, taking *sara* as ' manœuvre,' 'with staves, with a noose, from a platform, from a screen, from a dug-out, and in lotus-formation.' The last word is so used at *JA.* ii, 406, etc.

[1] Four qualities are given above, § 181. *Cf. G.S.* i, 263.

[2] Or ' smasher.'

Mallikā the queen[1] came to visit the Exalted One, and on coming to him saluted the Exalted One and sat down at one side. As she sat thus Mallikā the queen said this to the Exalted One:

' Pray, lord, what is the reason, what is the cause why in this world some women-folk are ill-favoured, deformed, of a mean appearance, and are .poor, having little of their own, of small possessions and are of small account ?[2]

Again, lord, pray what is the reason, what is the cause why in this world some women-folk are ill-favoured . . . but yet wealthy, of great riches, of great possessions and of great account ?

Again, lord, pray what is the reason, what is the cause why in this world some women-folk are well-favoured, well-formed, lovely to look upon, amiable, possessed of the greatest beauty of complexion, and yet are poor, having little of their own, of small possessions and are of small account ?

And yet again, lord, pray what is the reason, what is the cause why in this world some women-folk are well-favoured, well-formed, lovely to look upon, amiable, possessed of the greatest beauty of complexion, and are moreover wealthy, of great riches, of great possessions and of great account ?'

' In this case, Mallikā, a certain woman is ill-tempered, of a very irritable nature.[3] On very little provocation she becomes cross and agitated. She is upset and becomes stubborn, she shows temper and ill-will and displeasure. She is no giver of charity to recluse or brāhmin, nor gives food, drink, clothing, vehicle, flower, scent, ointment, bed, lodging or light. Moreover, she is jealous-minded,[4] she is jealous of

---

[1] *Cf. Ud.* v, 1. Acc. to the legend she was a poor flower-girl who gave her only cake to the Buddha as his first meal for the day. The immediate fruit of this gift was, acc. to the Buddha's prophecy, that she became that very day the queen of the rājah Pasenadi. She was plain-looking.

[2] *Appesakkho* (*mātugāmo* is masc.). *Sinh.* text and *Comy.* have the adj. feminine throughout. *Comy.* ' of small retinue.'

[3] *Upāyāsa-bahulo.*

[4] Text *issamānikā*; *Comy.* and *Sinh.* text *issāmanikā, =issāy sampayutta-cittā. Comy.*

other folk's gain, of the honour, respect, reverence, homage and worship paid to them. She is revengeful[1] and harbours a grudge. Such an one, if, deceasing from that life, she comes back to this state of things, wherever she is reborn, is ill-favoured, ill-formed, of a mean appearance and poor, having little of her own, of small possessions, and is of small account.

Herein again (in the second case), Mallikā, a certain woman is ill-tempered, of a very irritable nature. On very small provocation . . . she shows temper and ill-will and displeasure. But she is a giver of charity to recluse and brāhmin . . . she gives bed, lodging and light. However, she is not jealous-minded, she is not jealous of other folk's gain, of the honour, respect, reverence, homage and worship paid to them. She is not revengeful, nor does she harbour a grudge. Such an one, if, on deceasing from that life, she comes back to this state of things, wherever she is reborn, is ill-favoured, ill-formed, of a mean appearance; but she is wealthy, of great riches, of great possessions and is of great account.

Herein again (in the third case), Mallikā, a certain woman is not ill-tempered, not of a very irritable nature. Even on great provocation she becomes not cross and agitated. She is not upset, does not become stubborn, does not show temper, ill-will and displeasure. Yet she is no giver of charity to recluse and brāhmin . . . nor does she give bed, lodging and light. But she is jealous-minded. She is jealous of other folk's gain, of the honour, respect, reverence, homage and worship paid to them. She is revengeful and harbours a grudge. Such an one, if, deceasing from that life, she comes back to this state of things, wherever she is reborn, is well-favoured, well-formed, lovely to look upon, amiable, possessed of the greatest beauty of complexion. But she is poor, having little of her own, of small possessions and is of little account.

Herein again (in the fourth case), Mallikā, a certain woman is neither ill-tempered nor of a very irritable nature. Even on great provocation she becomes not cross and agitated. She

---

[1] *Upadussati.* So Childers (not in *A. index* or *P. Dict.*).

is not upset, does not become stubborn, does not show ill-will and displeasure.   Moreover, she is a giver of charity to recluse and brāhmin.   She gives one food, drink, clothing, vehicle, flowers, scent, ointment, bed, lodging and light.   She is not jealous-minded, she is not jealous of other folk's gain, of the honour, respect, reverence, homage and worship paid to them. She is not revengeful nor does she harbour a grudge.   Such an one, deceasing from that life and coming back to this state of things, wherever she is born, is well-favoured, well-formed, lovely to look upon, amiable, possessed of the greatest beauty of complexion.   She is wealthy, of great riches, of great possessions and is of great account.

Now, Mallikā, these are the reasons and causes why a certain woman is ill-favoured . . . and of small account; ill-favoured . . . but of great account; well-favoured . . . and of small account; well-favoured . . . and of great account.'

At these words queen Mallikā said this to the Exalted One:

' Suppose, lord, that *I* in another birth was ill-tempered and of an irritable nature, becoming cross and agitated even on slight provocation; that I became upset thereat and stubborn, showed ill-will and displeasure.   That same I (might now be) ill-favoured, ill-formed and of mean appearance.

Suppose, lord, that in another birth I gave gifts of charity to recluse and brāhmin . . . bed, lodging and light, that same I now might be wealthy, of great riches, of great possessions.

Suppose, lord, that in another birth I was not jealous-minded, I was not jealous of other folk's gain, nor of the honour, respect, reverence, homage and worship paid to them.   I was not revengeful nor did I harbour a grudge.   That same I am now of great account.

Now again, lord, in this rājah's family there are maids of the nobles, maids of the brāhmins and of the householders too.   Over them I hold supremacy.   Lord, from this day forth I will indeed become good-tempered, not irritable.   Even on great provocation I will not become upset nor stubborn. I will not show ill-will nor displeasure.   I will give to recluse and brāhmin food and drink . . . bed, lodging and light.   I will not become jealous-minded.   I will not be jealous of other folk's gain, nor of the honour, respect, reverence, homage and worship paid to them. I will not be revengeful nor will I harbour a grudge.

It is wonderful, lord ! It is marvellous, lord ! Lord, may the Exalted One accept me as a woman disciple from this day forth so long as life may last, as one who has gone to him for refuge.'

§ viii (198). *The self-tormentor.*

' Monks, these four persons are found existing in the world. What four ?

Herein, monks, a certain person is a self-tormentor, given to the practice of self-torment. Herein again a certain person is a tormentor of another, given to the practice of tormenting another. Yet again a certain person is a tormentor both of self and another, and given to that practice. And yet again, monks, a certain person is a tormentor neither of self nor of another, not given to the practice of tormenting self and another. He who torments neither self nor another in this very life is no more hungry,[1] he is allayed, he has become cool, one who has penetrated bliss, he dwells with self that has become Brahmā.[2]

And how, monks, is a person a self-tormentor, one given to the practice of self-torment ?

In this case a certain one[3] goes naked, he has loose habits, he licks his hands clean, he will have none of your " Come in, your reverence !" or " Stop a bit, your reverence !" He refuses food brought to him, he refuses special food, he refuses an invitation to a meal. He refuses food straight from the pot or straight from the pan, or within the threshold of a door, or among the firewood,[4] or among the rice-pounders. He refuses food when a couple are eating, or from a pregnant

---

[1] *Nicchāto = nittaṇha. Cf. K.S.* iv, 136.

[2] *Brahma-bhūtena attanā viharati.*

[3] *Dial.* i, 227; as at *A.* i, 295 (*G.S.* i, 273); *M.* i, 342 = *F. Dial.* iv, 248; *Pugg.* 56. *Cf. Kathā-vatthu,* I, i, § 74, 236, and Introduction above.

[4] *Daṇḍa-m-antaraṃ.* What sort of sticks ? See *Dial.* iii, 228 *n. Comy.* at *A.* i = *DA.* ii, 354 expl. 'lest it be put there specially for me'

woman, from a woman giving suck, or from one having inter-course with a man.   He refuses food from a mixed collection, or where a dog stands by, or where flies are swarming.   He eats neither fish nor flesh, drinks no liquor or intoxicant, not even rice-gruel.

He asks an alms from one house only, he is an eater of one mouthful; or maybe he begs from two houses, eats two mouth-fuls . . . begs from seven houses, eats seven mouthfuls only. He exists on just one little dole of food or on just two or more or seven such doles.   He takes food only once a day or once in two days . . . or once in seven days.   Thus he lives given to the practice of taking food by rule, even to the interval of half a month.

He feeds on vegetables, on millet, on raw rice, on scraps of leather, on water-plants, rice-powder, burnt scum of rice, flour of oil-seeds, on grass and cowdung.   He just exists on forest roots and fallen fruit.

He wears coarse hempen clothes, cloth of different fibres, discarded corpse-cloths, rags from a rubbish heap, tree-bark fibre, antelope skins, strips of antelope skin, clothes made of *kusa* grass, made of wood shavings, blankets made of human hair, made of horsehair, made of owls' wings.

He is a plucker out of hair and beard and given to this practice.   He remains standing and refuses a seat.   He squats down and keeps a squatting posture.   He is a " bed-of-thorns " man, he makes his bed on spikes.   He lives given to the practice of going down to the water to bathe even a third time in the evening also.   Thus in divers ways he lives given to these practices which torment the body.

Thus, monks, a person is a self-tormentor and given to that practice.

And how, monks, is a person a tormentor of another and given to that practice ?

Herein a certain person is a butcher, a pig-killer, a fowler, deer-stalker, a hunter, a fisherman, a bandit, an executioner, a jailer, or (one of) any others who follow a bloody calling.[1]

---

[1] *Cf. A.* iii, 383.

That, monks, is how a person tortures another and is given to such practice of torture.

And how, monks, is a person a tormentor of both self and another and given to the practice of tormenting self and another ?

Herein, monks, a certain person is a rājah or nobleman who has been consecrated, or a brāhmin of a great house.   Having built a new mote-hall[1] on the east side of a town, he gets his head and beard shaved, dons a shaggy skin, smears his body with ghee and oil, scratches his back with a deer's horn and enters the mote-hall together with his chief wife and brāhmin chaplain.   There he makes his bed upon the bare[2] grass-covered ground.   Then the rājah lives on the milk from one teat of a cow with calf of like colour; his chief wife lives on the milk from the second teat; the brāhmin chaplain lives on the milk from the third teat, while that from the fourth they offer as sacrifice to the fire.   The calf is fed with what is left. Then he says: " Let so many bulls be slain for the sacrifice; let so many cows, so many heifers, so many goats, so many rams, (let so many horses)[3] be slain for the sacrifice.   Let them cut down so many trees for sacrificial posts; let them mow so much *kusa* grass for the sacrifice."[4]

Then whosoever are called his slaves, messengers or work-men, scared by fear of the rod, with tearful faces set about their preparations.   That, monks, is how a person is a self-tormentor, given to the practice of tormenting both self and others.

And how, monks, is a person neither the one thing nor the other, given neither to the practice of tormenting self nor to that of tormenting others ?

---

[1] *Comy.* takes it to mean *yañña-sālaŋ* (hall of sacrifice).

[2] Text *anantarahitāya* (from *antaradhāyati*); *Sinh.* text *antarahitāya*; *Comy. anattharahitāya* (?) (editorial correction), expl. as *asanthatāya*, 'without coverlet.'   My MSS. of *Comy.* have *anantarahita,* =' uncovered ' (with nothing between).   P. *Dict.* refers to *Vin.* i, 47, ii, 209; *M.* ii, 57.

[3] Only in Burmese MSS.

[4] *Barihisa.*   For the passage *cf. D.* i, 141; *M.* i, 344.

He who torments neither self nor another in this very life is no more hungry, he is allayed, become cool. He is one who has penetrated bliss, he lives with a self that has become Brahmā.

In this case, monks, a Tathāgata arises in the world, an Arahant, a Fully Enlightened One, perfect in knowledge and conduct, a Wellfarer, a world-knower, unsurpassed driver of men to be driven, teacher of devas and mankind, a Buddha, an Exalted One. He makes known this world with its Devas, its Māras, its Brahmās, with its host of recluses and brāhmins, of devas and mankind, himself having thoroughly understood and realized it. He teaches Dhamma that is lovely in youth, lovely in middle age, lovely at the end of life, both in the spirit and the letter. He makes plain the God-life entirely complete and fully purified. Then a housefather or one of a household or one born in some family or other hears that Dhamma, and so hearing acquires faith in the Tathāgata.

Possessed of this faith so acquired he thus reflects: Oppressive is this household life, a way of dust.[1] The way of going forth is of the open air. It is no easy thing for one living the household life to practise the God-life in all its completeness, in utter purity like a polished shell. How if I were to get my beard shorn and, donning the saffron robe, were to go forth from home to the homeless ? Then he, some time later on, abandoning the whole mass of his wealth whether small or great, abandoning his circle of kinsmen whether small or great, gets his beard shorn, dons the saffron robes and goes forth from home to the homeless.

He, having thus gone forth, having entered upon the way of life in the training followed by monks, abandoning the slaying of creatures, abstains therefrom. He lives as one who has laid down the rod, who has laid down the knife, who has scruples, is kind and has compassion for every living thing. Abandoning the taking of what is not given, he abstains therefrom. He lives as one who takes only what is given, who waits for what is given, he lives with a self[2] that has become pure, not

---

[1] So *Comy.*, but adds that the *Great Commentary* takes it as *uṭṭhān' aṭṭhānaŋ* (impossibility of rising from) *rāga-rajādīnaŋ*.   [2] *Cf.* p. 3.

by stealth. Abandoning the unchaste life he lives chaste, lives a life aloof, abstaining from the sexual act, from dealings with womenfolk.[1] Abandoning falsehood he abstains therefrom, he speaks the truth, joins truth[2] to truth, unswerving, reliable, no deceiver of the world. Abandoning slanderous speech he abstains therefrom. When he hears something at one place he spreads it not abroad elsewhere to cause dissension among these folk. When he hears something at another place he spreads it not abroad elsewhere to cause dissension among these folk.

Thus he reconciles those who are at variance and confirms the friendly. He delights in harmony, finds pleasure herein, rejoices in harmony and utters words that make for harmony. Abandoning bitter speech he abstains therefrom. Whatever speech is blameless, pleasing to the ear, affectionate, speech that goes to the heart, is urbane, delights many folk, pleases many folk,—such speech does he utter. Abandoning idle babble he abstains therefrom. He is one who speaks in season, speaks of facts, speaks sense, speaks according to Dhamma, speaks according to Vinaya. He speaks words worth treasuring up, that are seasonable, reasonable,[3] discriminating and concerned with profit.[4]

He is one who abstains from injury to seed-life and plant-life;[5] lives on one meal a day, refrains from food at night, abstains from food at unseasonable hours, from flowers, scents, unguents, adornments and finery, from shows of nautch-dancing and singing, from beds high and broad, from taking gifts of gold and silver, from taking gifts of uncooked grain, of uncooked flesh, from gifts of women and girls, female and male slaves, of goats and sheep, fowls and swine, elephants, cattle, horses and mares. He abstains from gifts of fields, cultivated or waste, from buying and selling, sending messengers

---

[1] *Gāma-dhammā.* This word used to be trans. ' the village, or pagan, practice,' but *cf. mātu-gāma.*

[2] *Sacca-sandho. Comy.* at *A.* i, 212, *saccena saccaṇ sandahati.*

[3] *Sāpadesaṇ,* also acc. to *Comy.* ' with illustration.'

[4] *Pariyanta-vatiṇ; cf. supra,* § 22.

[5] *Bīja-gāma bhūta-gāma; cf. Dial.* i, 6, iii, 40; *K.S.* v, 394.

or going as such, from cheating with scales, copper vessels or measures, from taking bribes to pervert justice, from cheating and crooked ways.[1] He abstains from cutting, flogging, binding, highway robbery, plundering and deeds of violence.

He is content with a robe sufficient to protect the body,[2] with alms-food enough for his belly's need. Wherever he may go he takes these with him. Just as, for instance, a bird upon the wing, wherever he may fly, flies with the load of his wings,— even so a monk is content with a robe . . . and takes these with him. Possessed of this Ariyan mass of morals, he experiences in himself the bliss of blamelessness.

Seeing an object with the eye[3] he is not misled by its outer view nor by its lesser details. Since coveting and dejection, evil, unprofitable states, might flow in upon one who lives with the faculty of eye uncontrolled, he applies himself to such control, sets a guard over the faculty of eye and attains control thereof. Hearing a sound with the ear or with the nose smelling a scent or with the tongue tasting a savour or with body contacting tangibles, or with mind cognizing mental states, he is not misled by their outer view nor by their lesser details. But since coveting and dejection, evil, unprofitable states, might flow in upon one who lives . . . he sets a guard over the faculty of mind, attains control thereof. Thus possessed of this Ariyan restraint of faculties he experiences in himself unadulterated bliss.[4]

In going forth and returning he acts composedly.[5] In looking in front and looking behind . . . in bending or relaxing . . . in wearing his robe and bearing outer robe and bowl . . . in eating, drinking, chewing and tasting . . . in easing himself, in going, standing, sitting, sleeping, waking, in speaking and keeping silence he acts composedly.

---

[1] Reading *sāci-yoga*, with my *Sinh.* MSS., for *sāvi-* of the rest; *SA. yāci-* (on *S.* v, 473); *Pugg.* A. 240.

[2] *D.* i, 71 = *Pugg.* 58; *Dial.* i, 81. *Comy.* has more to say on the topic of alms than on any spiritual matter.

[3] *Cf. K.S.* iv, 63, etc.   [4] *Avyāseka = kilesehi anāsitta. Comy.*

[5] Here *Comy.* refers to *DA.* i, on *Sāmañña-phala-sutta*, pp. 184-193; *cf. K.S.* iv, 142.

He, possessed of this Ariyan mass of morals and this Ariyan restraint of the faculties and this Ariyan mindfulness and composure (and this Ariyan contentedness),[1] resorts to a secluded lodging-place, a forest, the root of a tree, a hill, ravine, grotto or cave, a charnel-field, a jungle-path, an open space, a heap of straw. After his meal, when he has returned from his alms-round he sits down cross-legged, keeping his body erect and fixing his attention in front of him. Then abandoning the hankering after the world, he abides with heart freed therefrom; having regard for the welfare of every thing that lives he purges his heart of the taint of ill-will. Abandoning sloth-and-torpor he remains freed therefrom, wide-awake,[2] mindful, composed, and purges his heart of sloth-and-torpor. Abandoning distraction-and-flurry he abides undistracted at heart in the inner self, he purges his heart of distraction-and-flurry. Abandoning doubt-and-wavering, he abides as one who has transcended them; no longer questioning this or that in things profitable, he purges his heart of doubt-and-wavering.

Thus abandoning these five hindrances, these taints of the heart which cause the weakening of wisdom,[3] aloof from sense-desires (*as at* § 194), he attains and abides in the first, second, third and fourth musings.

Then with heart calmed and purified, cleansed and flawless, void of taints, grown soft and pliable, fixed and come to utter peace, he bends down[4] his mind to the knowledge of how to destroy the āsavas. He comes to know as it really is: This is Ill. . . . This is the practice going to the ending of Ill. He comes to know as it really is: These are āsavas. This is

---

[1] Not in *Sinh.* texts.

[2] *Āloka-saññī. Comy.* ' with consciousness calm to recognize light, whether by night or by day.' *Cf. Dial.* iii, 44, ' conscious of light,' probably wide awake.

[3] I trans. at *K.S.* v, 80, ' which weaken insight,' but this is wrong. *Cf. Comy. ad S.* v, 97, *paññā dubbalā hoti.* Here *Comy.* has *paññāya uppajjituŋ na denti,* ' do not give wisdom a chance to arise.' These *nīvaraṇā* are also called (*S.* v, 97) ' causing blindness, sightlessness, nescience, ending wisdom, causing distress, not conducive to Nibbāna.'

[4] *Cf. D.* i, 84; *A.* iii, 17.

the arising of āsavas. This is the ending of āsavas. This is the practice going to the ending of āsavas. In him, thus knowing, thus seeing, his heart is released from the āsava of sense-desire; his heart is released from the āsava of becoming; his heart is released from the āsava of ignorance.[1] By release comes the knowledge: I am released.[2] He comes to know: Destroyed is rebirth. Lived is the God-life. Done is what was to be done. There is no beyond to this state of things.

Thus, monks, a person is neither a tormentor of self nor of another, nor given to the practice thereof. He, being neither of these, in this very life hungers no more, he is allayed, become cool, he abides in the experience of bliss with a self that has become Brahma.[3]

So, monks, these are the four persons found existing in the world.'

§ ix (199). *Craving.*

' Monks, I will teach you craving that ensnares,[4] that floats along,[5] that is far-flung,[6] that clings[7] to one, by which this world is smothered,[8] enveloped, tangled like a ball of thread, covered as with blight,[9] twisted up like a grass-rope, so that it overpasses not the Constant Round (of rebirth), the Down-

---

[1] The three, not the (? later) four āsavas.

[2] Texts *vimuttasmiŋ vimuttam iti,* but *DA.* i, 225 reads *vimuttasmiŋ vimutt' amhī ti,* which I follow.

[3] The foregoing formula of the recluse-life occurs in the same context at *Majjhima,* i, 344 *f.,* and at iii, 33 *f.* in a different context. A short version occurs in the former context at *Majjhima,* ii, 159.

[4] *Jāliniŋ. Cf. Dhp.* 180, *yassa jālinī visattikā taṇhā n' atthi* (=*S.* i, 107). The four words used here describe the process of a fisherman's circular cast-net, a familiar picture in the East.

[5] *Sarita. Cf. UdA.* 424, *saŋsār' aṇṇavaŋ taṇhā-saritañ ca.*

[6] *Visaṭa* = *patthaṭa. Comy.* ' the metaphor is that of the net (*jāla*).'

[7] *Visattikaŋ* (*visatta,* clinging). Here *Comy.* gives the right derivation, but adds the other popular one from *visa* (poison) of *SA.* i, 175, *visa-phala.*

[8] *Uddhasta* = *dhaŋsita.*

[9] *Cf. D.* ii, 55; *S.* ii, 92, iv, 158 *n.,* reading *tantākula-jātā, guḷā-guṇṭhika-jātā* (*J.P.T.S.,* 1919, p. 49).

fall, the Way of Woe, the Ruin. Do ye listen to it carefully. Apply your minds and I will speak.'

' Yes, lord,' replied those monks to the Exalted One. The Exalted One said this:

' And of what sort, monks, is craving that ensnares . . . in which this world is smothered . . . ?

There are these eighteen thoughts which are haunted[1] by craving concerning the inner self and eighteen which are haunted by craving concerning what is external to self. Now of what sort are the former ?

Monks, when there is the thought: I am,—there come the thoughts: I am in this world: I am thus: I am otherwise: I am not eternal:[2] I am eternal:[3] Should I be:[4] Should I be in this world: Should I be thus: Should I be otherwise. May I become: May I become in this world: May I become thus: May I become otherwise: I shall become: I shall become in this world: I shall become thus: I shall become otherwise. These are the eighteen thoughts which are haunted by craving concerning the inner self.

And of what sort, monks, are the eighteen thoughts which are haunted by craving concerning what is external to self ?

When there is the thought: By this[5] I am,—there come the thoughts: By this I am in the world: By this I am thus: By this I am otherwise: By this I am not eternal: By this I am eternal: By this should I be: By this should I be in this world: By this should I be thus: By this should I be otherwise:

---

[1] *Vicaritāni*. These are discussed in full at *Vibhanga*, 392 *ff.*, followed by *Comy.*, but there are differences of readings. The editors of both texts have confused the readings. See next *n.*

[2] *As' asmi* (*Sinh.* text has *ay' asmi* ?). It is Skt. *asat*, and in the next phrase *sat*. *Comy.* and *Vibh.* expl. thus: *nicco 'smi, dhuvo 'smi, sassato 'smi, avipariṇāma-dhamm' asmī ti* (which is just the opposite of what it means).

[3] Text *sāt' asmi* (but *sat' asmi* lower down). *Sinh.* and *Comy. sat' asmi* ; *Vibh.* explains *ucchijissāmi, na bhavissāmi* (wrong, see above).

[4] *San* (Skt. *syam*). *Comy.* and *Vibh.* take this as equal to *siyaŋ*. Text *santi* throughout for *san ti*. The pointing of our text is most confusing here.

[5] *Iminā*=*rūpena, viññāṇena*, etc. *Comy.*

By this may I become: By this may I become in this world:
By this may I become thus: By this may I become otherwise:
By this I shall become: By this I shall become in this world:
By this I shall become thus: By this I shall become otherwise.
These are the eighteen thoughts which are haunted by craving
concerning what is external to self.[1]

Now these . . . are called " the thirty-six thoughts haunted
by craving."

Thus such thirty-six thoughts of past, thirty-six thoughts
of future, such thirty-six thoughts of present time make up
one hundred and eight thoughts which are haunted by craving.[2]

Verily, monks, this is that craving that ensnares, that floats
along, that is far-flung, that clings to one, by which this world
is smothered, enveloped, tangled like a ball of thread, covered
over with blight, twisted up like a grass-rope, so that it overpasses not the Constant Round, the Downfall, the Way of Woe,
the Ruin.'

§ x (200). *Affection.*

' Monks, these four things are born. What four ?

Of affection is born affection, of affection is born ill-will.
Of ill-will is born affection, of ill-will is born ill-will.

And how is affection born of affection ?

In this case, monks, one person is dear, pleasant, delightful
to another person. Then others treat[3] that one as dear,
pleasant and delightful. The former thinks: He who is dear,
pleasant and delightful to me is treated by others also as dear,
pleasant and delightful. So he conceives affection for them.
Thus, monks, is affection born of affection.

And how, monks, is ill-will born of affection ?

In this case, monks, one person is dear, pleasant and delightful to another. Then others treat that one as not dear,

---

[1] In these two classes our *Comy.* thus regards *ajjhattika* as the self,
bāhira as the body or mental states, whereas *Vibhanga* uses *bāhira*
as applying to *parapuggala*, thus: *I* am thus, but *so-and-so* is different.
He is a brāhmin, *I* am not, etc.

[2] *Comy. aṭṭha-sataŋ ; Sinh.* text *aṭṭhañ ca taṇhā . . . sataŋ.*   Text
strangely reads *aṭṭhārasa taṇhā sataŋ.*

[3] *Samudācaranti,* ' associates with ' (instrum.).

not pleasant, not delightful.   The former thinks: He who is to
me dear, pleasant and delightful is treated by others as not
dear, pleasant and delightful.   So he conceives ill-will towards
them.   Thus, monks, is ill-will born of affection.

And how, monks, is affection born of ill-will ?

In this case, monks, a certain person is not dear . . . to
another.   Others also treat him as not dear. . . .   Then the
former thinks: This person is not dear . . . to me; others
also treat him as not dear, pleasant and delightful, so he conceives affection for those others.   Thus, monks, is affection
born of ill-will.

And how, monks, is ill-will born of ill-will ?

In this case, monks, a certain person is not dear, pleasant
and delightful to another.   But others treat him as dear,
pleasant and delightful.   The former thinks: This person is
not dear . . . to me, but others treat him as dear, pleasant
and delightful.   So he conceives ill-will for those others.
Thus, monks, is ill-will born of ill-will.   These four things[1]
are born.

Now, monks, at such time as a monk, aloof from sense-
desires . . . attains and abides in the first musing, the affection
that is born of affection exists not at all, nor yet does the ill-
will that is born of affection, nor yet the affection that is born
of ill-will, nor yet the ill-will that is born of ill-will.

At such time as a monk, by calming down thought directed
and sustained . . . attains and abides in the second musing
. . . these four do not exist.   (At such time as a monk, by
the fading out of zest . . . attains and abides in the third
musing . . . these four do not exist.)[2]

At such time as a monk, by the destruction of the āsavas,
attains the heart's release, the release by wisdom that is
without the āsavas, in this very life of himself thoroughly
comprehending it, and abides therein, the affection that is
born of affection is abandoned by him, cut down at the root,
made like a palm-tree stump, made not to exist, made of a

---

[1] Text wrongly *pemāni.*
[2] All texts omit the third *jhāna.*

nature not to recur in future time . . . (and it is the same
with the other three).

This monk is said neither to attract nor to repel, neither
to smoulder nor to blaze up, and is not bemused.[1]

And how does a monk attract ?

Herein a monk regards body as the Self or regards the
Self as having bodily form, or regards body as in the Self or
the Self as in the body. He regards feeling as the Self, or
the Self as having feeling. . . . He regards perception . . .
the activities . . . he regards consciousness as the Self, or
the Self as having consciousness; or consciousness as in the
Self, or the Self as in consciousness. That is how a monk
attracts.

And how does a monk not attract ?

Herein a monk regards not body as the Self . . . nor the
Self as in consciousness. That is how a monk does not
attract.

And how does a monk repel ?

Herein a monk reviles again him who reviles, annoys again
him who annoys, quarrels again with him who quarrels. That
is how he repels.

And how does a monk not repel ?

When reviled he reviles not again, when annoyed he annoys
not again, he quarrels not again with him who quarrels.
That is how he repels not.

And how does a monk smoulder ?

Monks, where there is the thought: I am,—there is also the
thought: I am in this world; I am thus; I am otherwise; I
am not eternal; I am eternal.[2] Should I be; Should I be in
this world; Should I be thus; Should I be otherwise. May I
become; May I become in this world; May I become thus;
May I become otherwise. I shall become; I shall become in

---

[1] *Cf. S.* iii, 89 = *K.S.* iii, 75, *pajjhāyati*, for which *Comy.* and *Sinh.*
text read *apajjhāyati*. *Cf. M.* i, 334, *jhāyanti, pajjhāyanti, nijjhāyanti,
apajjhāyanti*, trans. by Lord Chalmers (to bring out the force of the
prefixes): ' they trance, and en-trance, and un-trance and de-trance.'
Comy. ' with the pride of " I am." '

[2] Here *text* has rightly *sat' asmi* for *sāt' asmi* (above).

this world; I shall become thus; I shall become otherwise. That is how a monk smoulders.[1]

And how does a monk not smoulder ?

Where the thought: I am,—is not, the thought: I am in this world (and the rest) are not. That is how a monk smoulders not.

And how does a monk blaze up ?

Where there is the thought: By this I am,—there is also the thought: By this I am in this world. . . . By this I shall become otherwise. That is how a monk blazes up.

And how does a monk not blaze up ?

Where there is not the thought: By this I am,—the thoughts: By this I am in this world (and the rest) are not. That is how a monk blazes not up.

(And how is a monk bemused ?)

Where there is the conceit: I am (and the rest) . . . a monk is bemused.[2]

And how is a monk not bemused ?

Herein the conceit of "I am" is abandoned in a monk, cut down at the root . . . made of a nature not to arise again in future time; that is how a monk is not bemused.'

(THE FIFTH FIFTY SUTTAS)

CHAPTER XXI.—THE WORTHY MAN.[3]

§ i (201). *The precepts.*

'Monks, I will teach you the unworthy man and the still more unworthy man. I will teach you the worthy man and the still more worthy man. Do ye listen to it carefully. Apply your minds and I will speak.'

'Yes, lord,' replied those monks to the Exalted One. The Exalted One said:

---

[1] *Cf. M.* i. 144 (the simile of the ant-hill which smoulders by day and blazes up at night). This refers to a man's imaginings. At *S.* iii, 89 the word used is *sandhūpeti.*

[2] This section is not in the texts.

[3] *Sappurisa. Cf. Pugg.* iv, pp. 38-9.

' And of what sort, monks, is the unworthy man ?

Herein a certain person is one who takes life, steals, is a wrong-doer in sense-desires, is a liar, is given to the use of liquor fermented and distilled, causing negligence. This one is called " the unworthy man."

And of what sort, monks, is the still more unworthy man ?

Herein a certain person is one who takes life and so forth, and further encourages another to do the same. This one is called " the still more unworthy man."

And of what sort, monks, is the worthy man ?

Herein a certain person is one who abstains from taking life, from stealing and so forth. This one is called " the worthy man."

And of what sort, monks, is the still more worthy man ?

Herein a certain person not only himself abstains from taking life and so forth, but also encourages another to abstain from so doing. This one is called " the still more worthy man." '

§ ii (202). *The believer.*

' Monks, 1 will teach you the unworthy man and the still more unworthy man. I will teach you the worthy man and the still more worthy man. Do ye listen to it.' . . . The Exalted One said this:

' And of what sort, monks, is the unworthy man ?

Herein a certain person is one who believes not, who is shameless, reckless, of small learning, indolent, of distracted mindfulness, and weak in wisdom. This one is called " the unworthy man."

And of what sort is the still more unworthy man ?

Herein a certain person is one who himself believes not and encourages another to unbelief; who is himself shameless and encourages another to be shameless; who is himself reckless and encourages another to be reckless; who is himself of small learning and encourages another to be so; who is himself indolent . . . of distracted mindfulness . . . weak in wisdom, and encourages another to be the same. This one is called " the still more unworthy man."

And of what sort is the worthy man ?

Herein a certain person is a believer, modest, conscientious, of wide learning, of ardent energy, of good memory and strong in wisdom.   This one is called "the worthy man."

And of what sort, monks, is the still more worthy man ?

Herein a certain person is possessed of faith and encourages another to possess faith; is himself modest and encourages another to be modest; is himself conscientious and encourages another to be so; is himself widely learned . . . of ardent energy . . . of settled mindfulness . . . strong in wisdom and encourages another to be the same.   This one is called "the still more worthy man." '

§ iii (203).   *Destroyer of beings.*[1]

' Monks, I will teach you the unworthy man, the still more unworthy man; the worthy man and the still more worthy man.   Do ye listen to it. . . .

And of what sort is the unworthy man ?

Herein a certain person takes life and so forth and is of slanderous, bitter speech, and an idle babbler.   This one is called "the unworthy man." ' (*The more unworthy man does the same, but encourages another to do so ; the worthy man abstains and encourages another to abstain.*)

§ iv (204).   *The ten deeds.*

(*The same, with the addition of* he is covetous, of a malicious heart, and has wrong view.   *The worthy man abstains and encourages another to do so.*)

§ v (205).   *The Eightfold Way.*

' Monks, I will teach you the unworthy man. . . .

And of what sort is the unworthy man ?

Herein, monks, a certain one has wrong view, wrong aim, wrong speech, action, livelihood, effort, mindfulness and wrong concentration.' (*The still more unworthy man encourages others to be like himself ; the worthy man has right view and the rest, and encourages another to have it.*)

---

[1] The *uddāna* calls this *satta-nāso.*

§ vi (206). *The Tenfold Way.*

(*The same with the addition of* wrong knowledge and wrong release . . . right knowledge and right release.)

§ vii (207). *The wicked* (a).

' Monks, I will teach you the wicked and the more than wicked; the goodly and the more than goodly man.   Do ye listen to it. . . .

And of what sort is the wicked ?

Herein a certain one takes life and the rest, and is covetous, of a malicious heart and has wrong view.   This one is called " the wicked."

And of what sort is the more than wicked ?

(*He is the same but encourages another to be like himself.*)

And of what sort is the goodly ?

(*He abstains and encourages another to do so*) . . . and has right view.'

§ viii (208). *The wicked* (b).

(*The same qualities as in* § 206.)

§ ix (209). *Of wicked nature* (a).

' Monks, I will teach you the one of wicked nature and the one of more than wicked nature; the one of goodly nature and the one of more than goodly nature.   Do ye listen. . . .'

(*The same qualities as in* § 207.)

§ x (210). *Of wicked nature* (b).

(*The same qualities as in* § 208.)

CHAPTER XXII.—CORRUPTING.

§ i (211). *The company.*[1]

' Monks, there are these four corrupters of a company. What four ?

In this case a monk is immoral, of a wicked nature, a defiler of a company.   A nun is immoral . . . a male disciple

---

[1] *Cf. G.S.* i, 65, 222, 264 *ff.*; *supra*, § 20, *parisa-kkasāvo* and *parisāya mando*; here *Comy. parisa-dūsanā.*

. . . a female disciple is immoral, of a wicked nature, a defiler of a company. These are the four. . . .

Monks, there are these four who illumine a company. What four ?

In this case a monk is moral, of a goodly nature, illuminating a company.

A nun . . . a male disciple . . . a female disciple is of a like nature. These four illuminate a company.'

§ ii (212). *View.*

' Monks, possessing four qualities one is put into purgatory according to his deserts.[1] What four ?

By bad conduct in deed, word, thought, and wrong view. These are the four.

Monks, possessing four qualities one is put into heaven according to his deserts. What four ?

By good conduct in deed, word, thought, and right view. These are the four.'

§ iii (213). *Ingratitude.*

' Monks, possessing four qualities one is put into purgatory according to his deserts. What four ?

By bad conduct in deed, word, thought, ingratitude, that is ungratefulness.[2] These are the four.

Monks, possessing four qualities one is put into heaven according to his deserts. What four ?

By good conduct in deed, word, thought, gratitude, that is gratefulness. These are the four.'

§ iv (214). *Taking life.*

(*The same for* Taking life, stealing, wrong conduct in sense-desires and falsehood, and their opposites.)

---

[1] *Yathābhataŋ nikkhitto ;* cf. *supra,* § 19.

[2] *Akataññutā akatavedita ;* both words are the same in meaning aco. to *Comy.*

§ v (215). *The Way* (a).

(*The same for* Wrong view, wrong aim, wrong speech and wrong action, and their opposites.)

§ vi (216). *The Way* (b).

(. . . Wrong livelihood, effort, mindfulness and concentration, and their opposites.)

§ vii (217). *Modes of speech* (a).

(. . . One who says he has seen what he has not seen, has heard . . . sensed . . . cognized what he has not, and their opposites.)

§ viii (218). *Modes of speech* (b).

(. . . One who says he has not seen what he has, not heard . . . not sensed . . . not cognized what he has, and their opposites.)

§ ix (219). *Shameless*.

(. . . One who is an unbeliever, immoral, shameless, unconscientious, and the opposites.)

§ x (220). *Of weak wisdom*.

(. . . One who is an unbeliever, immoral, indolent, of weak wisdom.)

'Possessing these four qualities, monks, one is put into purgatory according to his deserts; but one who is a believer, moral, of ardent energy and strong in wisdom is put into heaven according to his deserts.'

CHAPTER XXIII.—GOOD CONDUCT.

§ i (221). *Good conduct*.

'Monks, there are these four bad habits of speech. What four ?

Falsehood, slander, bitter speech and idle babble. These are the four.

Monks, there are these four good habits of speech. What four ?

Speaking truth, not speaking slander, soft speech and wise speech.[1]　These are the four.'

§ ii (222). *View.*

'Monks, possessing four qualities the foolish, sinful, unworthy man carries about with him an uprooted, lifeless self, is blameworthy, is censured by the intelligent and begets much demerit.[2]　What are the four ?

By bad conduct of body, speech and thought, and wrong view.

Monks, possessing these four qualities the wise, prudent, worthy man carries about with him a self not uprooted, not lifeless, is blameless, not censured by the intelligent and begets much merit.　What are the four ?

By good conduct of body, speech and thought, and right view. . . .'

§ iii (223). *Ingratitude.*

'Monks, possessing four qualities the foolish, sinful, unworthy man carries about . . .　What are the four ?

By bad conduct of body, speech and thought, ingratitude, that is, ungratefulness.

Monks, possessing four qualities the wise, prudent, worthy man carries about a self not . . .　What are the four ?

By good conduct of body, speech and thought, gratitude, that is, gratefulness.'

§ iv (224). *Taking life.*

(*The same for* One who takes life, steals, is a wrong doer in sense-desires, a liar, *with the opposite for him* who abstains from these things.)

---

[1] Reading *mantā-bhāsā*, as at § 149, for text's *mantā-vācā*; *Sinh.* text *mattā-bhassaŋ.　Comy.* says nothing; but see *loc. cit.*

[2] As at p. 3.

§ v (225). *The Way.*

. . . Who has wrong view, wrong aim, speech and action. . . .
. . . Who has right view and the rest.

§ vi (226). *Modes of speech (a).*

. . . Who says he has seen what he has not, has heard
what he has not, has sensed and cognized what he has not.
. . . Who says not that he has heard, seen, sensed, cognized
what he has not.

§ vii (227) *Modes of speech (b).*

. . . Who says he has not seen . . . what he has. . . .
. . . Who says he has seen . . . what he has seen. . . .

§ viii (228). *Shamelessness.*

. . . Who is an unbeliever, immoral, shameless, unconscientious. . . .
. . . Who is a believer, moral, modest, conscientious. . . .

§ ix (229). *Weak in wisdom.*

. . . Who is an unbeliever, immoral, indolent, weak in
wisdom. . . .
. . . Who is a believer, moral, of ardent energy, strong in
wisdom. . . .

§ x (230). *Poets.*[1]

' Monks, there are these four poets.   What four ?
The imaginative, the traditional, the didactic and the
extempore poet.   These are the four.'

---

[1] Possibly inserted to make up the ten suttas of each vagga. *Cf.*
Dial. i, 22 *n.*; *Buddhist India,* 184; *DA.* i, 95; *SA.* i, 286; *UdA.* 205.
They are as follows:
Cintā-kavi, ' he who composes after thinking.'
Suta-kavi, ' who writes down what he has heard said—*e.g.,* myths
and legends.'
Attha-kavi, ' he who writes of the meaning of a thing.'
Paṭibhāna-kavi, ' who writes of his own invention, like the elder
Vangīsa.' *Comy.*

CHAPTER XXIV.—THE DEED.[1]

§ i (231). *In brief.*

'Monks, these four deeds I have myself comprehended, realized and made known. What four ?

There is a dark deed with a dark result; a bright deed with a bright result; a deed that is both dark and bright, with a dark and bright result; and the deed that is neither dark nor bright, with a result neither dark nor bright, which being itself a deed conduces to the waning of deeds.[2] These four deeds . . . I have made known.'

§ ii (232). *In detail.*

'Monks, these four deeds I have myself comprehended, realized and made known . . . (*as above*).

And of what sort, monks, is the deed that is dark, with a dark result ?

In this case, monks, a certain one plans planned bodily action[3] joined with harm . . . planned action of speech . . . planned action of thought, joined with harm. He thus planning harmful action of body, speech and thought, is born into a world that is harmful. Thus born into a harmful world, harmful contacts contact him. Thus touched by harmful contacts he feels feeling that is harmful, that is sheer pain, just as do beings in purgatory. This, monks, is called " the dark deed with a dark result."

And of what sort, monks, is the bright deed with the bright result ?

In this case a certain one plans planned bodily action that is not joined with harm. . . . So planning . . . he is reborn into a world that is not harmful. So born into a harmless world harmless contacts touch him. He, thus touched by

---

[1] *Comy.* calls this *Magga-Vagga.*

[2] *Cf. Expos.* i, 118; *Netti,* 159 (which calls the last named *nibbedho*); *A.* iii, 384. *Cf.* also *K.S.* i, p. 118 *f.*

[3] *Kāya-sankhāraŋ abhisankharoti savyāpajjhaŋ. Cf. A.* i, 123, where *Comy.* has *rāsiŋ karoti*; but here *āyūhati, sampiṇḍeti.* At *G.S.* i, 105 I translated *savyāpajjhaŋ* by ' discordant,' which is not quite accurate. *Cf. S.* ii, 40 (*K.S.* ii, 31, 65, 82); *supra,* § 171.

harmless contacts, experiences feeling that is harmless, utter
bliss, such as do the Ever-radiant devas.[1] This, monks, is
called " the bright deed with a bright result."

And of what sort, monks, is the deed that is both dark and
bright, with a result that is both dark and bright ?

In this case a certain one plans planned action of body,
speech and thought that is joined with harm and harmlessness
. . . he is born into a world that is both harmful and harmless. . . . Touched by contacts both harmful and harmless
he experiences feeling that is both harmful and harmless,
a mixture of pleasure and pain,[2] such as for instance some
humans, some devas,[3] and some dwellers in purgatory[4] feel.
This, monks, is called "the deed that is both dark and bright,
with a result that is both dark and bright."

And of what sort, monks, is the deed that is neither dark
nor bright, with a result that is similar, which, itself a deed,
conduces to the waning of deeds ?

In this case, monks, the intention to abandon this dark
deed with its dark result, the intention also to abandon this
bright deed with its bright result, the intention to abandon
this bright deed ·with its bright result, the intention to
abandon this deed both dark and bright with a like result,—
this intention is called "the deed . . . that conduces to the
waning of deeds."

These four deeds, monks, I have myself comprehended,
realized and made known.'

§ iii (233). *Soṇakāyana.*

Now Sikha[5] Moggallāna, the brāhmin, came to visit the
Exalted One, and on coming to him greeted him courteously.

---

[1] *Cf.* § 123.

[2] Text *vokiṇṇaṇ sankiṇṇaṇ sukha-dukkhaṇ*, but as at *A.* i, 123, *Sinh.*
text and *Comy.* read only *vokiṇṇa-sukha-d.*

[3] *Comy.* ' The *Kāmāvacaras*, who are happy in their own sphere, but
unhappy when they observe the still greater happiness of higher Devas.'

[4] *Comy.* 'Petas with vimānas, also Nāgas, Supaṇṇas, elephants,
horses, etc., who are sometimes happy, sometimes wretched.'

[5] ' On the crown of his head he had a great tuft.' *Comy. Cf. Moliya*
of *S.* ii, 13.

. . . As he sat at one side Sikha Moggallāna the brāhmin said this to the Exalted One:

' Friend Gotama, the other day or a few days ago the youth Soṇakāyana came to me and said: " Gotama the recluse proclaims the ineffectiveness of all deeds.[1] In doing so, sir,[2] he has uttered annihilation of the world. Why, sir, it is in deed that the world is real.[3] It persists in (man's) continual effort in his deeds !" '[4]

' For my part, brāhmin, I know not the youth Soṇakāyana even by sight. Whence then such a talk (by me) ?

Now, brāhmin, these four deeds I have myself comprehended, realized and made known. What are the four ?' (*The whole of the previous sutta word for word.*)

§ iv (234). *Precepts.*

' Monks, these four deeds I have myself comprehended, realized and made known. (*As in* § 231.)

And of what sort, monks, is the dark deed with a dark result ?

In this case, monks, a certain one takes life, steals, is a wrongdoer in sense-desires, a liar, given to the use of liquor fermented and distilled which causes sloth. This is called " the dark deed with a dark result."

And of what sort, monks, is the bright deed with a bright result ?

In this case a certain one abstains from taking life and the rest. . . .

And of what sort, monks, is the deed both dark and bright with a result both dark and bright ?

In this case a certain one plans planned bodily action . . . (*as in* § 232).

---

[1] Taught by Makkhali; *cf. D.* i, 53; *S.* iii, 210; *A.* i, 286 (*n' atthi kammaṇ, n' atthi kiriyaṇ, n' atthi viriyaṇ*).

[2] *Bho,* as *Comy.* and *Sinh.* text for *kho* of our text.

[3] *Kamma-sacca=k. sabhāvo. Comy.*

[4] *K. samārambha-ṭṭhāyi=k. s. tiṭṭhati ; kammaṇ āyūhanto tiṭṭhati Comy.*

And of what sort, monks, is the deed neither dark nor bright, with a result neither dark nor bright, a deed that conduces to the waning of deeds ?

In that case, monks, the intention to abandon this dark deed with its dark result . . . is called "a deed that conduces to the waning of deeds."

These, monks, are the four deeds I have myself comprehended, realized and made known . . . (*as above*).

And of what sort, monks, is the dark deed with a dark result ?

In this case a certain one is a murderer of his mother, a murderer of his father, of an arahant, one who with evil intent draws the blood of a Tathāgata, one who causes dissension of the Order.   This is called . . .

And of what sort is the bright deed with a bright result ?

In this case a certain one abstains from taking life and the rest, he abstains from idle babble, from coveting and ill-will, and has right view.   This is called . . .

And of what sort is the deed both dark and bright with a like result ?

In this case a certain one plans planned bodily action that is joined with both harm and harmlessness. . . .

And of what sort is the deed that is neither dark nor bright, with a result neither dark nor bright . . . (*as in* § 232) ?

These four deeds I have myself comprehended. . . .'

§ v (235). *The Ariyan Way.*

' Monks, these four deeds . . . (*as in* § 232).

And of what sort, monks, is the deed neither dark nor bright, with a result neither dark nor bright, a deed which conduces to the waning of deeds ?

It is right view . . . right concentration.   This is called . . .'

§ vi (236). *Limbs of wisdom.*[1]

' Monks, these four deeds . . . (*as in* § 232).

And of what sort, monks, is the deed neither dark nor bright . . .?

---

[1] *Cf. K.S.* v, 50 *ff.*

The limbs of wisdom that is mindfulness, that which is dhamma-search, that which is energy, that which is tranquillity, that which is concentration, and the limb of wisdom that is equanimity. This is called . . .'

§ vii (237). *Blameworthy.*

' Monks, possessing four things one is put into purgatory[1] according to his deserts. What four ?

Bodily action that is blameworthy, action of speech, action of thought, and view that is blameworthy. Possessing these four things . . .

Monks, possessing four things one is put into heaven according to his deserts. What four ?

Bodily action . . . view that is blameless. Possessing these four . . .'

§ viii (238). *Harmful.*

(*The same for* bodily action and the rest, that is harmful and harmless.)

§ ix (239). *The recluse.*[2]

' In this teaching, monks, the recluse is to be found, also the second, third, and fourth (class of) recluse. Void of such recluses are the systems of those who teach contrary views.[3] Thus, monks, do ye rightly roar this lion's roar.

And of what sort, monks, is the recluse ?

Herein a monk, by the utter destruction of three fetters,[4] is a Stream-winner, one not destined to the Downfall, one assured, bound for enlightenment. This is the recluse.

And of what sort, monks, is the second recluse ?

Herein a monk, by the utter destruction of three fetters, by wearing down lust, hatred, delusion, is a Once-returner. Coming back to this world once more he makes an end of Ill. This is the second recluse.

---

[1] *Supra*, § 212.

[2] *Cf. D.* ii, 151; *M.* i, 63; *VM.* i, 141, 268 (*Path of Purity*, ii, 162, 307); *Types*, 88; *Expos.* i, 219, ii, 451; *SnA.* 161; *Vibh.* 244; *VibhA.* 323. *Idh' eva*, ' in this teaching.' *Comy.*

[3] *Comy.* refers to *Ito bahiddhā samaṇo pi n' atthi* of *D.* ii, 151.

[4] *K.S.* v, 347.

And of what sort, monks, is the third recluse ?

Herein a monk, by the utter destruction of the five fetters that lead to rebirth, is born apparitionally, there meanwhile to win release,[1] not destined to return from that world. This is the third recluse.

And of what sort, monks, is the fourth recluse ?

Herein a monk, by the destruction of the āsavas, attains the heart's release, the release by wisdom . . . in this very life of himself comprehending it, and realizing it, having attained thereto, abides therein. This is the fourth recluse.

Monks, in this teaching the recluse is to be found, also the second, the third and fourth recluse. Void of such recluses are the systems of those who teach contrary views. Thus, monks, do ye rightly roar this lion's roar.'

§ x (240). *Profit by the worthy man.*

' Monks, because of the worthy man four profits are to be looked for. What four ?

One grows in the Ariyan virtue, in the Ariyan concentration. in the Ariyan wisdom, one grows in the Ariyan release.[2] These are the four profits.'

CHAPTER XXV.—FEAR OF OFFENCE.[3]
§ i (241). *Offence (a).*

On a certain occasion the Exalted One was staying near Kosambī in Ghosita Park. Now the venerable Ānanda came to visit the Exalted One. . . . As he sat at one side the Exalted One said this to the venerable Ānanda:

' Pray, Ānanda, is that dispute settled ?'

' How can that dispute be settled, lord ? Bāhiya,[4] lord,

---

[1] *Tattha parinibbāyin* (sometimes called *antarā-p.*); *cf. supra*, § 169. This formula is peculiar to the Saṅyutta and Anguttara, and recurs some ten times.

[2] *Cf.* the fourfold laywoman's growth, *K.S.* iv, 169.

[3] Text omits *-bhaya* in title. *Āpatti, cf. A.* i, 84, 87, etc.

[4] This can hardly be the elder so called (or Bāhika), *KhpA.* 115 of *S.* iv, 63, v, 165; *A.* i, 24 (' best of those of quick comprehension '); *Ud.* i, 10, who is also called *Dārucīriya* (' bark-dress ').

who lives along with the venerable Anuruddha, stands in
every way for dissension in the Order. Things being so,
the venerable Anuruddha thinks it not worth while to utter a
single word.'

' But, Ānanda, when did Anuruddha ever interfere in disputes amid the Order ? Is it not yourself, Ānanda, and Sāriputta and Moggallāna who settle[1] whatsoever disputes may
arise ?

Now, Ānanda, there are these four probable results,[2] seeing
which a wicked monk delights in a dissension of the Order.
What are the four ?

In this case, Ānanda, a wicked monk is immoral, of a
wicked nature, impure, of suspicious behaviour, of covert
deeds.[3] He is no recluse, though claiming to be such, he is
no liver of the good life, though claiming to be such, he is
rotten within, full of lusts, a rubbish-heap of filth.

It occurs to him: Now if the monks know me to be immoral,
of a wicked nature . . . a rubbish-heap of filth, united they
will do me harm, but if at variance[4] they will do me no harm.
Seeing this first probable result a wicked monk takes delight
in a dissension of the Order.

Then again, Ānanda, a wicked monk has wrong view, he
holds an extreme view.[5] It occurs to him thus: If the monks
know me to be of wrong view, a holder of extreme view,
united they will do me harm, but if at variance they will do
me no harm. Seeing this second probable result, Ānanda,
a wicked monk delights in a dissension of the Order.

Then again, Ānanda, a wicked monk is a wrong-liver, he
gets his living by a wrong way of living. It occurs to him

---

[1] Text *vo yuñjati* (reconciles you); but *Sinh.* text and *Comy.* and my
MSS. *voyuñjati=anuyuñjati, anuyogaṃ āpajjati* (makes an effort, inter-
feres). So also *Comy.* on *S.* iii, 11, and *S.* iv, 80 (*voyogaṃ*). Anuruddha,
the clairvoyant, was apparently of a very retiring nature, ' a confirmed
recluse ' (*Sakya*, 183, 342; *Gotama the Man*, 256).

[2] *Atthavase=kāraṇa-vase. Comy.*

[3] *Cf. Udāna*, 52; *UdA.* 297; *S.* iv, 181; *K.S.* iv, 114.

[4] *Vaggā*, opp. to *samaggā. Cf. A.* i, 70.

[5] *Anta-gāhika*, as at *A.* i, 154; *G.S.* i, 138 *n.*—' *e.g.* of the annihila-
tionists.' *Comy.*

thus: If the monks know me to be a wrong-liver, united they
will do me harm, but if at variance they will do me no harm.
Seeing this third probable result, Ānanda, a wicked monk
delights in a dissension of the Order.

Then again, Ānanda, a wicked monk is desirous of gain and
honour, and longs not to be despised. It occurs to him:
If the monks know me to be desirous of gain and honour,
and that I long not to be despised, united they will do me no
honour, they will show me no respect, they will pay me no
regard nor reverence: but if at variance they will do these
things. Seeing this fourth probable result, Ānanda, a wicked
monk delights in a dissension of the Order. So these are the
four probable results. . . .'

§ ii (242). *Offence* (*b*).

' Monks, there are these four fears of offence. What four ?

Just as if men were to seize a bandit, a malefactor, and
show him to the rājah, saying: "Sire, this is a bandit, a malefactor. Let your honour visit him with punishment." Then
says the rājah to them: " Go ye, strongly bind this fellow's
arms behind him with a stout cord, shave him bald, and with
a harsh-sounding tamtam parade him from street to street,
from crossroads to crossroads. Then lead him forth by the
southern gate and at the south of the town chop off his head."
Thereupon those rājah's men . . . do just as they are bid.[1]

Thereupon to some bystander[2] it occurs thus: Truly a
wicked deed has this fellow done, worthy of execration, for
which he deserves to lose his head; inasmuch as the rājah's
men must bind his arms behind him with a stout cord, shave
him bald and with a harsh-sounding tamtam parade him from
street to street, from crossroads to crossroads, then lead him
forth by the southern gate and at the south of the town chop
off his head. Let me see to it[3] that *I* do no such wicked deed,

---

[1] The simile is at *S*. ii, 100, 128, iv, 343.

[2] *Thalaṭṭhassa = ekamante ṭhitassa. Comy.*

[3] *Assâhaŋ* for *assu* (strong particle) *ahaŋ*; see note below on *assa-
puṭaŋ.*

worthy of execration, for which I may deserve to lose my head.

Just in the same way, monks, in whatsoever monk or nun such lively consciousness of fear presents itself, in matters of grave offence[1] it must be expected that either he or she, being guiltless, will not fall into a grave transgression, or that if guilty he or she will make amends for the guilt as is fit and proper.

Just as if, monks, a man should don a black garment, let down his hair,[2] put a club on his shoulder, come before the public council[3] and say: " Sirs, I have done a wicked deed, one worthy of execration and cudgelling.[4] I submit to your worships' pleasure." Thereupon it occurs thus to some by-stander: Truly a wicked deed has this fellow done, worthy of execration and cudgelling; inasmuch as he dons a black garment, lets down his hair, puts a club on his shoulder, comes before the public council and says: " Sirs, I have done a wicked deed. . . ." Let me see to it that *I* do no such wicked deed, worthy of execration and cudgelling.

Just in the same way, monks, in whatsoever monk or nun such lively consciousness of fear presents itself, in matters calling for a decision of the Order[5] it must be expected that either, being guiltless, he or she will not come within the jurisdiction of the Order, or being guilty will make amends to the Order for guilt as is fit and proper.

Just as if, monks, a man should don a black garment, let down his hair, put a provision-bag[6] on his shoulder, come before

---

[1] *Pārājika-dhamma* (see below, *sanghādisesa-dh.*), an offence of the first class.

[2] Generally worn in a top-knot or ' bun ' (as in Ceylon).

[3] *Mahājana-kāya.*

[4] *Mosallaṃ* (only here), from *musala*, Skt. *musalya*, ' deserving a cudgelling.'

[5] *Sanghādisesa-dhamma*, an offence of the second class, a matter for a decision of the Order. *Cf. Vin.* ii, 38; *VM.* 22. Acc. to Childers, one to be dealt with by the Sangha *ādi*, in the beginning, and *sesa*, in the remaining stages.

[6] Text *assa-puṭaṃ. Cf. D.* i, 98, *assa-puṭena vadhitvā* (trans. at *Dial.* ii ' *killing* him with the ash-bag !' acc. to *DA. ad loc.*); but we should

the public council and say thus: " Sirs, I have done a wicked
deed, surely one deserving execration. I submit to your
worships' pleasure." Thereupon it occurs thus to some
bystander: Truly a wicked deed has this fellow done ! Indeed
it is worthy of execration; inasmuch as he dons a black
garment, lets down his hair, puts a provision-bag on his
shoulder, comes before the public council and says thus. . . .
Let me see to it that *I* do no such wicked deed, one worthy of
execration.

Just in the same way, monks, in whatsoever monk or nun
such lively consciousness of fear presents itself, in matters
calling for expiation[1] it is to be expected that either, being
guiltless, he or she will not fall into a state requiring expiation,
or, if guilty, will make amends for guilt as is fit and proper.

Just as if, monks, a man should don a back garment, let
down his hair,[2] come before the public council and say thus:
" Sirs, I have done a wicked deed, worthy of execration, worthy
of blame. I submit to your worships' pleasure." Thereupon
it occurs to some bystander: Truly a wicked deed has this
fellow done, one worthy of execration, worthy of blame, inasmuch as he dons a back garment, lets down his hair,
comes before the public council and says: " Sirs, I have done
a wicked deed. . . ." Let me see to it that *I* do no such
wicked deed, one worthy of execration, worthy of blame,—
just in the same way, monks, in whatsoever monk or nun such
lively consciousness of fear presents itself, in matters requiring

---

read at both places (as above, § 190) *aŋsa-puṭaŋ*—i.e., *punishing* him by
banishment; in which case he would take his food on his back. *Comy.*
takes it as ' ash-bag '! and Burmese texts even alter to *bhasma-puṭaŋ*
(see *P. Dict. s.v.*). There is evidently a vowel-confusion here in the
repetition below, where I propose to read *assu pi taŋ* (see on *assu* above),
and so translate. Could the original reading have been *assa puṭaŋ*,
' his cloth ' (Skt. *puṭaŋ* has this meaning) ? To put the cloth over the
shoulder is a mark of humility.

[1] *Pācittiya-dhamma* is a minor offence compared with the two above.
[2] It is to be noticed that the grievousness of each offence is marked
by the demeanour of the culprit. The first offence is clubbable, the
second requires banishment, the third does not go beyond requiring the
letting down of the hair.

confession¹ of guilt it is to be expected that either, being
guiltless, he or she will not fall into a state requiring confession or, if guilty, will make confession of guilt as is fit and
proper.

So these, monks, are the four fears of offence.'

§ iii (243). *Profit of the training.*²

' Monks, this God-life is lived for the sake of the profit of the
training, of further wisdom, of the essence of release, of the
mastery of mindfulness.

And how, monks, comes the profit of the training ?

Herein, monks, I have set forth for disciples the higher
practice of the training for the sake of giving confidence to
the wavering and for the increase in faith³ of the confident. As
a result of my doing so, monks, a disciple⁴ becomes one whose
deeds are consistent, congruous, not shady, not spotted.⁵ By
undertaking them he trains himself in the precepts of that
training.

Then again, monks, I have set forth for disciples the rudi-
ments⁶ of the training in the God-life for the utter destruction of
Ill in every way. As a result of my doing so, monks, a disciple
becomes one whose deeds are consistent, congruous, not shady,
not spotted; by undertaking them he trains himself in the
precepts of that training. Thus, monks, is the profit of the
training.

And how, monks, is there further wisdom ?

Herein, monks, I have set forth for disciples teachings for
the utter destruction of Ill in every way. As a result of my
doing so . . . those teachings are well scrutinized by wisdom.⁷
Thus there is further wisdom.

---

¹ *Pāṭidesanīyaka-dhamma.* A fourth class of offence requiring
merely confession.

² *Cf. Itiv.*, p. 40.

³ Text should read *bhiyyo-bhāvāya.*   ⁴ *So.*

⁵ *Cf. supra*, § 192.

⁶ *Ādibrahmacariyikā, K.S.* v, 354; *G.S.* i, 211.

⁷ *Samavekkhita* = *sudiṭṭha* (in my *Comy.* MS. has *ñāya-samapekkhā* (?)
= *samādhi-vipassanā*).

And how, monks, is there essence of release ?

Herein, monks, I have set forth for disciples teachings for the utter destruction of Ill in every way. As a result of my doing so . . . those teachings are realized[1] by release. Thus there is the essence of release.

And how, monks, is there mastery of mindfulness ?

By the thought: I shall complete the higher practice of the training where incomplete, or if complete I shall supplement it here and there by wisdom,[2]—mindfulness in the self is well set up. By the thought: I shall complete the rudiments of the God-life where incomplete, or if complete I shall supplement them here and there by wisdom,—mindfulness in the self is well set up. By the thought: The teaching not closely scrutinized I shall scrutinize, or if closely scrutinized I will supplement it here and there by wisdom,—mindfulness in the self is well set up. By the thought: The teaching not yet fully realized by release I will fully realize, or if fully realized I will supplement it here and there by wisdom,— mindfulness in the self is well set up. Thus, monks, is mastery of mindfulness.

Monks, this God-life is lived for the sake of the profit of the training, of further wisdom, of the essence of release, of the mastery of mindfulness. What I have said was said in this connexion.'

§ iv (244). *Postures.*[3]

'Monks, there are these four postures. What four ?

The posture of petas, that of the luxurious, that of the lion and the posture of the Tathāgata.

And of what sort, monks, is the posture of petas ?

Generally petas lie flat on their backs.[4] This is called "the peta-posture."

And of what sort, monks, is the posture of the luxurious ?

---

[1] *Phassitā* (contacted).   [2] *Supra*, § 194.

[3] *Cf. S.A.* i, 78; *UdA.* 403; *VibhA.* 345.

[4] *Comy.* says they are too meagre to lie on the side. As it calls petas 'just the dead,' it is possible that the posture of a corpse is thought of.

Generally the luxurious lie on the left side. This is called
" the luxurious posture."[1]

And of what sort, monks, is the posture of the lion ?

The lion, monks, the king of beasts, takes up a posture on
his right side, laying foot on foot[2] and folding his tail between
his thighs. On waking he straightens out the forepart of the
body and looks round to the hinder part. Then, monks, if
the lion, king of beasts,[3] sees any part of his body displaced or
disarranged,[4] thereupon, monks, the lion, king of beasts,[3] is
displeased. But if the lion, king of beasts, sees no part of his
body displaced or disarranged, then he is pleased. This,
monks, is called " the lion-posture."

And of what sort, monks, is the Tathāgata-posture ?

In this case, monks, a monk, aloof from sense-desires,
enters on and abides in the first . . . second . . . third . . .
and fourth musing. This is called the Tathāgata-posture.[5]
So there are these four postures.'

§ v (245). *Worthy of a cairn.*[6]

' Monks, these four are worthy of a cairn. What four ?

A Tathāgata, Arahant, a Fully Enlightened One is worthy
of a cairn; a Pacceka Buddha, a Tathāgata's disciple and a
rājah who rolls the wheel are worthy of a cairn.'

§ vi (246). *Growth in wisdom.*

' Monks, these four states conduce to growth in wisdom.
What four ?

---

[1] Reason not given.
[2] *Accādhāya* (not in *A. index* or *P. Dict.*); *cf. D.* ii, 134; *DA.* ii, 575.
[3] Here text twice reads *mahārāja.*
[4] *Visaṭaŋ=vijahitaŋ. Comy.*
[5] The usual description of a Buddha's posture is here omitted.
[6] Or *stūpa. Cf. D.* ii, 143=*Dial.* ii, 156. Here *Comy.* remarks:
' Why does the Exalted One permit a cairn for a wheel-rolling rājah
and not for an ordinary virtuous monk ? Because of its singularity.
Besides, if such were allowed *there would be no room in the villages and
districts of Ceylon, nor yet in other parts.* With the idea: They would not
be singular, he did not allow it.'

Association with a good man, hearing Saddhamma,[1] thorough work of mind,[2] and behaviour in accordance with Dhamma. These are the four.

Monks, these four states are of great service to one who has become human. What four ?' (*the same as the above*).

§ vii (247). *Modes of speech* (a).[3]

' Monks, these four modes of speech are un-Ariyan. What four ?

Speaking of things not seen as seen, of things not heard as heard, of things not sensed as sensed, speaking of things not cognized as cognized.'

§ viii (248). *Modes of speech* (b).

' Monks, these four modes of speech are Ariyan. What four ?

Speaking of things not seen as not seen, speaking of things not heard as not heard, of things not sensed as not sensed, of things not cognized as not cognized.'

§ ix (249). *Modes of speech* (c).

' Monks, these four modes of speech are un-Ariyan. What four ?

Speaking of things seen as not seen, of things heard as not heard, of things sensed as not sensed, of things cognized as not cognized.'

§ x (250). *Modes of speech* (d).

'Monks, these four modes of speech are Ariyan. What four ?

Speaking of things seen as seen, of things heard as heard, of things sensed as sensed, of things cognized as cognized.'[4]

---

[1] As at §§ 21, 22 notes. Here I take it to mean 'listening to the voice of conscience.'

[2] *Yoniso manasikāro.*

[3] *Cf.* § 226; *D.* iii, 232; *UdA.* 222; *Vibh.* 376, 387.

[4] Here *Sinh.* text adds an eleventh with *-vādī hoti* for *vāditā* (above).

CHAPTER XXVI.—HIGHER KNOWLEDGE.

§ i (251). *Higher knowledge.*

' Monks, there are these four states. What four ?

There are states to be comprehended by higher knowledge, states to be abandoned by higher knowledge, states to be made more of by higher knowledge and states to be realized by higher knowledge.

And of what sort, monks, are the states to be comprehended by higher knowledge ?

The five factors of grasping. These, monks, are called " states to be comprehended by higher knowledge."

And of what sort, monks, are the states to be abandoned by higher knowledge ?

Ignorance and the craving for becoming. These are called . . .

And of what sort, monks, are the states to be made more of by higher knowledge ?

Calm and insight. These are called . . .

And of what sort, monks, are the states to be realized by higher knowledge ?

Knowledge and release. These are called . . .

So these, monks, are the four states. . . .'

§ ii (252). *Quests.*[1]

' Monks, there are these four un-Ariyan quests. What four ?

Herein, monks, a certain one, being in himself subject to decay, seeks after that of which the nature is decay. Being in himself subject to disease, he seeks after that of which the nature is death. Being in himself subject to death, he seeks after that of which the nature is death. Being in himself subject to defilement, he seeks after that of which the nature is defilement. These are the four. . . .

Monks, there are these four Ariyan quests. What four ?

Herein, monks, a certain one, being in himself subject to

---

[1] *Cf. M.* i, 163.

decay, seeing the disadvantage of what is of a nature to decay, seeks after the undecaying, the unsurpassed rest after toil, even Nibbāna. Being in himself subject to disease, seeing the disadvantage in what is of a nature to be diseased, he seeks after the unailing, unsurpassed rest after toil, even Nibbāna. Being in himself subject to death, seeing the disadvantage in what is of a nature to die, he seeks after the deathless, unsurpassed rest after toil, even Nibbāna. Being in himself subject to defilement, seeing the disadvantage in what is of a nature to be defiled, he seeks after the undefiled, unsurpassed rest after toil, even Nibbāna.

So these, monks, are the four Áriyan quests.'

§ iii (253). *Sympathy*.[1]

'Monks, there are these four bases of sympathy. What four ?

Charity, kind speech, doing a good turn, and treating all alike.

These are the four. . . .'

§ iv (254). *Mālunkyā's son*.[2]

Now the venerable Mālunkyā's son came to visit the Exalted One, and on coming to him saluted the Exalted One and sat down at one side. As he sat thus the venerable Mālunkyā's son said this to the Exalted One:

'Well for me, lord, if the Exalted One would teach me Dhamma in brief ! Hearing which Dhamma from the Exalted One's lips I could dwell alone, remote, earnest, ardent and resolute.'

'Now, Mālunkyā's son, what am I to teach the young monks, when you,[3] a broken-down old man, far-gone in years, beg a teaching in brief of the Tathāgata ?'

---

[1] As above, § 32 (in gāthas). At *Dial*. iii, 145 rendered 'popularity.'

[2] *Cf. S*. iv, 72=*K.S*. iv, 42, where see *n*. There the teaching given is on the organs of sense. *Comy*. and *Sinh*. text read *Mālunkyā (brāhmiṇī)-putta. Cf. SA*. ii, 382. Text has Mālukya.

[3] *S*. iv reads *yatra hi nāma*=*yo nāma. Comy*. The old man had missed his chance in youth.

'Nay, lord, let the Exalted One teach me Dhamma in brief ! Surely I could understand the meaning of the Exalted One's words ! Surely I could become heir to the Exalted One's words !'

'Well, Mālunkyā's son, there are these four ways in which craving arises in a monk when it does arise. What four ?

It is because of the robe that craving arises; because of alms-food, lodging, because of failure or success to become this or that[1] craving arises in a monk when it does arise.

Now, Mālunkyā's son, when craving is abandoned in a monk, cut down at the root, made like a palm-tree stump, made not to become again, made of a nature not to arise again in future time, this monk is called " one who has cut off craving, broken the bond, by perfect comprehension of conceit has made an end of Ill." '[2]

Thereupon the venerable Mālunkyā's son, thus instructed by the Exalted One with this instruction, rose from his seat, saluted the Exalted One, and keeping his right side towards him went away.

Then the venerable Mālunkyā's son, living solitary, remote, earnest, ardent and resolute, in that very life himself comprehending and realizing that unsurpassed perfection of the holy life, for which clansmen rightly go forth from the home to the homeless, having attained it abode therein, so that he fully comprehended the meaning of: Cut off is rebirth, lived is the holy life, done the thing that should be done, there is no more of this state of things. And the venerable Mālunkyā's son was yet another of the arahants.[3]

§ v (255). *Profit of the family.*

'Whatsoever families, monks, having attained greatness of possessions, fail to last long, all of them do so because of these four reasons or one or other of them. What four ?

They seek not for what is lost, they repair not the decayed,

---

[1] *Itibhavābhava-hetu ; cf. supra,* § 9.
[2] *Cf. M.* i, 12; *S.* iv, 205.
[3] One of the eighty great disciples. *Comy.* (on *S.* iv, 72).

they eat and drink to excess, they put in authority[1] a woman
or a man that is immoral. Whatsoever families . . . fail to
last long, all of them do so because of these four reasons or
one or other of them.

Whatsoever families, monks, do last long, all of them do so
because of these four reasons or one or other of them. What
four ?

They seek for what is lost, repair the decayed, eat and drink
in moderation, and put in authority a virtuous woman or
man. Whatsoever families . . . do last long, all of them
do so because of these four reasons. . . .'

§ vi (256). *The thoroughbred* (a).[2]

'Possessed of four qualities, monks, a rājah's noble,
thoroughbred steed is worthy of the rājah, is the rājah's
possession, is reckoned an asset of the rājah. What four ?

Herein a rājah's noble, thoroughbred steed is possessed of
beauty, strength, speed and good proportions.[3] Possessed
of these four qualities a rājah's . . . steed . . . is reckoned
an attribute of the rājah.

Just in the same way, monks, possessed of four qualities
a monk is worthy of offerings . . . a field of merit unsurpassed for the world. What four ?

In this case a monk has beauty (of life), strength (of character), speed (of insight) and good proportions (of necessaries).

And how is a monk possessed of beauty ?

In this case a monk is virtuous, he lives restrained with the
restraint of the obligations, is proficient in the practice of
good conduct, seeing danger in the slightest faults he trains
himself in the precepts by undertaking them. In this way he
has beauty (of life).

And how is a monk possessed of strength ?

In this case a monk lives ardent in energy, ever striving to
abandon bad qualities, to acquire good qualities, strenuously

---

[1] As *seṭṭhi. Comy.*

[2] As at *A.* i, § 95, with three qualities.

[3] *Āroha-pariṇāha. Cf. A.* i, 288, lit. ' length of body and girth.'

exerting himself, not throwing off the burden in good qualities. In this way he has strength (of character).

And how is a monk possessed of speed ?

In this case a monk understands, as it really is, the meaning of: This is Ill. This is the arising of Ill. This is the ending of Ill. This is the practice going to the ending of Ill. In this way a monk is possessed of speed (of insight).

And how is a monk possessed of good proportions ?

In this case a monk is one who gets robe and alms-food, lodging, extras and necessary medicines for use in sickness. In this way a monk is possessed of good proportions (of necessaries).

Possessed of these four qualities a monk is worthy of offerings . . . a field of merit unsurpassed for the world.'

§ vii (257). *The thoroughbred (b).*

'Possessed of four qualities, monks, a rājah's noble, thoroughbred steed . . . is reckoned an attribute of the rājah.

(*The same as before, but in this case the monk's speed is thus defined :*)

In this case a monk, by the destruction of the āsavas . . . attains and abides in the first . . . second . . . third . . . and fourth musing.' (*Other qualities as before.*)

§ viii (258). *Powers.*[1]

' Monks, there are these four powers. What four ?

The power of energy, the power of mindfulness, that of concentration and the power of wisdom. These are the four. . . .'

§ ix (259). *Forest-dwelling.*

' Monks, if he possess four qualities a monk is not fit to resort to lonely spots and solitary lodging in a forest.[2] What four ?

Sensual thoughts, malicious thoughts, harmful thoughts,

---

[1] *Cf. K.S.* v, 223, with faith as the first.
[2] *A.* i, 60.

or if he be weak in wisdom, dull-witted, imbecile.[1] These are the four.

Monks, if he possess four qualities a monk is fit to resort to lonely spots and solitary lodging in a forest. What four ?

Thoughts of renunciation, thoughts not malicious, harmless thoughts, or if he be not dull-witted, not an imbecile. These are the four. . . .'

§ x (260). *Action.*

'Monks, possessed of four qualities the foolish, sinful, unworthy man carries about with him a lifeless, uprooted self, is blameworthy, is censured by the intelligent and begets much demerit. What four ?

Action of body that is blameworthy, action of speech and thought, and view that is blameworthy. These are the four.'

CHAPTER XXVII.—PATH OF ACTION.[2]

§ i (261). *Approving* (a).

'Monks, one possessing four qualities is put into purgatory according to his deserts. What four ?

He himself takes life and encourages another to do so, approves of taking life and speaks in praise thereof. Possessing these four qualities . . .

---

[1] *Eḷa-mūga*, a doubtful word not yet satisfactorily explained (*mūga*). At *M.* i, 20 *Comy.* expl. as equal to *mukha* ('by change of *kh* to *g*'!), 'dribbling at the mouth.' *Eḷa=lālā* (saliva) and gives *v.ll. -mūga, -mūka, -mukha. SA.* on *S.* v, 99 expl. as 'a stutterer' (*asampanna-vacano*). *AA.* on *A.* iii, 436; *DA.* i, 290; *A.* iv, 226 (the same phrase as here) have no remarks. Childers has 'deaf and dumb,' followed by *P. Dict.*; but this meaning, as Rhys Davids remarks at *Mil. Pañh.*, Trans. ii, 71, 'has not yet been confirmed by a single passage either in Pāli or Sanskrit,' and suggests 'as dumb as a sheep (*eḍa*)' or 'imbecile,' which I follow here. Perhaps our 'drivelling idiot' is the same word. *Cf. aneḷa-gala* (*eḷa=doso*) and *neḷagga*; *UdA.* 313, 369. Comy. on *M.* i, *loc. cit.*, points out that such people would be too timorous for forest life.

[2] Text miscalls this *Abhiññā-vagga*. There is no *uddāna* to this *vagga*, so I give my own titles to the suttas. *Cf.* § 212.

Monks, possessing four qualities one is put into heaven according to his deserts. What four ?

He himself abstains from taking life, encourages another to such abstinence and speaks in praise thereof. These are the four.'

§ ii (262). *Approving (b).*

(*The same for* Stealing or abstention from stealing.)

§ iii (263). *Approving (c).*

(*The same for* A wrong-doer in sense-desires or abstention.)

§ iv (264). *Approving (d).*

(. . . a liar or one who abstains.)

§ v (265). *Approving (e).*

(. . . a slanderer or one who abstains.)

§ vi (266). *Approving (f).*

(. . . of bitter speech or one who abstains.)

§ vii (267). *Approving (g).*

(. . . an idle babbler or one who abstains.)

§ viii (268). *Approving (h).*

(. . . is covetous or abstains.)

§ ix (269). *Approving (i).*

(. . . of a malicious mind or abstains.)

§ x (270). *Approving (j).*

(. . . one who has wrong view or right view.)

CHAPTER XXVIII.—PASSION (AND THE REST).[1]

' Monks, for the comprehension of passion four conditions must be made to grow. What four ?

Herein ⸋ monk dwells, as regards body,[2] contemplating body (as transient), by having restrained dejection as to the world arising from coveting. He dwells, as regards feelings . . . he dwells as regards mind . . . he dwells, as regards mind-states, contemplating mind-states (as transient), ardent, mindful and composed, by having restrained dejection as to the world arising from coveting. Monks, for the comprehension of passion these four conditions must be made to grow.

Monks, for the comprehension of passion, these four conditions . . .

Herein a monk starts desire,[3] strives, sets going energy, lays hold of thought and exerts effort to prevent the arising of bad qualities that have not yet arisen. He starts desire, strives, sets going energy, lays hold of thought and exerts effort to abandon bad qualities that have arisen. He starts desire . . . to cause the arising of good qualities not yet arisen. He starts desire . . . for the persistence of good qualities that have arisen, for their non-confusion, for their more-becoming, for their increase and development, for their perfecting. Monks, for the comprehension of passion these four conditions . . .

Monks, for the comprehension of passion these four conditions. . . .

Herein a monk cultivates that basis of psychic power[4] of which the features are desire, together with the co-factors of concentration and struggle. He cultivates that basis of psychic power of which the features are energy, together with the co-factors of concentration and struggle.

---

[1] *Sinh.* text makes four suttas of this. With it end the *First Fifty Suttas*; but in reality 271 according to our arrangement of the text.

[2] *Cf. K.S.* v, 119 *ff.* (Arisings of Mindfulness).

[3] *Cf. K.S.* v, 173 *ff.* (On the Faculties); Mrs. Rh. D.: *Gotama*, p. 222

[4] *Cf. K.S.* v, 225 *ff.* (On the Bases of Psychic Power).

He cultivates that basis of psychic power of which the features are thought, together with . . . He cultivates the basis of psychic power of which the features are investigation,[1] together with the co-factors of concentration and struggle. Monks, these four conditions . . .

Monks, for the full understanding, the utter destruction, for the abandoning, the destroying, for the decay of passion, for the utter passionless ending, giving up and renunciation of passion, these four conditions must be made to grow.

For the full understanding . . . and renunciation of anger[2] and malevolence, hypocrisy and spite, envy and grudging, deceit and treachery, obstinacy and impetuosity, pride and overweening pride, mental intoxication and negligence, these four conditions must be made to grow.'

---

[1] *Vimaṃsā ; cf. Sakya* (Mrs. Rhys Davids), p. 250.
[2] *Cf. G.S.* i, 86 *ff*.

HERE ENDS THE BOOK OF THE FOURS.

INDEX

I.—GENERAL

Index

265

II.—TITLES OF THE SUTTAS

Unthinkable, 89
Upaka, 189
Upavāna, 169
Uprooted, 3, 4

Vappa, 207
Vassakāra, 40, 186
Very far away, 58
View, 14, 139
Visākha, 59

Wanderers, 32
Weak in wisdom, 237
Well matched, 69
Withdrawn, 47
With some effort, 160
With the stream, 4
Worthy, 86
Worthy of a cairn, 250
Wrath, 54, 94
Wrong practice, 144

III.—SOME PĀLI WORDS IN THE NOTES

Akanittha, 137
Akukkuccaka-jāta, 212
Ajjhattika, 227
Attha-dhamma, 7. *Read* atthaŋ
. . . dhammaŋ. The older
meaning would be welfare . . .
dharma (sense of right).
Anantarahita, 220
Antarāyika, 9
Apaṇṇaka, 85
Appatta-mānasa, 100
Abbuda, 45
Alampetvā, 86
As'asmi, 226
Assa-puta, 246
Āpātha-dasa, 75
Āyatanaso, 76
Āloka-saññī, 224
Āvaranīya, 46
Āsava, 207

Itibhāvâbhāva, 11

Upavattana, 88
Ummagga, 184, 198

Eḷa-mūga, 257

Odhiso, 167
Oṇīta-patta-pāṇin, 71

Kaṇḍa-cittakāni, 213
Kamm'oja, 92

Gāma-dhamma, 222
Gūthâgata, 104

Nikattha, 140
Nekkhaŋ Jambonadassa, 8

Paccakkhāya, 33
Pajjhāyati, 29
Patipada, 96
Patta-kamma, 73
Papañca, 168
Parato, 18
Pariyāpuṇāti, 15
Palikhaṇati, 210
Putaŋsa, 192

Manta-bhāsa, 144

Yathābhataŋ, 19
Yuganaddha, 162
Yoniso, 85

Lekhanī, 212

Voyuñjati, 244

Saddhaṁma, 21
Sa-sankhāra-parinibbāyī, 160
Sangaha, 36
Sāci-yoga, 223
Sārambha, 201
Singī, 28
Susukā, 127
So maŋ pañhena, ahaŋ veyyāka-
raṇena, 167